COLLINS
COBUILD

COLLINS Birmingham University International Language Database

ENGLISH
GUIDES

4

CONFUSABLE
WORDS

Edwin Carpenter

**THE UNIVERSITY
OF BIRMINGHAM**

**COLLINS
COBUILD**

HarperCollins*Publishers*

HarperCollins Publishers
77–85 Fulham Palace Road
London W6 8JB

COBUILD is a trademark of William Collins Sons & Co Ltd

© HarperCollins Publishers Ltd 1993
First published 1993
Reprinted 1993

10 9 8 7 6 5 4 3 2

ISBN 0 00 370562-5

Computer typeset by Wyvern Typesetting Ltd

Printed in Great Britain by HarperCollins Manufacturing, Glasgow

The Author and Publishers would like to thank the following people for their help: Dora
Carpenter and Elizabeth Cane, who read the manuscript and provided valuable
comments; Deborah Kirby; Annette Capel, Lorna Heaslip, and Katy Shaw; and the
COBUILD team, in particular Stephen Bullon, Ann Hewings, and Jenny Watson.

Foreword

The *Guide to Confusable Words* is one of a series of COBUILD ENGLISH GUIDES to particular areas of difficulty for learners of English.

This Guide deals with words which may be confused. This may be because they look or sound similar, or because they have similar, but not identical, meanings. In some cases there may also be a difference in the grammar of the words. Often there are misleading similarities between words in English and words in other languages.

This book contains nearly 400 entries, covering over 900 items. Using real examples, the entries show the typical use of the words in modern English. The examples are taken from the Bank of English, a collection of modern English speech and writing drawn from a variety of sources. The computer files of the Bank of English currently contain approximately 200 million words.

I hope that we have selected useful information and that you find the book easy to use. Please write to me with any comments or suggestions about how to improve COBUILD publications.

John Sinclair
Editor in Chief: COBUILD ENGLISH GUIDES
Professor of Modern English Language
University of Birmingham

Corpus Acknowledgements

We would like to thank those authors and publishers who kindly gave permission for copyright material to be used in the Bank of English. We would also like to thank Times Newspapers Ltd, the BBC World Service, and National Public Radio of Washington for providing valuable data.

Introduction

This book deals with words which regularly cause problems because they are easily confused. It is fairly common to hear mistakes such as 'I'm so boring' (instead of 'I'm so bored') or 'An eventual solution would be...' (instead of 'A possible solution would be...'). The entries in this book are designed to help you when you are not sure which of two or more words is suitable for a particular context.

There are many reasons why certain words are confusable. For example, they may look similar when they are written down but have very different meanings, for example *quite* and *quiet*, or *suit* and *suite*. Or they might look similar and have closely related, but not identical, meanings, for example *altogether* and *all together*, or *breath* and *breathe*.

Some words not only look similar, but also sound the same when they are spoken, for example *practice* and *practise*, or *stationary* and *stationery*.

Other words do not look the same, but can be easily confused because they have similar, although not identical meanings, for example *baby*, *infant*, and *child*, or *job* and *work*.

Another area of confusion can be the grammatical differences between words which share a similar meaning or a similar form, for example *after*, *afterwards*, and *later*, or *its* and *it's*.

Differences between British and American English can also cause confusion.

The entries in this book deal with all these areas of confusion. The explanations are supported by real examples which show how the words are typically used in modern English.

How to use the book

The entry headings are printed in **bold**. They consist of two or more confusable items, separated by commas, for example:

everyday, every day
except, except for, unless, besides

Sometimes an item consists of more than one word, for example:

before, in front of

The entries are arranged according to the alphabetical order of the first item in each heading. For example, the first three entries in the letter E are:

earn, win, gain
east, eastern, easterly
eatable, edible

Where two entries start with the same item, they are arranged according to the alphabetical order of the second item, as in:

after, afterwards, later
after, behind

It is important to remember that some words (for example *actual*, *much*, and *shop*) appear in more than one entry. You can use the index to find out where they appear. The Index starts on page 241.

The Explanations

The entries contain explanations only for those meanings of words which are confusable, and not necessarily for all the meanings. For example, the entry for **square, place** begins:

A **square** is a flat open area surrounded by buildings in a town or city. Many such areas have **Square** in their names.

There is no mention of a *square* being a shape with four sides of the same length, because *square* and *place* are not confused when *square* has this meaning.

The Examples

All the explanations are supported by real examples which show how the words are used by speakers and writers of modern English. The examples are taken from the Bank of English and are printed in *italic*.

Grammar

Some entries contain information about the different grammatical functions of a word. Where this information is not a central part of the explanation, it appears towards the end of the entry, under the heading **Grammar**.

Other words

Some entries contain information about additional words which have a similar meaning to the words that are discussed in the

Introduction

main part of the entry. This information appears towards the end of the entry, under the heading **Other words**.

Pronunciation

Information about pronunciation is given where it helps to distinguish between confusable words.

The symbols used to indicate pronunciation are part of the International Phonetic Alphabet. Here is a list of the symbols used in this book:

vowel sounds:

ɑː	heart, start, calm
æ	act, mass, lap
aɪ	dive, cry, mind
aɪə	fire, tyre, buyer
aʊ	out, down, loud
aʊə	flour, tower, sour
e	met, lend, pen
eɪ	say, main, weight
eə	fair, care, wear
ɪ	fit, win, list
iː	feed, me, beat
ɪə	near, beard, clear
ɒ	lot, lost, spot
əʊ	note, phone, coat
ɔː	more, cord, claw
ɔɪ	boy, coin, joint
ʊ	could, stood, hood
uː	you, use, choose
ʊə	lure, pure, cure
ɜː	turn, third, word
ʌ	but, fund, must
ə	*the weak vowel in* butter, about, forgotten
i	*the weak vowel in* very, create
u	*the first weak vowel in* tuition

consonant sounds:

b	bed, rub
d	done, red
f	fit, if
g	good, dog
h	hat
j	yellow
k	king, pick
l	lip, bill
m	mat, ram
n	not, tin
p	pay, lip
r	run
s	soon, bus
t	talk, bet
v	van, love
w	win
x	loch
z	zoo, buzz
ʃ	ship, wish
ʒ	measure
ŋ	sing
tʃ	cheap, witch
θ	thin, myth
ð	then, loathe
dʒ	joy, bridge

Stressed syllables are indicated by an <u>underline</u> under the vowel symbol for the stressed syllable.

A

ability, capability, capacity

If someone has **ability**, a particular **ability,** or the **ability** to do
something, they can do it because they have the skill or the
knowledge that is needed to do it. You often use **ability** to say
that someone can do something well.

He had remarkable ability as an administrator.
There are four main factors which determine mathematical ability.
...the ability to bear hardship.

A person's **capability** is the amount of work they can do and how
well they can do it.

*The director has his own ideas both of the role and of the capability
of the actor.*
It was, in any case, beyond the capability of one man.

If someone has a particular **capacity,** a **capacity** for something,
or a **capacity** to do something, they have the characteristics
required to do it. **Capacity** is a more formal word than **ability.**

...their capacity for being inspired by heroes.
...his capacity always to see the other person's point of view.

able, capable

Both **able** and **capable** are used to say that someone can do
something.

When you say that someone is **able** to do something, you mean
that they can do it either because of their knowledge or skill or
because it is possible for them to do it.

Breslow wondered if he would be able to climb over the rail.
They must be able to use their profits for new investment.

Note that if you use a past tense, you are saying that someone has
actually done something.

We were able to reduce costs.

When you say that someone is **capable** of doing something, you
mean either that they have the knowledge and skill to do it if they
want or need to, or that they are likely to do it.

*Workers are perfectly capable of running the organizations which
employ them.*

able

She was quite capable of dropping off to sleep.

You can also say that someone is **capable** of a feeling or an action.

I think he's capable of loyalty and seriousness.
Bowman could not believe him capable of murder.

You normally use **'capable of'** when talking about what something such as a car or machine can do.

...water turbines, which are capable of producing more economical electricity.
The car was capable of 110 miles per hour.

If you describe someone as **able** or **capable,** you mean that they do things well and in an intelligent way. There is little difference between the two words when used in this way.

...the able and methodical King Charles V of France.
This very able man totally failed to see the possibilities of the telephone.
Newborn babies are more capable than was once thought.
Well, you certainly have a capable gardener there.

above, over

Above and **over** are both used to talk about position and height.

If something is higher than something else, but an imaginary line joining them is not vertical, you have to use **above.**

The trees rose above the houses.

If you go **over** something, you cross it and get to the other side.

Castle stepped over the dog.
...a soaring seagull swooping over Central Park.

If you are wearing two items of clothing one on top of the other, you can say that you are wearing one **over** the other.

Rudolph was wearing a sweater over a wool shirt, and a silk scarf.

You can use either **above** or **over** if something is higher than something else and an imaginary line could be drawn vertically joining them.

He opened a cupboard above the sink.
She leaned forward until her face was directly over the basin.

Above and **over** are also both used to talk about measurements.

You use **over** to say that a distance or period of time is longer than the one mentioned.

The plane flew at a height of over twelve thousand feet.
So we had this beautiful relationship for over a year.

You can use **above** or **over** when you are talking about a point that is higher than another point, especially a point on a scale.

The amount of tax you should pay is determined by what you earn above a certain figure.
Any money earned over that level is taxed at the rate of 59 per cent.
In each case I want to know the height of the man. Everybody above five feet eight inches is suspect.

Above and **over** are both used to talk about people's ranks and importance relative to others.

You use **above** to talk about people who are more important and in a higher position than other people.

...behaving as if she was in a position above even the staff, and certainly above us.

If someone is **over** you, they give orders or instructions to you.
...an officer set in authority over him.

account, bill

When you have an **account** with a bank, you leave your money in the bank and take it out when you need it.

The current account, sometimes called a cheque account, is the most widely used.

When you have to pay for things like electricity or a meal in a restaurant, you get a **bill**.

I'll want a copy of the phone bill.
Clive asked the waiter for the bill.

accuse, charge

If you **accuse** someone of doing something wrong, you say that they did it. For example, someone can be **accused** of being dishonest, or of a fault like laziness. If someone has done something that is against the law, they can be **accused** of a crime and put on trial in a court of law.

He himself was accused of incompetence.

accuse

And then you would start crying and accusing us of not caring if you died.
They were in great distress because they had been wrongfully accused of theft.
He is accused of killing ten young women.

When the police **charge** someone or **charge** them with committing a crime, they formally accuse them of it. The police **charge** a person with a crime when they have evidence that the person was responsible for it. You can also **charge** someone with things like not doing their duty or lying. You do not use 'charge' when referring to minor faults.

Colonel Burr was arrested by order of President Thomas Jefferson and charged with treason.
He was arrested and charged with committing a variety of offences.
He was declared not responsible for the criminal acts with which he had been charged.
Mr Horta charged the premier with being politically weak.

actual, real

You use **actual** to emphasize that the place, object, or person you are talking about is the correct or genuine one. For example, if you talk about the **actual** cost of something, you are talking about what it does cost rather than what it is expected to cost.

...turning from ratings in the polls to actual performance in elections.
We call the baby Doc. His actual name is Daniel.

You can also use **actual** when you are giving exact information about something, for example the time you take to do something rather than preparing to do it.

The actual boat trip takes about forty-five minutes.

You only use **actual** in front of a noun. You do not say that something 'is actual'.

Something that is **real** exists and is not imagined, invented, or theoretical.

...real or imagined feelings of inferiority.
Robert squealed in mock terror, then in real pain.

Note that you can use **real** after a link verb like 'be'.

What we saw was real.

actually, really

Actually and **really** are both used to emphasize statements. Both words can emphasize a whole clause or sentence, or just a word or group of words.

You use **actually** when you are saying what the truth is about something, in contrast to other things that might have been said or thought.

All of the characters in the novel actually existed.
Actually, all pollution is simply an unused resource.

You also use **actually** to emphasize something surprising. You put **actually** in front of the surprising part of what you are saying.

Tommo actually began to cry.
I was actually cruel sometimes.

Actually can be used to be precise or to correct someone.

No one was actually drunk.
We couldn't actually see the garden.

You use **really** in conversation to emphasize something that you are saying.

I really think he's sick.
I only wish your people really trusted me.

When you use **really** in front of an adjective or adverb, it has a similar meaning to 'very'.

This is really serious.
It was really good, wasn't it?
We're doing really well.

adhere, adherence, adhesion

If something **adheres** to something else, it sticks to it firmly.
Some sugar grains may adhere to the sides of the pan.

The noun from this sense of **adhere** is **adhesion**.
It stuck there for seconds only by tactile adhesion.

If someone **adheres** to a rule, they obey it. If someone **adheres** to a point of view, they support it strongly.
They mostly adhere to a diet which avoids meat.
The government has firmly adhered to the view that this is a matter for individuals to decide.

adhere

The noun from this sense of **adhere** is **adherence**.

...a rigid adherence to the laws of honour.
...their adherence to the philosophy of social democracy.

● You do not use 'adhere' to talk about becoming a member of an organization; you say you 'join' an organization.

admission, admittance

If you want to get into a private building or part of a building, you seek **admittance**. **Admittance** is a formal word and is sometimes used on signs.

How then was he to gain admittance?
Bernstein opened a door marked NO ADMITTANCE.

Admission has the same meaning, but is less formal. You do not usually use 'admission' on signs.

Marsha was insisting on admission to David's office.
To gain admission, one had to ring that bell at the main gate.

You always use **admission** when you want to talk about going into public places such as theatres and museums, or into a hospital as a patient, or being allowed into a university as a student.

...free admission to all national museums and galleries.
...priority cases for admission to hospital.
He applied for admission to Harvard.

● An **admission** is a confession, usually made rather reluctantly, that you have done something bad, unpleasant, or embarrassing.

The admission of guilt is hard.
They made no admission that the newspaper had been fooling the public.

admit, confess

If you **admit** something bad, unpleasant, or embarrassing, you agree, usually rather reluctantly, that it is true. You can **admit** that something is true, **admit** something, or **admit** to something.

I would be forced to admit that I had used Ewen Waite's gun.
He admitted that the mounting cost was a matter of serious concern.
Boylan began to play. Rudolph had to admit he played well.
Again the manufacturers, employers and government were reluctant to admit the danger.

She was obviously in considerable pain, but she wouldn't admit it.
She admits to being difficult to live with.

If you **confess** something, you say that you have done something
you should not have done. Usually you feel regret or
embarrassment when you **confess** something. You can **confess**
that you have done something, **confess** something, or **confess** to
someone.

Finally, the boy confessed that he had been lying throughout.
The mother could not be persuaded to confess her previous error.
It turned out that he'd confessed to Castle that he hadn't gone to the
dentist.

If someone **confesses** to something such as a crime, they say they
did it.

Bianchi had confessed to five of the murders.
They confess to murders they haven't committed.
Three days after Mr Profumo confessed and resigned, Stephen Ward
was arrested.

You can also use both **admit** and **confess** in expressions like 'I
admit', 'I must **admit**', 'I **confess**', and 'I must **confess**' when you
mention a fact that embarrasses you slightly or that you think
might upset the person you are speaking to.

Well, I'll admit he seems harmless.
I have to admit that this has been only partially successful.
This is not a neat household, I confess.
I must confess that, to put it plainly, I find him a bore.

advice, advise, suggest

If you tell someone what you think they should do, you give them
advice. **Advice** is a noun that cannot be made plural. You can
say instead that you give someone 'some **advice**'. **Advice** is
pronounced /ədvaɪs/.

She needs sound medical advice and help.
I'll give you some advice, Mike, don't try.

Advise is a verb. If you **advise** someone to do something, you say
that you think they should do it. You can **advise** someone, **advise**
something, **advise** someone to do something, or **advise** doing
something. **Advise** is pronounced /ədvaɪz/.

You could not help her or advise her.
I used to advise a simple and direct approach.

advice

David advised me to try to sleep.
You are advised to take out insurance.
If the doctor foresees complications, he will advise going to hospital.

If you **suggest** something, you mention it as an idea or plan for someone to think about. It is not necessarily the best idea or plan; it is simply something to be considered. You can **suggest** something, **suggest** doing something, or **suggest** that someone does something.

Your bank manager will probably suggest a personal loan.
I suggested inviting Denny, and Jim agreed.
Sometimes he would suggest that she stayed at home while he worked in the garden.
I suggest, my dear friend, that you leave this matter to me.

Other words

Instead of saying that you **suggest** something, you can say that you make a **suggestion**.

I made a few suggestions about how we could spend the afternoon.
The other governments greeted the suggestion with caution.

advocate, recommend

If someone **advocates** a particular action or plan, they say publicly that it is the right action or plan and that other people should adopt it. They are usually discussing a serious question that they know a lot about and that can affect many people. **Advocate** is pronounced /ˈædvəkeɪt/.

The socialist policies he advocates would mean a major reform of the Common Market.
The only positive step he took at this time was to advocate Winston Churchill's return to government as a Minister.
The report advocates a massive programme of aid to developing countries.

If someone **recommends** a particular action or plan, they suggest that it is the best action or plan. They may be discussing a serious question or a minor one, and they may be giving advice to one person, a few people, or many people.

He suffered severe headaches as a result of this injury, and his doctor recommended a rest.
The steps we've recommended above will help you get a view of your firm's interests.

8

They recommend that no more than one egg a day should be eaten.
We recommend that you take an adequate supply of currency and traveller's cheques.

affect, effect

If something **affects** a person or thing, it influences them or makes them change.

Fitness affects you mentally and physically, and how you feel affects everything from your relationships to your ability to cope.
One of the problems with noise is that it affects different people in different ways.
Emotional states can affect our hormone levels.

The noun from **affect** is **effect**. If something **affects** you, it has an **effect** on you.

...the effect of noise on people in factories.
...under the effect of the anaesthetic.

● If you **effect** something like a change or a repair, you cause the change to occur or the repair to be done. This is a fairly formal use, and is much less common than the use of **effect** as a noun.

She claimed that all her cures were effected solely by known medicines and by prayers.
Mrs Moffat had effected hasty repairs with tape and gummed paper.

afflict, inflict

Problems, illnesses, and misfortunes **afflict** people and cause them to suffer. You can also say that someone **is afflicted** with an illness, problem, or misfortune.

...the diseases that afflict the poor in poor countries.
Queasiness, headaches and languor afflicted her all day.
...those afflicted with the stark problem of how to keep on living.

When people **inflict** things like problems, pain, or damage on other people, they are deliberately doing something to make them suffer.

One ought not to inflict one's problems on other people.
The body must have been erect when this chest wound was inflicted.
He wanted to inflict a punishment on me.

after

after, afterwards, later

You use **after, afterwards,** and **later** to talk about things that happen at a time following the time of speaking or following a particular event.

You can use **after** as a preposition.

After dinner she got hold of the President and spoke to him.
He resigned after allegations that he was involved in drug-trafficking.

You can also use **after** as a conjunction.

I returned to England only recently, after spending two months in India.
His fame grew after he left the hospital.

In expressions like 'shortly **after**' and 'not long **after**', you can use **after** as an adverb.

Douglas came round to see me, and soon after I met him again at a friend's.
Shortly after, Fania called me.

Afterwards can also be used as an adverb when you do not need to mention the particular time or event.

Afterwards we went to a night club.
You'd better come up to my room afterwards and show me what you've got.

You can use **later** as an adverb to refer to a time or situation that is after the one that you have been talking about, or following the time of speaking.

I returned some three or four weeks later.
I'll go round and see Nell later.

You can use all these words after a phrase which mentions a period of time to say when something happens.

She wrote about it six years afterwards.
Ten minutes later Sutherland grabbed a microphone.
...five hundred years after his death.

● The words 'shortly', 'soon', and 'long' can be used with both **after** and **afterwards**.

He was back in the hotel shortly after six.
Soon afterwards, Ira came storming into the clinic.
...under a tree known long afterwards as the Queen's Oak.

● 'A little', 'much', and 'not much' can be used with **later**.

A little later, the faint blue glow of the emergency lights went out.
I learned all this much later.

after, behind

You use **after** to say that something happens at a later time than something else.

Eva was tidying up after lunch.
Send them on their way after just one meal.

If you are **behind** someone or something, they are in front of you and you are facing their back.

Alison came across and stood behind her.
The girl behind him is typing.
Sandy stared at me, his eyes widening behind his rimless glasses.

After and **behind** can also be used with verbs such as 'walk' or 'run' which express movement. If you walk or run **behind** someone, they are in front of you and stay in front of you.

He walked behind me for a long way.

If you walk or run **after** someone, you try to reach where they are, perhaps so you can talk to them or in order to catch them.

Thomas ran after him, yelling to him to stop.

after all, at last, finally, in the end, lastly, last of all

You use **after all** when you are mentioning an additional point which confirms or supports what you have just said.

They did not expect heavy losses in the air; after all, they had superb aircraft.
They didn't bother to tie me up. After all, there were four, five, six of them there, mostly with handguns.

You also use **after all** to say that something is the case or may be the case in spite of what had previously been thought.

Could it be true, after all, that money did not bring happiness?
Perhaps it isn't such a bad village after all.

You do not use 'after all' to talk about what happens at the end of a long period. You use **at last, finally, in the end,** or **last of all**.

after all

You use **at last** or **finally** to say that something happens after you have been waiting for it or expecting it for a long time.

You can use **at last** at the end of a sentence.

The storm that had threatened for so long broke at last.

Finally usually comes either at the beginning of a sentence or in front of a verb.

After another search on the map they finally located it.

You also use **finally** to talk about an act or result that is last in a series of things.

Trotsky lived in turn in Turkey, France, Norway, and finally Mexico.
Let's come finally to the question of pensions.

You use **in the end** when you are talking about a situation that comes about after a long time or after a long process.

'Perhaps the police got him in the end,' Sam said.
The performance was quite a success in the end.
In the end, Peter seemed quite happy and so did I.

You use **lastly** to talk about the last of a series of people or things.

Then I went through the bathroom and lastly the bed-sitting room.
Lastly he jabbed the knife hard into the trunk of the tree.

You use **last of all** to emphasize that there is nobody or nothing else after the person or thing you mention.

In rapid succession his friends' faces appear and disappear: last of all he sees Lewis Seidel's maddening smile.
Last of all came the cat.

agenda, diary

An **agenda** is a list of things that people want to discuss or deal with at a meeting.

It was possible to place it on the agenda for discussion by the next international congress.
Among the major topics on the summit agenda: interest rates.

A **diary** is a book that has a blank space or page for each day of the year. You use a **diary** for writing down arrangements or appointments or your comments on what has happened on a particular day.

He scribbled an appointment for 10.30 in his desk diary.
My diary tells me that summer begins on 22nd June.

● Sometimes **agenda** is used to refer to important matters that are being widely discussed, especially by politicians. You will most often find it being used in this way by journalists.

Telecommunications has moved to the top of the political agenda.

Other words

Many people no longer use ordinary diaries, but have 'personal organizers'. These have sections that deal with the separate areas in someone's life, for example their special interests, their personal accounts, or important telephone numbers. People sometimes call a personal organizer a 'Filofax'; 'Filofax' is a trademark.

ago, before, for, since

You use **ago** to connect a time in the past with the moment of speaking. If you are speaking on Friday and you say that something happened two days **ago**, you mean that it happened on Wednesday.

The land was acquired by the University two years ago.
I discovered a few days ago that Weiss was Houdini's real name.

You use **before** to connect a time in the past with a more recent time in the past. If you are talking about what you did last Wednesday and you say that you met someone two days **before**, you mean that you met them last Monday.

She said that, about six months before, she had gone to see an aunt who lived in Stoneyvale.
...a woman he had first met twenty minutes before.

You use **for** to say how long a period lasts in the past, present, or future. If you say that you have been doing something **for** two days, you mean that you have spent the last two days doing it all the time or part of the time.

She sat down and remained absolutely still for nearly half an hour.
He had disappeared for three weeks after that.
It will ruin us for several years.

You also use **for** to say how much time passes without something happening. If you are speaking on Friday and you say that you have not done something **for** two days, you mean that the last time you did it was on Wednesday.

ago

I hadn't seen him for four years.
He couldn't bring himself to eat their food, and he hadn't eaten for days.

You use **since** to say when a period started. If you are speaking on Friday and you say that you have been doing something **since** Wednesday, you mean that you have spent the last two days doing it.

She had been a manager of Fairacre School since the reign of King Edward the Seventh.
She has been working with the group since it began.
Brazil is to have its first civilian president since the military regime was set up 17 years ago.

You also use **since** to say either when the last time was that something happened, or how much time passes without something happening. If you are speaking on Friday and you say that you have not done something **since** Wednesday, or that it is two days **since** you did something, you mean that the last time you did that thing was on Wednesday.

Probably she hadn't touched food since breakfast.
It was a shamefully long time since either she or Tusker had been to church.

alike, likely

If people or things are **alike,** they are similar to each other. If people do the same things, they act **alike.**

Dolly and Molly were really very much alike.
Supermarkets tend to look alike.
We think and talk alike.

If something is **likely,** or if it is **likely** to happen, it will probably happen. If someone is **likely** to do something, you expect them to do it.

Nuclear war would be less likely under a non-nuclear policy.
The argument is likely to prove long and exhausting.
...the sort of questions you are likely to ask.

alive, living, lively

Someone who is **alive** has not died and their life continues. You use **alive** after a link verb like 'be', or occasionally after a noun. You do not use 'alive' in front of a noun.

She didn't say whether he was still alive.
I am the happiest man alive.

A **living** person, animal, or plant has life and is different from
someone who is dead or something that does not have life.

...or see living artists at their work.
*Baboons, even the smaller living species, are very formidable
creatures.*

Someone who is **lively** is active and enthusiastic. Behaviour and
activities can also be described as **lively**.

Before her marriage she had been lively and alert and carefree.
The debate promises to be lively.

all, both, every, each

You use **all** to consider a whole thing or group, complete with its
parts or members. You can talk about 'all bread', 'all the bread',
or 'all of the bread', and 'all books', 'all the books', or 'all of the
books'. You can also talk about 'all people', 'all the people', or 'all
of the people'.

Note that when **all** is used to consider a group, it implies that the
group has more than two members.

*Our task, and the task of all education, is to understand the present
world.*
All their equipment is good.
But remember: most of mankind is not all of mankind.
All green plants depend on light.
...a list of all the biggest countries in the world .
She thought of all the women Marsha had told her about.
He wanted all of the people to be there.

You can also say that people or things **all** do something.

*...the big table where we all ate from different plates and odd
patterned cups and saucers.*

You use **both** to refer to two people or things. You can talk about
'both boys', 'both the boys', or 'both of the boys'.

...the assassination of both Kennedy brothers.
Both the kings under whom he served had financial difficulties.
Both of the diplomats blushed when the company thanked them.

You can also say that people or things **both** do something.

Tony and Nigel both laughed noisily.

all

You use **every** to indicate that you are referring to all the members of a group and not just to some of them. Note that **every** implies that the group you are considering has more than two members. You only use **every** with a singular noun.

He listened to every news bulletin on the radio.
Every house had to be cleaned.
We are still so far from granting an equal chance to every child.

You use **each** to talk about every person or thing in a group. You use **each** rather than 'every' when you are thinking about the members of a group as individuals. Note that **each** can refer to both members of a pair. You only use **each** with a singular noun.

The treatment is different in each case.
It may be impossible to give each child a room to himself.
Each apartment has one or two twin-bedded rooms.

You can also say that people or things **each** do something or that **each** of them does something.

We each carried a blue marking pencil.
There will be the benefit of the lower rates of tax for each of them.
Each of the boys stood to earn as much as he used to.

alone, lonely, lone

If someone is **alone,** there is nobody with them. If someone does something **alone,** nobody does it with them. They may be happy or sad to be **alone.** Note that you do not use 'alone' in front of a noun.

Again he feels he is alone.
I quite like travelling alone, actually.

If someone is **lonely,** they are sad that there is nobody with them or that they do not have any friends.

It will be so dull and lonely here without you.
We started it mainly with the aim of helping lonely people.

If you talk about a **lone** person or thing, there is only one person or thing of that kind present, when you might expect there to be more. Note that **lone** is always used in front of a noun.

In an American suburban street a lone pedestrian is more conspicuous than a lone motorist.
Suddenly a lone figure came struggling out of the swamps.

alternate, alternative

Alternate actions, events, or processes keep happening regularly after each other. The adjective **alternate** is pronounced /ɔːltɜːnət/.

A pattern of **alternate** black and white stripes has a black stripe, then a white stripe, another black stripe, another white stripe, and so on. If something happens on **alternate** days, it happens on one day, then does not happen on the next day, then happens again on the day after it, and so on. Things can also happen in **alternate** weeks, months, or years.

Frost splits rock, so does alternate intense heat and cold.
He played alternate balls left- and right-handed.
These courses are available in alternate years.

You use **alternative** to describe something that can be used, had, or done instead of something else. For example, an **alternative** plan is a plan that could be used instead of another one. If you look for an **alternative** route, you know about one route but you want another one, perhaps because the first one is closed.

Propose alternative solutions and test them.
There was no alternative site for a third London airport.

Alternative can also be used as a noun, meaning something else that can be chosen instead.

The other alternative was to wait until July.
There was absolutely no alternative but to go ahead.

You can also say that someone has two or more **alternatives,** meaning that they have two or more courses of action to choose from. This use is now quite common, although in the past it was considered incorrect.

If a man is threatened with attack, he has five alternatives: he can fight, flee, hide, summon help, or try to appease his attacker.

You can also talk about an **alternative** lifestyle or an **alternative** society, meaning one which is different from the traditional one and which some people think is better.

...the supporters of Alternative Schooling.

● Some English speakers use **alternate** to describe something that can be used, had, or done instead of something else. This is not very common; you normally use **alternative**.

...the development of alternate energy sources.

17

alternate

● **Alternate** can also be used as a verb. When you **alternate** between two things, you regularly do or use one thing and then the other. When **alternate** is a verb, it is pronounced /ɔːltəneɪt/.

They alternated between patronising us and ignoring us.
The post of president should alternate between a Greek and a Turk.

When one thing **alternates** with another, the two things regularly occur in turn.

The Third World suffers from an annual cycle of drought alternating with flood.

Other words

Instead of saying that you do something on **alternate** days or during **alternate** weeks or years, you can say you do it 'every other' day, week, or year.

We only save enough money to take a real vacation every other year.

alternately, alternatively

You use **alternately** to say that two actions or processes keep happening regularly after each other.

Each piece of material is washed alternately in soft water and coconut oil.
The little girl had alternately sulked and made scenes.

You use **alternatively** to give a different explanation from one that has just been mentioned, or to suggest a different course of action.

Or alternatively was he short of cash because he had never been to the Rosses' house at all?
Alternatively, change seats at once.

altogether, all together

You use **altogether** as an adverb to emphasize that something has stopped or has been done or finished completely. If you say that something stops **altogether,** you mean that it stops completely; if you say that you have given something up **altogether,** you mean that you no longer do it at all.

Quite soon she stopped trembling altogether and began to look round at them.
This does not mean that people should go without breakfast altogether.

You can also use **altogether** to emphasize a quality in someone or something. If you say that two things are **altogether** different, you mean that they are completely different. If you say that something is **altogether** more interesting, you mean that it is much more interesting, and if you say that something is **altogether** too slow, you mean that it is much too slow.

Your sources of supply are altogether different from those of a normal retail business.
What troubled me was altogether vaguer and deeper.

You can also use **altogether** to sum up a situation you have been discussing and make a final judgement.

Altogether our playground is a good one.
Altogether, caution and courage are necessary.
Yes, it's quite a pleasant place altogether.

You also use **altogether** to show that an amount is a total. If you say that something cost a hundred pounds **altogether,** you mean that the total cost was a hundred pounds; if you say that ten people were present **altogether,** you mean that there were a total of ten people present.

Altogether there must have been about twenty babies.
Altogether I went back to her about seven times.
You will get £340 a week altogether.

You use **all together** to say that a group of people or things are together or do something together, and that none of them is missing. You can also talk about bringing people **all together** if you bring everyone to a particular place.

It had been so long since the days when we were all together – at home, secure, sheltered.
Each organ depends on the other and all together make up the whole.
When we have enough, we pour it all together in a pot and heat it.
Students may be accommodated all together on a vast campus.

always, already, ever

If something **always** happens, it happens regularly or on all possible occasions; if something is **always** the case, it is true at all times.

I would always ask for the radio to be turned down.
He's always been an active person.
No matter what she did, she would always be forgiven.

always

A man always remembers his first love.

If something has **already** happened, it has happened before now. By using **already,** you are often suggesting that it is surprising that it has happened, or that you expected it to happen later.

Hasn't the government in fact already shown some readiness to compromise?
He had already eaten more than he wanted.

You use **ever,** especially in negative sentences, questions, and 'if'-clauses and with superlatives, to talk about any time in the past, present, or future.

The weeks dragged on, but no one ever came.
Will I ever see France?
We could have got ourselves into a precarious situation if we had ever launched ourselves on the climb.
That's the nicest thing anybody's ever said to me.

amend, emend

If you **amend** something, you change it so that it is more correct or appropriate. Laws, documents, and statements are often **amended.**

...the power to amend legislation.
I merely asked if you wished to amend your statement.

If you **emend** a piece of writing, you change it so that a mistake is corrected. **Emend** is far less common than **amend;** you say that editors **emend** old literary texts.

Other words

Instead of using the verbs **amend** and **emend,** you can use 'make an **amendment**' and 'make an **emendment**'.

Madison sent me a copy of the proposed amendments to the constitution.

amiable, amicable

If someone is **amiable,** they are friendly and pleasant to be with. You can also describe someone's behaviour or a conversation as **amiable.**

He was an amiable, amusing fellow.
He raised a finger in amiable warning.

You use **amicable** to describe how people behave or feel when they are polite and co-operate with each other instead of arguing or fighting.

Kathy and Vim had their amicable divorce.
...after a week of amicable talks.

Other words

Instead of saying that someone is **amiable,** you can say that they behave **amiably.**

The Customs man smiled amiably.

Instead of describing something such as a dispute as **amicable,** you can say that it is settled or conducted **amicably.**

The vast majority of disputes are settled amicably.

anger, fury, rage

You feel **anger** when someone does something that is cruel or that frustrates you. You can feel **anger** about things like insults or delays.

Impatience is the first reaction against a setback and can soon turn to anger if you're not careful.
There was anger at the suffering inflicted by the bombing.

If you feel **fury** or **rage,** you have intense feelings of anger which are hard to control and can be violent. You can also be 'in a **fury**' or 'in a **rage**'.

I nearly smashed the phone in fury.
Thomas flew into a cold fury, which Fanny observed with terror.
So great was their rage that they began to destroy everything in sight.
In a rage I went to his desk, took all his books and hurled them out of the window.

anniversary, birthday

An **anniversary** is a date when people remember and celebrate what happened on the same date in a previous year. A married couple celebrate their **anniversary** on the date of their wedding. People also celebrate the **anniversaries** of important political events or of the founding of organizations.

We went to Hull for our anniversary.
...the sixty-sixth anniversary of the end of the First World War.

You do not use 'anniversary' to talk about the date when you were born. If you were born on January 1st, your **birthday** is on January 1st every year.

I always treat her to a gift on her birthday.
...soon after his ninetieth birthday in November 1964.

announce, proclaim, declare, pronounce

If you **announce** some news, you tell people about it publicly or officially.

All that remained was to announce their engagement and fix the date of the wedding.
On 1 April he announced a full public review of the project.
They always announce the results on the radio.

You can also say that you **announce** news when you tell it to a few people in a very serious or important way, even if the news itself is not very important.

'I've made up my mind to come back,' announced Mrs Pringle majestically.
When he returned, he announced that he had broken seventeen windows.

To **proclaim** something important means to state publicly that something is the case or that something will happen. Governments and newspapers, for example, can **proclaim** something.

General Blanco had been authorized to proclaim an armistice.
The Public Safety Act allowed the Government to proclaim a state of emergency at any time without giving reasons.
The paper proclaimed in big banner headlines: 'END OF WAR IN EUROPE'.
They proclaim adherence to a religious ethic but do not live by it.

To **declare** something like war or independence means to state officially that it has just begun.

War was declared on the enemy.
The decision of whether or not to declare independence still hung in the balance.
Starting tomorrow we will declare a hunger strike.

If you **declare** something to be the case, you officially state that it is the case.

India declared self-sufficiency in wheat in 1976.

At his trial he was declared innocent.
Hamburg had been declared an open city.

If you **declare** your position or intentions, you state them
openly.

*They argued that the party should publicly declare its opposition to
the plans.*
*My opponent has declared his intention to petition the Election
Court.*

If you **declare** something, you say it firmly and definitely.

He declared that Jed was the murderer of Moira Page.
Gertrude had declared that Anne needed a holiday.
'Yes,' she declared, 'we must be off.'

If you **pronounce** something to be the case, you state officially or
with authority that it is the case.

*In the end she was pronounced cured, and released after about three
years.*
He was pronounced guilty of robbery.
*When she left at sixteen, any inspector of schools would have
pronounced her a poorly educated girl.*

To **pronounce** something means to say it in a way that shows
that you feel very sure about what you are saying.

'The letter is a forgery,' she pronounced.
'That is good,' Baranovich pronounced at last.

annoyance, irritation

You feel **annoyance** when someone does something that you do
not like, or when you cannot do what you want to do.

*To his considerable annoyance, Francis did not accept the idea
immediately.*
*'Why didn't you tell me?' Jimmie failed to keep the annoyance out of
his voice.*

Irritation can be used with the same meaning as **annoyance**.
However, it is more often used if something you do not like goes
on for a long time.

I still felt an increasing irritation as I watched her.
*They remain a source of constant irritation to both mother and
father.*

another, other, others

Another thing or person of a particular kind means one more thing or person of that kind. **Another** is usually followed by a singular count noun or the pronoun 'one'.

Rick pulled out another camera.
I imagine somebody like you could have easily found another job.
She had one plateful and then went back for another one.

You can use **another** with 'few' or a number that is larger than one.

Within another few minutes reports of attacks began to come in.
The woman lived for another ten days.
They raised another £15,000 for Roskill.

Another thing or person also means a different thing or person from the one you have been talking about.

It all happened in another country.
He mentioned the work of another colleague, John Lyons.

Another can also be used as a pronoun.

She ate in one place, and I ate in another.
...one tin of pink paint and another of brown.

When you want to refer to more than one type of person or thing, you use **other**. **Other** is followed by a plural count noun, or occasionally by an uncount noun.

Other boys were appearing now.
There was certainly other evidence.

When you are talking about two people or things and have already referred to one of them, you refer to the second one as **the other** or **the other one**.

They had two little daughters, one a baby, the other a girl of twelve.
He blew out one of his candles and moved the other one.

When you are talking about several people or things and have already referred to one or more of them, you usually refer to the remaining ones as **the others.**

Jack and the others paid no attention.
First, concentrate on the important tasks, then move on to the others.

When you have been talking about some people or things of a particular type, you refer to more people or things of this type as **others.**

Some writers are greater than others.
One policeman was stabbed and three others received minor injuries.

Other is also used after determiners such as 'the', 'some', or 'any' and after numbers. When it is used in this way it is usually followed by a singular or plural count noun.

He was stopped by a policeman who had posted himself on the other side of the door to our room.
Chris is crying hard and people look over from the other tables.
I love my son like any other mother does.
The Hogans were there, and three other couples all from the English Department.

apart, away

If two people or things are **apart,** there is a distance between them. You can also use **apart** to say what the distance between them is. For example, they might be three metres **apart** or fifty centimetres **apart.** You use **apart** when you are thinking about people or things together or as a unit, although there is a distance between them.

Stand with your feet just slightly apart.
I was sitting somewhat apart from the rest.
300 black women got together from places as far apart as Birmingham, Brighton and Leeds.
Main crop potatoes should be planted 14 inches (35 cm) apart.

If something is **away** from another person or thing, it is at a distance from them. You can also use **away** to say what the distance between them is. For example, if something is two kilometres **away,** you mean that it is two kilometres from yourself or from somewhere you have mentioned. You use **away** when you are thinking about the people or things separately and not as a unit.

I have to inspect a building in a little village away from the main roads.
Fleet Street is only a few yards away.
And there, some twenty miles away, was the Central Tower of Paine.

● If you say that someone is **away,** you mean that they are not at work or not at school because they are ill or on holiday.

apologize

apologize, excuse oneself

If you **apologize** to someone, you say that you are sorry for doing something that they disapprove of, that upsets them, or that causes them trouble.

He apologized for interrupting her and quickly left.
Indeed not more than a week after her terrible accusations she apologized to Michael for what she had said.
'If I hurt you, I'm sorry.'—'Don't apologize.'

If you **excuse yourself,** you give reasons to justify something that you have done and that other people might disapprove of. These reasons are often not very good ones.

She was late for work every morning and excused herself by saying that she had overslept.
What a fool he'd been to send her that expensive scarf to excuse himself for not having kept the appointment.

● Note that you also **excuse yourself** when you explain that you have to leave someone to go somewhere else.

The doorbell rings. Lewis excuses himself and pushes through the crowd.

apparently, obviously

You use **apparently** to emphasize that you are repeating information that you have heard, but that you do not know is definitely true.

Mr Andersen is here and would like to see you for a few moments. Apparently it's rather urgent.
Did she really believe this? Apparently she did.
Apparently artists and directors alike donate their services.

You can also use **apparently** when you are describing how something seems to be, even though you are not sure that it is really like that.

There are cases where two apparently opposing views may both be correct.
He was systematically circling the block, stopping each time, apparently to make sure I was still upstairs.

You use **obviously** to emphasize that something is easily seen, noticed, or recognized.

He had obviously already taken his shower, as his hair was dark with water.

Fontane was obviously irritated but trying to be polite for Lucy's sake.
She was looking at him darkly and obviously wanting to speak.

You can also use **obviously** to introduce something that is easily understood.

This will obviously take some time and cost a great deal of money.
Obviously parents need to be sensible.

approve, approve of

If someone in authority **approves** a plan or action, they formally agree to it and say that it can happen. For example, if a committee **approves** a decision, it allows the decision to be acted on.

At least the idea is now accepted and has even been approved by Parliament.
Benn was reluctant to approve projects in case they might not be commercially viable.

If someone in authority **approves** something such as a building or a product, they say that they are satisfied with it and allow it to be used or sold. For example, if a drug **is approved,** doctors are allowed to treat patients with it.

...premises which have been approved by the local authority.

If you **approve of** an action or event, you are pleased that it has happened or is going to happen.

I don't like the whole idea, I didn't approve of this meeting.
His return to the office was widely approved of.

If you **approve of** a person or something such as a book or film, you like and admire them.

Do you think your father will approve of me?
He did not approve of my pictures.

argument, dispute

An **argument** is a disagreement between people who may or may not know each other. People are sometimes calm during an argument, but they can become angry.

He and David had been drawn into a ferocious argument.
Money is notorious for causing arguments in marriage.

argument

A **dispute** is a serious argument which can last for a long time.
Disputes often take place between organizations, political parties,
or countries. When used as a noun, **dispute** is pronounced
/dɪspjuːt/ or /dɪspjuːt/.

*Disputes over land boundaries, water rights, and debts are
commonplace.*
A similar dispute divided the party in 1975.

You can also talk about a **dispute** between individuals.

*Their dispute raged for a week, Cindy becoming bitchier as it
progressed.*

Dispute is also used as a verb. If you **dispute** a fact or a claim,
you state strongly that you think it is wrong. The verb **dispute** is
pronounced /dɪspjuːt/.

Some learned historians today dispute his conclusions.
He disputed the legality of the invasion.

arrive, reach

You use both **arrive** and **reach** to talk about coming to a
particular place, often during or at the end of a journey.

If you have already mentioned the place you are travelling to, you
can simply say you **arrive.** If you want to mention the place, you
use **arrive,** followed by 'at' or 'in' and the place name.

He was nearly the last to arrive.
They were due to arrive at London Airport at about one o'clock.
That was how I came to arrive in Lexington.

You can use **arrive** to emphasize being in a place rather than
travelling to it.

When I arrived in England I thought I knew English.

Reach is always followed by a noun or a pronoun referring to a
place.

The weather broke a few days after we reached Zermatt.
Guerrero knew that Flight Two would never reach its destination.

You can use **reach** to emphasize the effort or the long journey
required to get somewhere.

To reach it in nine days might not be easy.

Arrive at and **reach** can also be used to say that someone
eventually makes a decision or finds the answer to something.

It took us several hours to arrive at a decision.
They were unable to reach a decision.

arrogant, proud

You can describe someone as **arrogant** if they think that they are better than other people and behave in an unpleasant way towards them.

My husband was an arrogant, bullying little drunkard.
I think it would be arrogant if I tried to give any advice.

You can describe someone as **proud** if they have strong feelings of self-respect.

...millions of decent, proud, hard-working people.
He was a poor, but very proud old man.

You can also say that someone is **proud** of something they have or something they have done. This means that they think it is good and are pleased about it.

He was proud of his son-in-law.
We were all tired but proud of our efforts.

Proud can also be used with a similar meaning to **arrogant**. Someone who is **proud** thinks that they are better than other people and ignores the feelings or advice of others.

She was too proud to apologize.
She was proud and defiant.

artist, artiste

An **artist** is a person who draws, paints, or produces sculpture, either as a job or as a hobby.

Giotto had, more than any artist before him, the ability to make his figures look solid.
He took to sketching and thought of a career as an artist.

An **artist** is also a writer, or a performer or entertainer such as a musician, actor, or dancer.

Any artist wants an audience.
There are few film artists who can equal this Renaissance man for sheer cultural depth.

Artiste is an old-fashioned word for a professional entertainer such as a dancer, musician, or circus performer. Note that 'artiste' is not used to refer to classical musicians.

artist

He was the strong man in the acrobatic troupe, often taking the place of the usual artiste as bottom man in the 'human pyramid' act. Bal always called himself an artiste. He was a very small-time actor.

ashamed, embarrassed

If someone is **ashamed,** they feel guilty because they believe they have done something wrong or done something that other people will disapprove of. They are afraid of moral disapproval.

She was too ashamed to tell the family of Oliver's crimes.
Inside, she felt ashamed about being a failure.
But almost as my temper flared, I felt ashamed of my lack of control.

If someone is **embarrassed,** they feel upset because they think they have done something which makes them seem foolish. They think that other people will laugh at them or criticize them if they find out. They are afraid of social disapproval.

'Did you check the engine?'—'No,' Brody said, embarrassed.
I was extremely embarrassed that I had not learned a little Spanish before the trip.
She talked about how reluctant, even embarrassed, she had always been to express her deep feelings.

ask for, demand

You use **ask for** when you are reporting requests. When someone says that they want to be given something, you report this using **ask for.** For example, if a woman says 'Can I have an orange juice?', you report this as 'She **asked for** an orange juice'.

She asked for a drink of water.
No good artist who asked him for money was ever disappointed.
Robertson decided to ask for a job.

You use **demand** when reporting that someone has asked for something in a very forceful way and is determined to get it. For example, if a thief says 'Hand over the money', you report this as 'He **demanded** the money'.

They were demanding the resignation of the government.
...the fear that women may demand equal rights.
The policeman demanded to see their identity cards.

You can also use **demand** when you yourself are asking for something in a very forceful way.

I demand to see a doctor.
'I demand to know the meaning of this!' he screamed.

asleep, sleeping

You use **asleep** and **sleeping** to describe people when they sleep.

You only use **asleep** after a link verb like 'be' or in the phrase 'to fall **asleep**'.

Don't make any noise, Guy's asleep.
It is good, too, for babies to get used to falling asleep in their own bed.

When you use **sleeping** as an adjective, it comes in front of a noun.

The house was full of sleeping children.
Ginny stood looking down at her sleeping mother.

assent, consent

If you give your **assent** to something that has been proposed, or if a proposal has your **assent,** you agree to it.

Haldane acted in these talks with the full assent of Grey and the Foreign Office.
'Cocoa all round?' People murmured assent.
There is at least grudging assent to his rule.

If you give your **consent** to something, you give the permission that is needed for it to happen or be done.

I had to ring the education office to get official consent.
They ask for no-one's consent to come, they just arrive.
Have you the husband's consent to take this child out of the country?

You can also say that when a number of people all agree that something is the case, or that something should be done, they do it **by consent.**

The question of whether ordinary people can govern themselves by consent is still on trial.
By common consent they stopped.

Grammar

Assent and **consent** can also be used as verbs.

They all assented to the proposition.
If he and Belinda were to run away together, her father would consent to the marriage in order to avoid a scandal.

31

assignment, assignation

An **assignment** is a job that someone has been told to do, usually by an employer or a teacher.

John had an assignment as a photographer.
This was a straightforward public-relations job, an easy assignment for beginners.
She hastily set them another assignment before letting the class go.

An **assignation** is a secret meeting, usually between lovers. **Assignation** is an old-fashioned word.

The couple had made the assignation on the beach.

assist, attend

If you **assist** someone, you give them the help they need. For example, a nurse can **assist** a doctor, a guide can **assist** someone who needs information, or you can **assist** someone who has fallen by picking them up.

Two of his men assisted the midwife and the baby was born.
I enclose a simple map that may assist you.
He assisted her to the stool.

You use **attend** to talk about being present at an event such as a class or a meeting. You do not use 'assist' in this way.

Each day he walked several miles to attend his lectures.
I stopped off in London to attend a conference.

assurance, insurance

'Life **assurance**' is a system by which you pay money regularly to a company that then pays money to your relatives when you die. This sort of agreement is also often called 'life **insurance**'.

...all the developments in taxation, life assurance and investment.
A special form of life insurance would be well suited to this purpose.

You do not use 'assurance' to refer to a similar system by which you pay money to a company that then repays you if your property is lost, stolen, or damaged. A system like this is called **insurance**.

You should look into insurance to cover against theft or fire at your home.
The manager can advise you on travel insurance and probably arrange cover.

assure, ensure, insure

If you **assure** someone that something is true, you tell them it is definitely true, especially when they are worried or doubt that it is true. You can also **assure** someone of something, for example, a fact, your sincerity, or the importance of something.

He had been able to assure them that the schools would not close.
'You're wearing a wig.'—'I can assure you I'm not!'
A top official summoned some Americans to his office to assure them of their safety.

If you **ensure** that something happens, you do what is necessary to make it happen. Note that in American English, **ensure** can also be spelled **insure**.

The accounts department will ensure that your tax is paid.
Eating these foods ensures that they get enough vitamin C.
He would do whatever was necessary to ensure victory.

In British and American English, **insure** is normally used to talk about protecting against risks. If you **insure** your property, you pay money to an insurance company that agrees to pay money to you if your property is lost, damaged, or stolen. You can also **insure** yourself.

Insure your baggage before you leave home.
If you bring your bicycle you must have it insured against theft.
He insured himself against all eventualities.

avenge, revenge

If you avenge a wrong or harmful act, you hurt or punish the person who did it. **Avenge** is always a verb. You **avenge** a person who has been killed, **avenge** a murder, or **avenge** yourself.

When a man was killed, it was his family's duty to avenge him.
He muttered time and time again that he would avenge his father's death.
...a cold-blooded desire to avenge himself on all humanity.

If someone takes **revenge,** or does something **in revenge,** they hurt someone because that person has hurt them or someone they care about. **Revenge** is usually a noun.

What if Stein took revenge upon Breslow's daughter?
He will be safe from the dead man's relative who seeks revenge.
I suppose a more sensual woman would have taken a lover in revenge.

avenge

• **Revenge** is occasionally used as a verb. If you **revenge** yourself on someone who has hurt you, you hurt them in return.

That was how he could revenge himself on those people who had mocked and robbed him.

avoid, evade

If something is unpleasant or causes you trouble, you can try to **avoid** it or **evade** it.

If you **avoid** a place or a person, you do not go near them. If you **avoid** doing something, you do not do it, either because it is a bad thing to do or because you do not want to do it. If you **avoid** something such as illness or a problem, you take action in order to prevent it affecting you.

Why have you been avoiding me?
Try to avoid carrying more cash around with you than is necessary.
Human beings will avoid pain like any other animal.

If you **evade** something such as a duty, you manage not to do it. If you **evade** a problem, you do not deal with it. If you **evade** someone, you do not let them catch you or find you.

It might also be used as an excuse for evading our responsibilities.
Again Gordon evaded the question. 'I can't tell you that.'
Tim tried to hold her arm but she evaded him.

• Note that if you **avoid** tax, you find a legal way of paying less; if you **evade** tax, you do not pay it when you should.

Most private forest buyers are using it as a way of avoiding tax on large sums of money.
The real delinquents are people like you evading your tax.

B

baby, infant, child

A **baby** is a young human being during the very first months and years of life. Some people refer to three-year-olds as **babies,** but usually a **baby** is too young to walk or talk. English speakers often use the pronoun 'it' instead of 'he' or 'she' when talking about a baby.

When a baby is born the spine is curved backwards from head to pelvis.
...the ghastly non-stop racket that a healthy baby makes when it wants its food.

Infant is a fairly formal word which means the same as **baby.** Doctors and people writing about how to care for babies often call them **infants. Infant** can be used before another noun in expressions such as '**infant** health'. You do not normally call a baby an **infant,** but some writers use the word for stylistic effect or to suggest that the baby is behaving in an unpleasant way.

The human infant is uniquely helpless and slow to mature.
...infant foods.
In half a minute Mrs Taylor was back, carrying the screaming infant in her arms.

A **child** is a human being at any stage between birth and becoming an adult, especially before becoming a teenager.

The teachers adapt their understanding and method to suit the child.
Adults find it very hard to realize that young children have no regard for property.

Note that someone's **child** is their son or daughter of any age.

...grown-up children.

● In British English, an **infant** school is a school for children between the ages of five and seven. In a primary school, the **infants** are the children between the ages of five and seven.

back, backwards

You use **back** to talk about returning to a point where someone or something has been before. If you **go back,** you return to the place you left; often this place is mentioned.

I had lent my apartment to a friend for the weekend and when I got back I found that the reading lamp would not work.
Days later, I came back to the spot.
No, I'm not going back inside.

If someone moves **backwards,** they move in the opposite direction to the one that they are facing.

He was jerked off his feet and dragged backwards.
So the hummingbird can hover and even fly backwards.

back

You use either **back** or **backwards** to talk about moving to a position behind you without turning round.

Then they stepped back, laughing with triumphant pleasure.
'And the Russians, of course,' he said, rocking back comfortably on his stool.
She stepped backwards onto a coffee cup.
Stuart moved backwards into a corner.

back, rear

The part of a building or a vehicle that is furthest from the front can be called either the **back** or the **rear**.

Rear is often used in technical descriptions. For example, car manuals talk about the **rear** of a car.

He decided to approach the house from the rear instead of going to the front door.

It is more usual to use **back**. For example, in ordinary conversation people talk about the **back** of a car, not the 'rear'.

...in the back of the dark cab, with the lights of the city streaking past.
Lang and Colonel von Tempelhof sat in the back.

Both words are also used as adjectives.

There was a rear entrance into the post office.
...a suitcase on the back seat.

You use **back** to talk about the part of an object that is at the opposite end to the front. You do not use 'rear'.

He pulled his cap down more warmly over his ears and the back of his head.
Mimi had Carter held by the back of his trousers.

● Your **back** is the part of your body that is behind you, from your neck to your bottom.

● Your **rear** is your bottom; this is a humorous use.

bag, baggage, luggage

Both British and American speakers can refer to everything that travellers carry as their **bags**. American speakers can also call any individual suitcase or similar item a **bag**.

'Let me carry those for you,' he said as I picked up the bags.

She got out on the sidewalk and the porter took her bags.
It was a fact that an airline passenger's bag could not be counted on to arrive safely at Pine Bluff, Arkansas.

Speakers of British English normally use **luggage** when they are talking about everything that travellers carry. However, they sometimes use **baggage** when they are talking about travelling in a technical way, for example when discussing airports or travel insurance.

There are also coin-operated lockers in which you may leave luggage.
If you lose any of your luggage, enquire at once at the Lost Property Office.
Your baggage, clothing and personal effects are covered up to one thousand pounds.

In American English, **luggage** refers to empty bags and suitcases. **Baggage** refers to bags and suitcases with their contents.

He pulls in behind a Citroen with a Paris license, takes out his baggage, and locks the car.

Note that there is no plural form of **baggage** or **luggage**.

bar, pub

A **bar** is a place where you can buy alcoholic and non-alcoholic drinks. A **bar** can be part of a larger building such as a hotel or theatre, or in America it can be a separate building.

He called for the menu and ordered in the bar while they were finishing their drinks.
Willie paid for the drinks and they left the bar.
He eventually selected a small bar calling itself the Pussycat Go-go.

A **pub** is a building where you can buy alcoholic and non-alcoholic drinks. Most **pubs** are in Britain and Ireland. They often contain two or more **bars** and have an important role in the social life of the people nearby. Pubs are rarely found in America.

The Black Friar, lavishly appointed with Art Nouveau decoration, is the best pub of its kind in London.
We all met in the pub during the lunch break.

Both **pubs** and **bars** have a counter where drinks are poured and this is also called a **bar**.

He ordered a whisky and drained it standing at the bar.

base

base, basis

The **base** of an object is its lowest part, where it begins, or where it touches the ground or a surface.

We reached the base of the volcano.
...a small hole at the base of the cylinder.

A **base** for a system of ideas or a subject of study is the foundation from which other ideas or more advanced studies are developed.

...the compulsory base on which post-school education rests.
Society is natural and has a spiritual base.
Marx came to describe the economy as a base, or structure, upon which a superstructure was erected consisting of such elements as law, politics, philosophy, etc.

The **basis** of or for something is the central and most important part of it, from which it has been or can be further developed.

The court is quite satisfied that there is no basis for these criticisms.
This figure has been adopted as the basis for the Government's longer-term planning in higher education.
This was the basis of the final design.

The word **bases** is pronounced /beɪsɪz/ when it is the plural of **base** and /beɪsiːz/ when it is the plural of **basis**.

...lamps with bases like blunt instruments.
It is possible to explain the biological bases for man's seemingly altruistic behaviour.

bath, bathe

A **bath** is a long, low container that you fill with water and sit in to wash yourself. Bath is pronounced /bɑːθ/.

He leaped out of the bath and grabbed a towel.
The bathroom had two basins, a huge bath and more towels than I had ever seen.

If you **bath** someone, or give them a **bath,** you wash them in a bath.

She will show you how to bath the baby.
I wonder if you'd give the children a bath?

You do not say that people 'bath' themselves. British speakers say that someone has a **bath** and American speakers say that someone takes a **bath** or, more formally, that they **bathe**. Bathe is pronounced /beɪð/.

I had a bath and then I shaved.
Welch was about to take a bath.
I found myself running up the stairs to bathe.

In British English, when someone **bathes,** they swim or play in a
lake or river or in the sea. This use is rather old-fashioned. It is
more common to say that someone 'swims' or 'goes for a swim'.

He loved to stay at Oxford and bathe in the river.
It is dangerous to bathe in the sea here.

Bathe can also be used with a direct object, when it means to
gently wash something. For example, you can **bathe** a wound or
bathe someone's eyes.

She really wanted to bathe his eyes because they looked bloodshot.

Other words

American speakers of English call a **bath** a 'bathtub' or 'tub'.

I spent hours in the warmth of the bathtub.
I lowered myself deeper into the tub.

because, as, since, for

You can use **because, as, since,** or **for** to give an explanation for
something or to explain why you say something.

Because is the most commonly used word for giving a reason or
motive for something. If someone asks a question beginning with
'Why?', you can reply using **because.**

'I said I wouldn't go.'—'Why?'—'Because I didn't want to leave you.'
'Why shouldn't I come?'—'Because you're too busy.'

If you have said that something is the case and you want to say
why it is the case, you usually add a reason clause beginning with
because.

*She finally walked off and caught the bus, because she could not
really afford to pay both Eileen and a taxi.*
I couldn't see Helen's expression, because her head was turned.

You can also use **as** or **since** to introduce a reason clause,
especially in writing.

*A brief note on The National Portrait Gallery's character is
necessary, as the word 'Gallery' can be misleading.*
*I realized it wouldn't be in my interests to deceive him since I
planned to deal with his bank for many years.*

because

The reason clause is sometimes put first.

As they have been on the winning side, they may have temptations to extend their borders.
Since evaporated milk is about twice the strength of fresh milk, you always dilute it with at least an equal amount of water.

If you want to say that there is a special reason for something, you can use words like 'especially' or 'particularly' in front of **as** or **since.** When you do this, you put the reason clause after the main clause.

I was frightened when I went to bed, especially as my room was so far up.
It was nice to have someone to talk to, particularly as it looked as if I was going to be there all night.

In stories, **for** is used to explain or justify something that has just been said. This is an old-fashioned use.

After a while he seems to feel the need of company again, for he suddenly scrambles back into the kitchen.
The diet we gave her seemed satisfactory, for she grew well.

become, become of

You use **become** to talk about changes and developments. If you **become** ill, you start to be ill after being healthy. If something **becomes** necessary, it is necessary now but was not necessary before.

When that happens, people become jealous.
When Uncle Nick was told about this, he became very quiet.
In less than a year Long Beach became the most crime-free town of its size in the United States.

If you ask what **has become of** somebody or something, you want to know what has happened to them.

He was a most diligent little man. The librarian wondered whatever had become of him.
What then becomes of the country's concept of national security?

before, in front of

You use **before** to talk about something that happens at an earlier time than something else.

I woke well before dawn.
He thought for a moment before he spoke.

If someone or something is **in front of** a particular thing, they are further forward than it is.

He stood there, in front of the desk, chewing at his moustache.
Stopping in front of the aluminium gate, she got out and unlocked the chain.

You can use **before** to mean the same as **in front of.** This is a formal or old-fashioned use.

He saw now suddenly before him the face of Guy.
The tea had been set before them.

begin, start, commence

If you **begin, start,** or **commence** something, you do it from a particular time.

There is little difference in meaning between these words, but **commence** is used in formal English. It is not used in conversation.

I had been asked to chat to the kids before they began lessons for the day.
As they saw him coming they began to dance.
The meeting, then, is ready to begin.
He tore the list from the pad and started a fresh list.
Mrs Bixby put a hand up to her mouth and started backing away.
The war started between England and France.
Students may commence a two-year Training Study in a chosen activity.
The space-probe commenced taking a series of photographs.

Start has some special meanings which are not shared by 'begin' or 'commence'. You can use **start** to say that someone makes an engine or machine begin to work. You can also use **start** to say that someone creates a business or other organization. In stories, **start** is used to say that someone begins to move in a particular direction.

He couldn't get his engine started.
He scraped up enough money to start his Hollywood restaurant.
They started down the street together.

Grammar

Note that **commence** cannot be used with a 'to'-infinitive. You can **begin** to do something, or **start** to do it, but you cannot 'commence' to do it.

41

believe, believe in

If you **believe** something, you are convinced that it is true, even if you cannot prove it logically. You can **believe** a claim, **believe** that something will happen, or **believe** that something should be done.

No one ever believes the official answer.
I believed that I was at the beginning of a great adventure.
The Government believes that such powers are essential.

If you **believe in** God, you believe that God exists. If you **believe in** ghosts, you believe that there are ghosts. If you **believe in** something such as a system, you think that it works. If you **believe in** doing something, you think that it is the right thing to do.

It's natural to think of Europeans who believed in ghosts as ignorant.
Elaine believes in love.
The Kirks are a modern couple, and believe in dividing all tasks equally down the middle.

beside, besides

If one thing is **beside** another, it is next to it or at the side of it.

His mother sat beside him, clutching her handbag.
Beside the shed was a huge wire birdcage.

Besides means 'in addition to' or 'as well as'.

What languages do you know besides Arabic and English?
Is there anything else wrong besides her heart?
The farm possessed three horses besides Clover.
Besides its own publications the works have handled many other magazines.

Besides can also be used as an adverb meaning 'in addition to the thing just mentioned'.

He needed so much else besides.

between, among, amongst

You use **between** to talk about anything that separates two people or things, for example a distance, space, object, person, point, or place.

...an area between Mars and Jupiter.

...the wide expanse of short grass between the lake and the great house.
...the Orange River boundary between the Free State and the Eastern Province.

You use **among** or **amongst** to talk about a person or thing that is surrounded by more than two other people or things. **Amongst** is less common.

The house stood unfenced in green grass among grazing black-faced sheep.
Stephanie moved amongst the guests, thanking people for things.

Note that if someone or something is **between** things or people, the things or people are on either side of them. If someone or something is **among** or **amongst** things or people, the things or people are all around them.

He sat silently for a while, staring down at the glass between his hands.
The canvas bag was standing on the floor between us.
...the sound of a wood pigeon cooing among the trees.

● You can talk about relationships **between** or **among** people or things. You can also talk about arguments or discussions **between** or **among** people. You use **between** when there are two people or things. You normally use **among** or **amongst** when there are more than two.

This raised important questions about the relationship between the state and the public sector.
...the similarities between the two situations.
She had already caused considerable rivalry among the men.
There is a striking similarity among the wall paintings throughout these regions.
...an argument between his mother and another Polish woman.
...an opportunity to discuss policy and educational issues amongst themselves.

big, large, great

Big, large, and **great** can all be used to talk about size. They can all be used in front of count nouns, but only **great** can be used in front of uncount nouns.

Big is the word you usually use in conversation.

'Where?'—'Over there, by that big tree.'
Ellen had a big bag of eggs.

big

Large is more formal than **big**.

Except in large cities, specialist bookshops for children's literature are few.
Countries which are planning to build medium-sized and/or large wind turbines over the next few years include France and Holland.

You can use **big,** but not 'large', to suggest that something is important or impressive.

Chicago is to him the Big Town.
...his influence over the big advertisers.

You normally use **great** to emphasize the importance of someone or something.

...the great English master of classical architecture, Inigo Jones.

However, **great** can also be used to emphasize size and impressiveness.

...the beach of a great curving bay in the west of England.
Gardens lay wasted in order that great office blocks and car parks might take their place.

Both **big** and **great** can be used to emphasize the intensity of something. **Great** is preferred in formal writing.

You must find this a big change from the Navy, Mr Rutland.
Most of them act like big fools.
He switched from one task to another with great difficulty.
Effective analysis and recognized techniques can bring about a great improvement.

You use **large** or **great** to describe amounts. You do not use 'big'.

She made a very large amount of money.
...drugs taken in large quantities.
Young people consume great quantities of chips.

blame, fault

If someone gets the **blame** for something wrong, they are criticized by other people for being responsible for it.

He had to take the blame.
The blame for this situation lies solely with the government.
The point is to find out who was responsible. Whether they deserve blame is a separate matter.

A **fault** is a bad feature of a person's character or a system.

I knew my past much better than she did – and my faults.

His only fault was a tendency to repeat himself.
Computer faults are commonplace.
...the National Health Service, with all its faults.

If you want to say that someone is responsible for something that is wrong, you can say either that they are **to blame** for it or that it is their **fault.**

In this way, attention is drawn away from who is to blame for these attacks.
I know you love me and that none of this is your fault.

If you say that someone who is in a difficult situation 'has only themselves **to blame**', you mean that it is entirely their fault.

He has only himself to blame for his predicament.

Blame is also a verb. If you **blame** someone or something for something wrong or bad, you say that they are responsible for it or that they caused it.

I was blamed for the theft.
Violence at school is blamed on immigrants.

bonnet, hood

In British English, the metal cover over the engine at the front of a car is called the **bonnet.**

Slowly he climbed out, unlocked the boot and laid the rucksack on the bonnet.
I unlocked the boot and laid the tools on the bonnet.

In American English, this cover is called the **hood.**

Patrick gets out of the car, opens the hood, and peers into it.
...the raised hood, under which I had bent to watch the mechanic at work.

In both British and American English, a **bonnet** can also be a type of hat tied under the chin. In former times, **bonnets** were worn by women, but nowadays only babies' hats are referred to as **bonnets.**

Rhoda was wearing a bonnet and a kind of long travelling cape.

In both British and American English, a **hood** is also a part of a coat or jacket which can be pulled up over your head to protect you from bad weather.

The weather had turned so cold that I had to bicycle with the hood of my anorak pulled up over my little orange hat.

border, boundary, frontier

A **border** is a line that separates two countries or other political regions such as states or counties.

Stanley wanted to spend the night across the Florida border.
...his parents' crumbling ancestral home somewhere on the Welsh border.
So, legally or illegally, they crossed the border.

A **boundary** is a line that separates any two areas, for example towns, farms, or countries.

Matthews showed us a fine old hedge which once marked the parish boundary.
In international law, three miles is generally taken to be the boundary of a country's airspace.

You refer to a border as a **frontier** when it is guarded and separates countries which have different political systems or are in dispute about something.

Military activity on the frontier diverted troops from their internal security role.
I have to get off the train at the frontier and cross on foot between the guard posts.

A **frontier** can also be a limit beyond which nobody has explored or established political rights.

Space will not be the last frontier, it will simply be the next frontier.

bored, boring

If you are **bored** with what you are doing, you are not interested in it and wish that you were doing something else.

We were all bored with the prospect of another day's school.
I could never be bored with football.

You can also say that you are **bored** when you feel that you have nothing to do and wish that you were doing something.

She said she was bored just hanging around the house with the kid.
Bored, he joined an amateur theatre group for something to do in the evenings.

An activity or person that is **boring** makes you feel bored.

For me the most boring task is cleaning the machine.

Later on, when a lecturer was boring, one could entertain oneself with one's own thoughts.
'Was it a boring journey?' I asked.

borrow, lend

If you **borrow** something that belongs to someone else, you take it, usually with their permission. You intend to return it some time in the future.

Early the next morning he borrowed his hostess's car.
Jeremy had to borrow a cloth from the barman.
Father, I need to borrow five thousand dollars.

If you **lend** something you own to someone else, you allow them to have it or use it for a period of time. The past tense and past participle of **lend** is **lent. Lend** is often followed by two objects.

Betty lent him some blankets.
He had lent Tim the money.
I'd be grateful if you wouldn't lend them to students.

Both **borrow** and **lend** can be used without objects, especially when you are talking about money.

So the poor had to borrow from the rich.
Banks will not lend to them.

Other words

The noun related to **lend** is **loan.**

The government had to make a further loan of £3.3m to save the industry.

The verb **loan** has a similar meaning to **lend. Loan** is used mainly in American English.

I'll loan you fifty dollars.

box, carton, crate

A **box** is a square or rectangular container used for packing objects. **Boxes** are usually made of cardboard or wood. Some are open, some have a separate lid, others close with a set of overlapping flaps.

He packed up his stock in cardboard boxes.

In American English, a **carton** is a cardboard box used for packing things.

box

Hi-fis should be specially packed in the cartons in which they arrived.

In British and American English, a **carton** is also a closed cardboard or plastic container used for food or drink.

I drank more milk from the carton I had opened.
...eating ice cream directly out of the carton.

A **crate** is a box made from thin strips of wood.

...a large wooden crate.

A **crate** is also a box divided up into sections for individual items and made of wood, plastic, or metal.

Empty bottles chinked as the milkman put them into his wire crate.

brand, make, type

The **brand** of a product such as soap or tea is the name given to it by the firm that makes it. One firm may make several brands of a particular product. **Brands** are usually products which do not last for a long time.

There used to be so many different brands of tea.
Stein was most particular about soap and he had used this particular brand for over twenty years.

The **make** of a car or of an electric appliance such as a radio or washing machine is the name of the company that makes it. You use **make** to refer to products which last for a long time.

...tests on different makes of car to establish resistance to bodywork stress.
She can spot the make of typewriter a secretary is using.

If you talk about what **type** of product you want, you are saying what features it should have and what quality it should be. You do not only talk about **types** of goods; you can also talk about **types** of people or abstract things.

You will have to decide which type of pram to choose.
With a certain type of actor that method can be quite effective.
It's a new type of bank account for young people and children.

Note that if you ask someone what **type** of car they have, they could reply, for example, 'a saloon' or 'an estate'. If you ask what **make** of car someone has, they could reply, for example, 'Ford' or 'Toyota'.

bread, loaf

Bread is a type of food made from a mixture of flour, water, and yeast, and baked in an oven.

Her diet consisted of bread and a handful of lentils.
Garroway broke off another piece of bread and chewed at it.

Bread that has been baked in one large piece is called a **loaf.** The plural of **loaf** is **loaves.**

...a loaf of fairly fresh bread.
I like to get hold of a new loaf and tear the end crust off it and eat it.

● You do not talk about 'breads' unless you mean different types of bread, for example breads made with different types of flour.

breath, breathe

Your **breath** is the air that you take into your lungs and let out again, or the way air flows in and out of your lungs. If you **take a breath,** you make air go into your lungs. **Breath** is a noun and is pronounced /breθ/.

She took a deep breath.
He bent down and blew on the coal steadily with his own breath.
She paused for breath.

When you **breathe,** you make air flow in and out of your lungs. You **breathe** in to make the air go in, and you **breathe** out to make the air go out. Breathe is a verb and is pronounced /briːð/.

Just breathe deeply and try to relax.
Breathe in a relaxed way, expanding your abdomen fully as you breathe in.

briefly, shortly

You use **briefly** to talk about things that happen for only a short period of time. For example, if you see someone **briefly,** you do not see them for very long. If you stay somewhere **briefly,** you stay there just for a short time.

The two men had met briefly once before.
The Duke proposed to stay there briefly to rest his troops.

If you explain something **briefly,** you use very few words or give very few details.

briefly

She told them briefly what had happened.
Stephanie wrote briefly and delicately to Mrs Orton, suggesting a visit.

You use **shortly** and not 'briefly' to say when something happens. If something happens **shortly** after something else, it happens soon after it.

Shortly after the break I was driven back to the hotel.
She died shortly afterwards.
When I informed her we were shortly to sail for New York, she looked distressed and bewildered.

You can also say that something happens **shortly** before something else. This is a slightly old-fashioned use.

It happened shortly before my seventeenth birthday.

● If you speak **shortly** to someone, you speak in an impatient or slightly angry way.

'Good-bye, and thanks!' said Miss Jackson somewhat shortly, pushing open the wet gate.
'Naturally,' I said shortly.

bring, take

If you **bring** a person or thing with you when you come to a place, you have them with you.

Why haven't you brought me here before?
Be friendly and hospitable when your child brings others home to play.
Please bring your calculator to every lesson.

If you ask someone to **bring** you something, you are asking them to carry or move it to the place where you are.

Bring me a glass of Dubonnet.
Bring down a pair of nice, warm socks and a towel for Mr Jordache.

If you **take** a person or thing with you when you go to a place, you have them with you.

She gave me some books to take home.
It's a lovely house – he took me over to see it the other day.
There are limits on the amount of money you can take abroad.
She took the suitcase inside and left it in the corridor.

British, English

British describes people and things that come from anywhere in the United Kingdom, which includes England, Wales, Scotland, and Northern Ireland.

Some British scientists have dismissed this evidence as 'poor science'.
If you hold a current British passport, a visa is not required for entry into Greece.

British is also used to describe anything to do with the administration of the United Kingdom and in the names of national organizations.

Mr Georgiadis is a naturalized British citizen of Greek origin.
...a lecture at the British Association for the Advancement of Science.

The **British** are the people who live in the United Kingdom.

Compromise is one of the basic principles and virtues of the British.

English describes people and things that come from England.

Mr Jumperwala told her some amusing anecdotes about the English aristocracy.
...the pleasures of the English countryside.

The **English** are the people who live in England.

...in 1850 when the English, like the Californians of today, had more money than sense.

Note that you should not use 'English' to describe people or things from other parts of the United Kingdom.

brought, bought

Brought is the past tense and past participle of the verb **bring**. If you say 'He **brought** his dog', you mean that he had his dog with him when he came.

My secretary brought my mail to the house.
He was glad someone had brought a camera.

Bought is the past tense and past participle of the verb **buy**. If you say 'She **bought** a newspaper', you mean she obtained a newspaper by paying money for it.

I bought myself a piece of chocolate cake.
She bought a piano.

bus, coach

In British English, a **bus** is a large vehicle which takes passengers on journeys in a town or city, or to towns or villages not far away. **Buses** can have either one or two floors or 'decks'. They stop at '**bus** stops'.

You can take the Victoria line to Walthamstow and walk or catch a bus to the door.
I'm waiting for the bus back to town.

In British English, a **coach** is a comfortable bus which takes passengers on long journeys between towns and cities, either as a regular route, or as a special journey for a school or a group of holidaymakers.

You may be able to travel by coach from Victoria Coach Station.
...various excursions, including coach trips and day trips to nearby Turkey.

In American English, both types of vehicle are referred to as **buses.**

Each day plain-clothes men rode the buses and subways.
...riding effortlessly over the plain in a Greyhound bus.

Other words

In informal British English, a bus with two decks is called a **double-decker bus** or a **double-decker.**

...the large number of double-decker London Transport buses.

by, from

When you are talking about the author of a book or play, you say that the book is **by** someone or written **by** someone.

...three books by a great Australian writer.
...a collection of pieces by Mozart.

When talking about the person who has written you a letter or sent a message to you, you say that the letter or message is **from** that person.

A few days later in Chicago the Capones received a message from Vito Corleone.

C

café, cafeteria, wine bar

A **café** is a place where you can get light meals, cakes, and drinks. In Britain **cafés** do not usually sell alcoholic drinks. In **cafés** your order is usually brought to your table by a waiter or waitress.

We went down to the café to have tea and sandwiches.
Paul Gazengel opened up his café as usual, although there was almost no business.

Note that **cafés** in France and the rest of Europe sell alcoholic drinks.

...the glasses of wine which he consumed in the café before dinner.

A **cafeteria** is a place which serves meals. Customers take their food from a counter on a tray and pay for it at a cash desk. Colleges, offices, and factories often have a **cafeteria** where students and employees can eat.

...a breakfast of boiled eggs and orange juice and coffee at the dorm cafeteria.

In Britain, a **wine bar** is a place which serves wine by the glass. Unlike a pub, it does not usually sell beer, but it does sell non-alcoholic drinks. It usually also serves meals. You can either drink at the bar or have your order brought to your table by a waiter or waitress.

She works three evenings a week in a wine bar.
I usually go to a wine bar just along the road.

can, could, be able to

Can, could, and **be able to** are all used to talk about a person's ability to do something. They are followed by the infinitive form of a verb.

You use **can** or a present form of **be able to** to talk about ability in the present. **Can** is more common, especially in speech.

You can all read and write.
I'm no writer but I can draft a lecture or a report that's reasonably lucid.
The rattlesnake is able to detect the presence of a small ground squirrel.

53

can

You use **could** or a past form of **be able to** to talk about ability in the past.

He could run faster than anyone else.
He was able to answer a few questions.

You use **be able to** and not 'could' to say that someone managed to do something at a particular time.

After treatment he was able to return to work.
Dr Brancale had been able to get to Boston only late the night before.

You use 'will' or 'shall' with **be able to** to talk about ability in the future.

He will be able to provide accurate, detailed information for you.
One day, perhaps, I'll be able to explain.

If you want to modify a statement about someone's ability, you often use **be able to** after a modal such as 'may' or 'should'. You do not use 'can' or 'could' after another modal.

We may be able to save him.
A man in good health should be able to go without external oxygen for at least a minute.
I might be able to help you.
You would not be able to drive to inland cities alone here.

After verbs such as 'want', 'hope', or 'expect' which must be followed by a 'to'-infinitive, you use **be able to** and not 'can' or 'could'.

I hope to be able to have wonderful touring holidays.
You're foolish to expect to be able to do that.
As a driver you have to be able to drive, obviously.

Can and **could** are also used to talk about possibility. You do not use 'be able to' in this way.

You use **could** when you are saying that something is possible on a particular occasion.

Don't eat it. It could be a toadstool.
300,000 jobs could be lost.

You use **can** when you are saying that, in general, something is possible.

Such shifts in opinion can sometimes have a snowball effect.
Too much salt can be harmful to a young baby.
The press tell me he can appear insecure when dealing with them.

To talk about possibility in the past, you use **could have** followed by a past participle.

It could have been worse.
He could have been doing research on his own.

Can is also used to talk about what is allowed by rules, or what someone is willing to let another person do. When you are referring to what was allowed in the past, you use **could** rather than 'can'.

No student can be admitted to a first degree until he has completed full-time attendance for at least three university sessions.
They can leave at any time.
We could go to any part of the island we wanted.

Can and **could** are often used for asking permission or for making requests.

Can I take out a card please?
Could we put this fire on?
Can you send me three new men out there right now?

Could, but not 'can', is used for making suggestions.

You could phone her and ask.
'Well, what shall we do?'—'You could try Ebury Street.'

canal, channel

A **canal** is a long, narrow stretch of water that has been specially built, usually to enable barges or ships to sail inland.

In summer, boat trips go east down the canal to Regent's Park.
...the construction of a canal linking the Pacific and Atlantic oceans.

A **channel** is a route in the sea or in a large river along which ships can sail.

The Russian tankers finding their way up the channel occasionally lodge fast.
The main channels had been closed by enemy submarines.

A **channel** is also a small passage along which water can flow.

The river had now assumed a new character, racing through a single channel between tree-clad banks.
...irrigation channels.

cancel, postpone, delay

If you **cancel** an arrangement or an appointment, you stop it from happening. You usually do not make any new arrangements.

The airport closed again. All flights were cancelled to and from Glasgow.
The performances were cancelled because the leading man was ill.

If you **postpone** an arrangement or an appointment, you make new arrangements for it to happen at a later time.

The flight has been postponed until eleven o'clock.
Could you postpone your departure for five minutes?

If you **delay** something that has been arranged, you make it happen later than planned.

Try and persuade them to delay some of the changes.
The flight had been delayed one hour, due to weather conditions.

If something **delays** you, you start or finish something later than you planned.

Suppose there is some accident which delays you.
I'm afraid I was slightly delayed.

Other words

English also uses a number of phrasal verbs to express the idea of doing things at a later time or not at all. For example, if you **cancel** a meeting, you can also say that you 'call it off'. If you **postpone** a meeting, you 'put it off'. If a meeting **is delayed,** it is 'held up'. Phrasal verbs are more common in speech than in written English.

capacity, capability

The **capacity** of something is the amount that it can hold or produce.

The pipeline has a capacity of 1.2 million barrels a day.
In all countries military security requires economic capacity to be developed.

A person's **capacity** is their ability to do something well.

Monty, as I soon realised, had no more capacity for figures than Jeremy had.
If a man is self-employed, he can adjust his performance to his capacities.

The **capability** of a country, machine, or person is their ability to do a particular thing.

This constitutes a strong argument for maintaining a retaliatory capability.
The Tornado, with its ultralow flying capability, presented the Warsaw Pact with severe problems.
Every advance in medical capabilities is an increase in our moral responsibility.
She may worry about her capabilities as a parent.

carefree, careless, careful

If you are **carefree,** you do not have any cares or worries and therefore feel happy and able to enjoy life.

Before her marriage she had been lively and alert and carefree.
He was aware of a glorious carefree feeling of joy.

If you are **careless,** you do something badly because you are not giving enough attention to it.

...if your courier is careless and leaves the coach unlocked.
He was careless and inefficient and drank too much.

If you are **careful,** you do things properly and with a lot of attention. **Careful** is the opposite of **careless.**

I showered slowly, being careful not to wet my sore face.
He watched all this with the most careful attention.

carpet, rug

A **carpet** is a thick heavy covering for a floor. It is usually large and covers most of the floor. A 'fitted **carpet**' covers the floor completely.

The floor was visible through the holes in the carpet.
He asked what the marks were on the stair carpet.

A **rug** is a fairly small carpet which can easily be moved. **Rugs** are often placed on top of a large carpet.

It was sparsely furnished, with a few brightly coloured rugs.
...Oriental rugs.

carry, lift

When you **carry** something, you move it from one place to another without letting it touch the ground.

carry

They carry the packing case up the stairs and into the bedroom.
The students carried banners.

When you **lift** something, you move it upwards with your hands.
After you have **lifted** it, you may **carry** it to a different place.

He jumped out of the cab to lift the two heavy suitcases from the boot.
The colonel lifted his cup, glared at it, set it down again.

carry, wear

When you **carry** something, you move it from one place to another without letting it touch the ground.

'I can't carry any more wood,' said Eric. 'I'm tired.'
The man got up and sauntered through, carrying an open beer can.
I carried my dancing shoes in a little box.

When you are dressed in your clothes you say that you **are wearing** them. You do not say that you 'carry' clothes or shoes when you are dressed in them.

She wore a plaid shirt, blue jeans and sneakers.
He is a dynamic little man who wears a bow tie.
He wore green suede shoes.

cave, cavern, cellar, basement

A **cave** is an opening in rock, for example in the side of a cliff or a mountain, and can be large or small. In prehistoric times, people lived in **caves**.

...a large collection of caves known as the Blue Grotto.
The cliffs are riddled with caves and almost every one shows some sign of ancient habitation.

A **cavern** is a very large cave, usually underground.

Gradually the underground caverns fill up with deposits.

Areas below ground in buildings are called **cellars** or **basements**. **Cellars** are often used for storing things that are no longer wanted or that are not used very often.

I decided to return the unwanted books to the cellar.

A **basement** is designed to be used regularly or lived in. Department stores often have **basements,** and some restaurants and bars are in **basements**.

*He stopped outside the door leading down to the basement, where
Dr Firmius lived.*

certainly, surely

You use **certainly** to emphasize that what you say is definitely
true.

*He had probably been employed at Cluny and he certainly worked
at Vezelay.*
It's certainly not accidental spillage.

You use **surely** for emphasis, especially when you are objecting to
something that has been said or done, or when you are expressing
surprise that other people do not agree with you.

But surely, Hamo, you care about what happens to your work?
*Academics tend to use 'journalism' as a dirty word, but surely some
of the best writers have been journalists.*
*Eva Crane must surely be one of the world's best known experts on
bee keeping.*

Both British and American speakers of English use **certainly** to
agree to a request, or to agree with what someone has said.
American speakers also use **surely** in this way.

*'Would you agree that it is still a difficult world for women to live
in?'—'Oh, certainly.'*
*He asked if he might be allowed to hear one of her records. 'Why
surely, Daniel!'*

cheque, check

In British English, the forms that people use to pay money from
their bank accounts are called **cheques.**

Mrs Bradley wrote a cheque and gave it to the vicar.

In American English, this word is spelled **check.**

She had been receiving a check for six hundred dollars a month.

● In American English, a **check** can also be a bill in a restaurant.

I signaled to the waitress for the check.

childish, childlike

You can describe an adult or a young person as **childish** when
they act in an immature way, as if they were still a young child.

childish

She hoped that he wouldn't settle into one of his gloomy childish moods and spoil the day.
I thought her nice but rather childish.

You can describe an adult or young person as **childlike** if they shows some of the attractive qualities that children have, especially simplicity and sincerity.

...his childlike charm.
She was a dear old thing, but childlike and eccentric.

Other words

Instead of saying that an adult or young person is **childish,** you can say that they behave **childishly.**

Even the competent adult may become childishly helpless or demanding when ill.

Note that neither 'childish', 'childishly', nor 'childlike' is normally used to describe ordinary things to do with children. Instead you use **children's** or **for children.**

Good children's bookshops are few.
There are special shampoos for children.

chips, crisps, french fries

In British English, **chips** are pieces of potato cut like short sticks that are fried and served hot. They are called **french fries** in American English.

Then I'd get the tea ready, which was usually ham and chips, or kippers.
He ordered his lunch from Room Service—a club sandwich with french fries on the side.

Very thin slices of potato that have been fried until they are hard and crunchy are called **crisps,** or occasionally **potato crisps,** in British English and **potato chips** in American English.

I can't open this packet of crisps.
...a bowl of dip surrounded with a selection of salty biscuits and potato crisps.
We had a packet of potato chips and American Ice Cream Sodas.

choose, elect

If you **choose** something or someone from a group of things or people, you decide which one you want.

She stared for a moment at the clothes hanging in the closet, then chose a simple, severe blue suit.
A prince in my position is free to choose men to serve him for their ability.

If someone **chooses** to do something, they do it because they want to or because they feel it is right.

Most visitors to these parts choose to travel by bicycle or to walk.
They could fire employees whenever they chose.

If a group of people **elect** someone to represent them or to do a particular job, they choose them by voting for them rather than for another person.

They elected a man from the southern Bendel state as their chairman.
They met to elect a president.

If you **elect** to do something, you choose to do it. This is a formal use.

They may elect to opt out of the scheme.

church, chapel

A **church** is a building used for religious services by most major Christian denominations.

This is one of my favourite London churches.
Half a century ago nearly everyone in Britain went to church at Christmas.

A **chapel** is a separate area within a church or cathedral, or a building in a place like a school or hospital, where some Christian services are held.

He turned away and went into one of the side chapels, where candles were burning.
I was working late in my school chapel, preparing for a special service the next day.

In Britain, a **chapel** is also a small church used by some Protestant Christians, such as Methodists or Baptists.

The funeral was held in the Methodist chapel.
The Baptists, of course, have got their own burial ground behind the chapel.

civic, civil, civilian

Civic is used to describe people or things that have an official or important status in a particular town or city.

...a civic leader from the local Pakistani community.
The City Council announced plans to build a 100 million dollar civic centre.

Civic is also used to describe duties, rights, and feelings that people have because they are members of a particular community.

She was determined to carry out her civic responsibilities.
There followed a remarkable burst of civic pride and enthusiasm.

The **civil** institutions of a country are those which are not connected with the armed forces.

Civil flying had virtually ceased.
They have their own regional systems of military and civil administration.

The **civilians** in a country are people who are not members of the armed forces.

Most of the work I did in the army could have been done by a civilian.
Brazil is to have its first civilian president since the military regime was set up 17 years ago.

Other words

Civil rights are the rights people have in a society to equal treatment and equal opportunities, whatever their race, sex, or religion may be.

The American battle for civil rights helped the battle for women's liberation.
...the civil rights movement.

A person's **civil liberties** are the rights they have to say, think, and do what they want as long as they respect other people's rights.

Here too there has been a similar attack on civil liberties.

claim, demand

If someone **claims** money, they ask for it because it legally belongs to them.

People have to show their passports to get medical treatment, to claim welfare benefits, even to send their children to school.

You should claim your pension 3 or 4 months before you reach pension age.

If someone **demands** money, they ask for it in a forceful and sometimes aggressive way, even if they do not deserve it or have a right to it.

My mother used to watch at a window in case a landlord turned up and demanded money we hadn't got.
They are demanding still higher wages.

claim, pretend

If you **claim** that something is true, you say that it is true, although you may not be able to prove it or to make people believe you.

'Did he really kill six men?' Kay asked. 'That's what the newspapers claimed,' Mike said.
He claimed that he found the money in a forest.
He claimed to be a Scot but had a powerful Liverpool accent.

If you **pretend** that something is true, you try to make people believe that it is true, although you know that it is not.

The rest of us stood around for a while trying to pretend nothing had happened.
He could pretend, perhaps, not to recognise them.
'You don't want to spend your life with me,' Joyce said, 'so why pretend?'

classic, classical, classics

Something that is described as **classic** is an absolutely typical example of its kind.

It is a classic example of what I can only call Masculine Logic.
Otto broke off, shaking his head in the classic manner of one baffled beyond all hope of illumination.

You also use **classic** to describe something such as a book or film which is of a very high quality and has become a standard against which similar things are judged.

...one of the classic works of the Hollywood cinema.

In this sense, **classic** can also be used as a noun.

...a great classic of Brazilian literature.
...cheap paperback editions of the classics.

classic

Classical describes things that are traditional in their form, style, or content, and that have existed for a long time. **Classical** things are often contrasted with modern things.

...the company's American-style blend of modern and classical dance.
...a central flaw within classical Marxism.

Classics is the study of the language and literature of Ancient Greece and Rome.

Guy had studied classics and philosophy at Oxford.

● Note that **classical** is also the adjective related to **classics**.

Traditionally in Europe the subjects of study were classical languages, history and the natural sciences.

cloth, clothes, clothing

Cloth is material made from fibres such as cotton, wool, or nylon.

...machine-woven cloth.
...strips of cotton cloth.

A **cloth** is a piece of **cloth**. The plural is **cloths**.

Remove tea stains from china with a damp cloth.
Rinse out cleaning cloths after use and hang to dry.

Your **clothes** are the things you wear, such as shirts, coats, trousers, and dresses. Note that there is no singular form of **clothes**.

She laid the baby down and quickly started taking off its clothes.
He washed his summer clothes and put them away.

Clothing is a more formal word used to refer to a person's clothes, either in a general way, or when talking about specific types of clothes worn for particular jobs or by particular people.

He takes off his wet clothing.
...prison clothing.
They have to wear spacesuit-style protective clothing.

If you want to refer to one garment, you can talk about a piece of **clothing** or an article of **clothing**.

He has been identified as the man who visited Malta and bought a number of articles of clothing from a boutique.

coast, beach, shore

The **coast** is the area of land which lies alongside the sea. When you talk about a **coast,** you may mean just the land close to the sea, or a wider area inland.

To the north and south the coast is rock for the most part.
At this time sea kale was a relatively common plant around the coasts.
...a protest at official plans to site a third London airport on the Essex coast.

A **beach** is a flat area immediately next to the sea that is usually covered in sand or pebbles.

Tourists go there to walk on the beach.
Gradually the oil stains were cleaned from the beaches.

The **shore** is the area of land along the edge of the sea, a lake, or a wide river.

Bronzed men surfed into the shore on curling waves.
We could see the trees on the other shore.

coat, jacket

A **coat** is a piece of clothing with sleeves that you wear over the rest of your clothes when you go outside. **Coats** are usually quite long, often reaching down to your knees or below your knees.

Gertrude was wearing, under her coat, a brown light jersey dress.

A **jacket** is a piece of clothing like a short coat. Usually **jackets** reach down to your hips or waist. You can wear a **jacket** indoors or outdoors, and you can wear a **coat** over it.

He began to undress, hanging his jacket neatly on the back of a chair.

comic, comical

Comic is used to describe things which are intended to be funny. When **comic** has this meaning, it can only be used in front of a noun.

She was glad it was a comic film. She had seen it before.
Tim had nearly had a commission to illustrate a comic cookery book.

Both **comic** and **comical** can be used to describe something that is amusing and makes you want to laugh, usually because it is

comic

slightly silly. They can come either in front of a noun or after a verb such as 'be' or 'look'.

Her eyes rolled up in a blend of comic disgust, resignation and tolerance.
She would look up with the most comical expression.
Brooks's attention to detail can occasionally be comic.
It was almost comical to see the conflicting emotions flit across Frank's face.

Grammar

Comic is also a noun. A **comic** is an entertainer who tells jokes to make people laugh.

When the comic comes on they'll all laugh.

A **comic** is also a magazine, usually for children, that contains stories told in pictures.

He saw me reading a comic.

comment, mention, remark

If you **comment** on a situation, or make a **comment** about it, you give your opinion on it. You may express a careful thought, or you may just say a few words.

He knew his father expected him to comment on the meal.
'It's going to be pretty cold if you have to stay there all night,' he commented.
'I'll believe it when I see it,' was Mrs Pringle's comment.

If you **mention** something, you say it, but you do not spend very long talking about it. You have usually not been discussing it before.

She casually mentioned: 'I thought I had something of interest for you.'
Johnny mentioned that he might be in New York right after the holidays.

If you **remark** on something, or make a **remark** about it, you say what you think or have noticed about it, often in a casual or informal way.

Visitors generally remark on how well the children look.
Mr Nixon hastened to remark that he was not against television.
Gerald Sutton's first remark was: 'Your pals have found you.'

complement, compliment

You use **complement** to talk about making something complete, good, or effective. For example, if one food **complements** another, or is a **complement** to it, they go well together. If two people **complement** each other, they have personalities that are suited to each other.

As oregano comes from the Mediterranean, it is a perfect complement to aubergines and peppers.
Her interests and my interests complement each other: there is no conflict.

The 'full **complement**' of a group, set, or amount is every item or person that it normally includes or should include.

He lacks a full complement of teeth.
...a full complement of one thousand passengers and crew.

If you **compliment** someone, or pay them a **compliment,** you praise them or say something that shows admiration.

Thomas tried a smile, to compliment Mrs Jardino on her rough humour.
When he pays his compliment to you, show no reaction whatever.
Frank took the invitation as a great compliment.

comprehend, understand

If you **comprehend** something, you know what its meaning is or why it is the way it is. **Comprehend** is only used in fairly formal or literary language, and usually with a negative to say that someone cannot **comprehend** something.

Her face was blank and numb as though she could no longer comprehend the reality around her.
He could not comprehend how Grant had ever been selected for this mission.

It is much more usual to say that someone **understands** a situation or a problem.

'And because I can go no further, you must go alone. Do you understand?'
Morris felt he understood more deeply, now, what McLuhan was getting at.

comprehensive, understanding

Something that is **comprehensive** includes everything that is needed. For example, a **comprehensive** study examines every

comprehensive

detail of a subject; **comprehensive** plans consider every possibility.

...a comprehensive insurance policy.
Chapter 4 examines the last attempt to implement a comprehensive anti-poverty programme in Britain.

You do not use 'comprehensive' to describe people who understand others and show them kindness and sympathy. You say that they are **understanding.**

Mrs Viccary turned out to be a delightful person, wise, tolerant and understanding.
I want so much to be as brave and as understanding as you are.

Other words

Instead of saying that something is **comprehensive,** you can say that it is done **comprehensively.**

We need designers able to deal with the design process comprehensively.

confused, confusing

If you are **confused,** you do not understand someone or something. People who are **confused** sometimes do no know how to behave in a particular situation.

She looked away, confused, not knowing what to say next.
Parents are apt to be confused about what psychiatrists and psychologists are for and what the difference between them is.
Many young people are confused about the causes of cancer.

Something that is **confusing** makes you feel confused.

The sizes in clothing are sometimes confusing and you may find the following information useful.
This word is confusing in that it has two rather different but related meanings.

Something that is **confused** does not have any order or pattern and is difficult to understand.

The figures are sometimes confused.
Further questioning revealed how confused and contradictory Carmichael's replies were.

conscience, consciousness

A person's **conscience** is the part of their mind that decides whether what they are doing is morally right or not.

My conscience told me to vote against the others.
Oddly enough his conscience was never troubled by the two men he had murdered.

A person's **consciousness** is their mind and thoughts.

Fantasies swam in and out of his consciousness.
If anything was imprinted on her consciousness that night, it would be the twinkling silver lights.

If someone loses **consciousness** in an accident, they become unconscious; when they regain **consciousness** they become conscious again.

Then he felt himself carried into the hospital and he lost consciousness.
He has regained consciousness after four days in a coma.

conscious, conscientious

Someone who is **conscious** is awake and able to know what is happening, and not sleeping or unconscious.

When I was allowed to go into the surgery he was conscious but too weak to move.
The patient was fully conscious during the operation.

If you are **conscious** of something such as a problem, you know that it exists.

She was conscious of her age and full of doubt about her worth.
He was conscious of his limited achievements.

If you take a **conscious** decision, you are aware of what you are doing.

Most large families expand unintentionally, without conscious planning.

If someone is **conscientious,** they do what they have to do properly and with care.

Conscientious parents sometimes worry so much about jealousy.
He's a very conscientious minister.

contest, competition

A **contest** is a struggle to win power or control, especially in politics. The noun **contest** is pronounced /kɒntest/.

...the contest for the deputy leadership of the Labour Party.

contest

A **contest** or **competition** is an event in which people take part in order to find out who is the best at something, especially in order to win a prize. They usually involve tests of knowledge, speed, skill, or talent.

The local radio station was sponsoring a contest to find the most popular high school athlete.
Her insurance company employers held sales contests for its staff, with merchandise prizes.
She won several competitions for rock-and-roll dancing.
...a magazine full of competitions and activities.

If only two people are involved, you usually use **contest.** For example, if you are talking about an event in a sport such as boxing or wrestling, you refer to it as a **contest.**

...the heavyweight contest between Muhammad Ali and the Canadian champion Trevor Berbick.

A **competition** is often more serious than a **contest,** with more complicated rules or more complicated things to do. It may take place over a longer period of time, and the entrants may have to do several different things.

...the 1981 Lorry Driver of the Year competition.
His greatest disappointment was that he didn't win the competition to do the Byron memorial in Hyde Park.

Grammar

Contest is also a verb. If you **contest** something such as a decision or a will, you object to it formally and oppose it, sometimes aggressively. The verb **contest** is pronounced /kəntest/.

I am going to contest the will.
We would hotly contest this idea.

If parliamentary candidates **contest** a seat, they try and win it.

There was a by-election contested by six candidates.

Competition is used most commonly as an uncount noun to describe a situation in which two or more people or organizations are trying to get something that only one of them can have. When they are in this situation, you can say that they are **in competition.**

As the population expanded, so did the competition for land.
Searle is likely to face some stiff competition from Tate & Lyle.
The two parties were not in competition with each other.

Note that 'contest' is not used in this way.

continual, continuous, constant

You use **continual, continuous,** and **constant** to describe things which continue to happen or exist without stopping.

...the necessity for continual change by managers and workers alike.
The world that people thought to be stable was instead undergoing continuous dynamic change.
This would keep society in a condition of constant change.

If you are describing something undesirable which continues to happen or exist without stopping, it is better to use **continual** than 'continuous'.

Continual police pressures were brought to bear against Card to get him to withdraw his statement.
Her continual demands on me were affecting my work.
It was sad to see her the victim of continual pain.

Continual is also used to describe things which happen repeatedly.

Nino Valenti's face was handsome though bloated by continual drinking.
The management refused to deal with him because of his continual disruptive activities.

You describe something as **continuous** when it happens all the time without any interruption at all, or seems to happen without any interruption.

After days of continuous rain in the area the Telle River was in flood.
The Kirks spent the summer in a state of continuous excitement.
When standing you sway slightly forwards and backwards continuously although you are unaware of it.

Note that **continual** is only used in front of a noun. **Continuous** can be used in front of a noun and after a verb such as 'be'.

He gave continual thought to these two questions.
The landscape has undergone continuous transformations.
These recordings are in sequence and continuous.

You describe something as **constant** when it happens all the time or is always there.

He was in constant pain.
He had to recognize the truth of Eva's constant criticism that he wasn't a man.

continual

Other words

You say that something happens **continually, continuously,** or **constantly.**

I shivered and sweated continually.
Bev and I studied continuously, either in the library or in our rooms.
For the first six weeks in Naples I was constantly cold.

control, manage

If you **control** something such as a country or an organization, you have the power to take all the important decisions about the way it is run.

The Imam of Yemen was an absolute ruler. He controlled the life of every subject.
The merchants controlled the network of marketing and supplies.
They want to control their own lives without being intimidated by anyone.

If you **manage** something such as a business, an organization, or a system, you are responsible for organizing it and seeing that the right things are done. You have the power to make decisions, but you may need the co-operation of other people.

...in the small business sector, where those who own the business often manage it as well.
Mrs Hughes manages the 400 acre dairy farm with the help of five men.

cost, costs, price

The **cost** of something is the amount of money you need to buy it, do it, or make it. For example, the **cost** of a holiday could include what you pay for travel, hotels, and restaurants.

You may be charged with the cost of the telephone call.
Although the total cost was over a million pounds the results were spectacular.

The **costs** of a business or a home are the sums of money that have to be spent regularly on running it. They include money spent on electricity bills, repairs, and taxes.

The company has one particular problem: energy costs.
Employers were free to cut costs and boost profits by forcing down wages.

The **price** of something is the amount of money you have to pay to buy it.

Members of Parliament were outraged by the price of cold drinks in Oxford Street.
Most restaurants now include the tip in the price of the meal.

country, countryside, provinces

Land away from towns and cities is called the **country** or the **countryside**.

Country is often preferred when you want to contrast this type of land with towns and cities.

The key members of the cabinet had farms in the country to which they liked to retire for the weekend.
She'd plenty of money and a big house somewhere in the country.
It was just like being in the country and not at all in a town like Twickenham.

Countryside is used especially when mentioning some of the particular qualities of country areas, such as the scenery.

The wreckage was strewn over a three-mile stretch of heavily wooded, hilly countryside.
The unspoilt countryside is mostly given over to farming.

Someone who lives in **the provinces** lives outside the capital of a country, normally in a town or city. **Provinces** is not used in conversation.

....his desire to leave the provinces for London.
No hotel in the country, either in the provinces or Paris, had taken in a guest of that name.

country, nation, state

A **country** is a geographical area recognized as a separate political unit. Most countries have their own independent governments. England, Wales, and Scotland, however, are separate countries, even though they are all part of the United Kingdom and are governed by the British Government. **Country** is used in a general way, not just when talking about the political status of a place.

In the last few days there have been riots all round the country.
I had already worked in a developing country.
Many Asian countries are still losing far more trees than are being replanted.

country

You use **nation** to refer to a country that has political independence, its own government, and its own social structures. **Nation** is used in more formal language, and is often used to talk about the people of a country. You do not use 'nation' simply to refer to a place. You use **country** instead.

...the biggest and most valuable assembly of works of art ever given to the nation by an individual.
Almost every western nation has had its era of revolution or civil war.
The whole nation should have recoiled with shock at the things that were done.

You use **state** to refer to a country when you are considering it in terms of its political organization and structure.

The Latin American states maintained their independence.
The peoples of the new states are by no means insensitive to the dangers of one-party rule.

States can also be administrative areas within a country.

...the oil-producing states of Texas and Oklahoma.
Haryana and Punjab were the fastest-developing states in India.

couple, pair

Both **couple** and **pair** refer to groups of two.

If you call two people a **couple,** you mean that they are married or have a close permanent relationship. You usually use a plural form of a verb with **couple.**

Some couples do not give themselves time to adjust to marriage.
In Venice we met a South African couple.

Two partners who dance or do other things together can also be called a **couple.**

On the discotheque floor the younger couples do not circulate.

Two people can also be called a **pair,** but they may not have a very close relationship. You often use **pair** in a humorous way or to show disapproval. When **pair** is used like this, you use a plural form of a verb with it.

They'd always been a devoted pair.
A pair of drunkards were trying to kill one another.

Two animals that mate with each other and produce young are called a **pair.**

Breeding pairs lay from three to eight eggs annually.

Two things that match each other, for example shoes or ornaments, are called a **pair**. When **pair** is used like this, the verb can be singular or plural.

She had put on a pair of long black gloves.
It is likely that a new pair of shoes brings more happiness to a child than a new car brings to a grown man.
He put on a pair of brown shoes which were waiting there for him.

You also talk about **a pair of** scissors, trousers, or other things made of two matching parts. You use a singular verb.

On a hook behind the door was an old pair of grey trousers.
Around his neck was a pair of earphones.

In conversation, **a couple of** things or people are two things or people. You use a plural verb with **a couple of**.

I walked two miles there and back for a couple of pails of water.
They've been helped by a couple of newspaper reporters.

Very often when people talk about **a couple of** things or people, they do not mean exactly two of them. They mean at least two but not very many.

They'll be coming out in a couple of minutes.
Somewhere amongst the group were a couple of teachers.

cry, shout, yell

If you **cry** or **cry out,** you call out loudly usually because of a strong emotion such as unhappiness, excitement, or fear.

'Come on!' he cried.
I heard Amy O'Shea cry out in fright.

If you **shout,** you speak in an extremely loud voice. You may shout in order to be heard in a noisy place, or because you are angry or excited.

I was very happy and shouted, 'Thank you!' to him but he only smiled and waved his hand.
They turn their radios on and shout across the room to one another.
That made Clarissa very angry indeed. She shouted, 'You make me sick!'

If you **shout** at someone, you talk angrily to them in a loud voice.

She scarcely glanced at the poor man; just shouted at him for spoiling her lovely evening.

cry

The negotiators shouted at each other across the table.

If you **yell,** you call out loudly, either using words or just making a noise. People usually yell because they are excited, angry, or in pain.

I threw back my head and yelled 'Help!'
I yelled out in pain and fell off the wall.
'Get out of my office!' yelled Mr Morris.

If you **yell** at someone, you shout loudly at them, usually because you are angry.

If she caught us eating, she would yell at us, and sometimes she told the boss.
I yelled at Richard to hang on.

cry, weep, sob

When someone **cries,** their eyes produce tears, because they are unhappy, afraid, or in pain.

She was now crying and moaning through her sleep.
One of her children fell in a game and started to cry.

If someone **weeps,** they are crying because of strong emotion. **Weep** is a literary word.

Her face felt raw with weeping. She was sick and dizzy with grief.
James wept when he heard the news.

When someone **sobs,** they cry in a noisy way, taking short rapid breaths. **Sob** is also a literary word.

Behind him he could hear Kairi sobbing in helpless, childish grief.
I began to sob with fear and nervous tension.

Grammar

Sob is also used as a noun.

She began to weep in gasping, choking sobs.

cure, heal, recover, recovery

When a doctor or a treatment **cures** a patient or a disease, or **cures** a patient of a disease, the patient gets better.

He took the boy to a special doctor and had his eye infection cured.
Dr Battacharya went in for acupuncture, and had once cured Mrs Bhoolabhoy of migraine for a whole week.

A **cure** is a medicine that cures a disease.

Nobody would deny the value of the work being done to find a cure for cancer.
...a possible cure for AIDS.

When an injury such as a cut or a broken leg gets better, you say that it **heals** or that it **is healed**.

I waited there six weeks, not knowing whether the leg would heal or not.
This ointment should heal the cut in no time.

If you say that someone **heals** a sick person, you mean that they make them better, usually by unconventional methods known as 'alternative medicine'.

Give the Lord a chance, Ginny. He healed my leg. He can heal your mother's blood.
He had been miraculously healed of his illness.

When a sick person **recovers, recovers** from an illness, or makes a **recovery,** they get better.

In time Johnnie recovered, thankfully without any permanent damage.
How long do people take to recover from sickness of this kind?
He made a quick recovery, but the operation hadn't been as successful as hoped.

cushion, pillow

A **cushion** is a fabric case filled with soft material, which you put on a seat to make it more comfortable. You can sit on it or use it to support your back or head.

She overturned the chairs and hurled the cushions about.
She tucked up her feet on a big divan covered with cushions.

A **pillow** is a type of cushion. You put your head on it when you go to bed.

She was lying on the bed, her head on the pillow.
I heard the chambermaid thumping pillows as my bed was made up for me.

custom, habit

A **custom** is something that people in a community do because it is a tradition, or because it is considered the right thing to do in society. For example, in Britain, celebrating Christmas and shaking hands are **customs**.

custom

'Harvest Festival,' I said firmly, 'is a good old Christian custom.'
I'm a stranger in this country, I don't know the customs that well.
They had done all that their religion and family customs had
required them to do.

You can also say that it is someone's **custom** to do something
when it is something they usually do. This is a fairly literary use.

She had risen at half past six as was her custom.

A **habit** is something that you do regularly, often without
thinking why you do it. **Habits** can sometimes be irritating or
pointless.

His tongue moistened his top lip. It was a habit of his.
She has a bad habit of mumbling.
I can't help it, I always tell everybody everything, it's a terrible
habit, it really is.

D

damp, moist, humid

If something like the ground or a house is **damp,** it is slightly
wet. If you make a cloth **damp,** you make it slightly wet, usually
so that you can clean something with it.

My old, discarded boots had been letting in water on even
moderately damp ground.
I see the way old people are treated. There are too many living in
damp, tumbledown houses.
Remove tea stains from china with a damp cloth dipped in
bicarbonate of soda.

If something like food or the air is **moist,** it is slightly wet in a
pleasant way. If someone's skin is **moist,** they are perspiring
slightly; if their eyes are **moist,** they look as if they are going to
cry.

Oil, butter, lard or margarine help to keep bread moist.
There's mountain air in this room. It's cool and moist and almost
fragrant.
He had glanced at her as she smiled in her sleep and had kissed her
on her moist brow.
His eyes, too, were serious and moist.

If the air in a place is full of water vapour, you can say that it is **humid.** When a place is **humid,** it is usually hot and unpleasant.

The air felt humid and oppressive, saturated with heat and moisture.
In the humid, disease-ridden jungle the costs of road construction are high.

dead, died

You use **dead** to describe a person, animal, or plant that is no longer alive; **dead** is an adjective.

His first wife is dead.
He thought of his dead companions.

You use **died** to say what has happened to a person, animal, or plant that has stopped living; **died** is the past tense and past participle of the verb **die.**

I pushed him. He fell and hit his head. And he died.
I'm trying to trace refugees whose relatives have died in England.

deceptive, deceitful, deceiving

Something that is **deceptive** encourages you to believe something that is not true.

Yet this apparent realism, even in his straightest drawings, is deceptive.
Beth knew that its fragile appearance was deceptive.

If someone is **deceitful,** they are deliberately trying to trick another person and make them believe something that is not true.

They had deserted me, the ungrateful, cunning, fickle, deceitful traitors.
The bureaucrats' evidence varied from the inept to the downright deceitful.

If you say that someone **is deceiving** you, you mean that they are deliberately trying to trick you and make you believe something that is not true. **Deceiving** is the continuous form of the verb **deceive.**

I fear he may have been deceiving you on this point, as, indeed, he has been deceiving you on another.
The quickest way to rattle him was to accuse him of deceiving the public.

deceptive

Other words

If you say something is **deceptively** easy or safe, you mean that it seems easy or safe, but that it is not really so.

It was a brilliant effort, made to look deceptively easy.
Instead, he said with a deceptively calm, almost cooing voice: 'Jerry, look at me.'

delighted, delightful

If you are **delighted** about something, you are very pleased and feel some excitement about it. If you say you would be **delighted** to do something, you mean you are very willing to do it.

Hawk was delighted at the way our training sessions were going.
Most children who find they have shocked their parents are delighted, at least secretly.
She said we would be delighted to see more of Canton.

If you find something **delightful,** you think it is very pleasant or attractive.

Really, they are delightful children to live with.
Thank you for a wonderful meal, and a truly delightful evening.

Other words

If you do something **delightfully,** you do it in a way that people like. You can use **delightfully** before an adjective; for example, if something is **delightfully** sweet, it is sweet in a very pleasant way.

She was sure that he would dance delightfully.
The result is a delightfully smooth, light soup.

deny, refuse

If you **deny** something, especially something that someone says, you say that it is not true.

He denied that there was any need for drastic reform.
This allegation was denied repeatedly by Government spokesmen.
I don't deny that art is political.

If someone **denies** you something you need or want, they do not allow you to have it.

All my life I had never denied my mother anything.
At times we've denied justice to groups with different religions or political views.

Hekima was denied the right to present the defence he had so carefully worked out.

If you say that someone **refuses** you or **refuses** you something, or that you have been **refused** something, you mean that they do not allow you to have something you have asked for, or do not allow you to do something you have asked to do.

He knows he can run to his Dad for money if I refuse him.
The Rajah was infatuated with her and could refuse her nothing.
They had been refused permission to return home.

If you **refuse** to do something, you deliberately do not do it, or say firmly that you will not do it.

She's one of those people who refuse to change their opinions.
Mr Benn refused to condemn them.

If someone **refuses** something you offer them, they do not accept it.

Anne was about to refuse the drink but then thought she had better accept it.
It was an offer Lever felt he couldn't refuse.

dependent, dependant

If you are **dependent** on someone or something, you need them in order to exist or survive. If children are **dependent,** they cannot manage without their parents. A relative whose needs are entirely paid for by another person is a **dependent** relative. If one country is **dependent** on another, it needs money or goods from the other country. Used in this way, **dependent** is an adjective.

The gift of material goods makes people dependent.
A secure child isn't made dependent by ordinary comforting.
...allowances for housekeepers, blind persons and dependent relatives.
West Europe was still heavily dependent on Middle Eastern Oil.

Your **dependants** are the people who you support financially, such as your children. In American English, this noun is usually spelled **dependent.**

If the borrower dies during that period, his (or her) dependants will be protected against losing their home.
You do not need to work to support yourself or your dependents.

describe

describe, characterize

If you **describe** someone or something, you say what they are like, for example by saying what someone looks like, how something works, or what you have experienced.

Gordon had casually remarked that a boy had done it, and described him. A few days later the arsonist was caught.
Ideally you would make your own vinegar and I describe how to do this on page 196.
He described the rest of his terrible ordeal.
And yet you describe him as respectable?
Northcliffe's official biographers describe his relationship with Lloyd George as one of friendliness.

If one thing **characterizes** another, it is very typical of it.

...the incessant demand for change that characterizes our time.

If you **characterize** someone or something, you describe them by picking out their main characteristics.

How would you characterize yourself?
The relationship was increasingly characterized as one of vigilant and stealthy hostility.

detract, distract, disturb

If one thing **detracts** from another, it makes the second thing seem less important or not as good.

Advertisers prefer television programmes not to be too involving, for fear of detracting from the impact of their advertisements.
To say all this doesn't detract from the achievement, of course.

You do not use **detract** to talk about bothering people. You say that you **distract** them or **disturb** them.

If someone **distracts** you, or if they **distract** your attention, they stop you from thinking properly about what you are doing and prevent you from concentrating.

Her band was playing in a pub when a man began trying to distract them and make trouble.
I soon found an infallible way to distract his attention if he became too excitable.
I spoke merely to distract his attention from the feast.

If someone **disturbs** you, they interrupt you when you are busy or want to be quiet or alone.

All I wanted was a quiet corner where I wouldn't disturb anyone if I just happened to snore.
The slightest sound would have disturbed him.

dinner, lunch, tea, supper

The meal eaten in the middle of the day is called **dinner** by some people and **lunch** by others. **Lunch** can be either a main cooked meal or a snack. **Dinner** is usually a cooked meal, and is the main meal of the day.

At one o'clock he went down the hall to the kitchen for lunch.
It is difficult to provide a rest-time after school dinner for these really small children.

The light meal or snack that some people have in the afternoon is called **tea.** Usually it consists of cakes or biscuits with tea to drink. It is sometimes called **afternoon tea** in cafés, restaurants and hotels. **High tea** is a larger meal served on special occasions or as an early evening meal.

Madeleine took tea with Madame.
He crept into the dining-room, where the table was laid for high tea.

The main meal of the evening is called **dinner, tea,** or **supper** by different people. People who call their midday meal **dinner** usually call their main evening meal **tea** and serve it early in the evening. People who call their midday meal **lunch** may call their main evening meal **tea, supper,** or **dinner. Dinner** may be a more formal meal than **tea** or **supper.**

Run out into the yard and let your father finish his tea in peace.
I wondered if you'd like to go into town with me for supper tonight.
I'd like to ask you round for dinner one evening.
There were only the three of us at dinner at Sissinghurst that night, my parents and myself.

Some people have a late evening snack which they call **supper.**

Supper consisted of a large jug of tea and a plate of cakes.

disappointed, disappointing

If you are **disappointed,** you are rather upset because something has not happened or because something is not as good as you hoped it would be.

He was very disappointed that John had not been accepted for the Grammar School at Caxley.

disappointed

I'm disappointed in you, Philip, really I am.

Something that is **disappointing** is not as good as you hoped it would be.

The results have generally been disappointing.
The food and service, I regret to say, were disappointing.

discreet, discrete

If you describe people or their behaviour as **discreet,** you mean that they are tactful and do not give away secrets about other people.

She is very discreet. She has never told me anything.
He followed at a discreet distance.

Jewellery or decorations that are described as **discreet** are simple and in good taste.

...her smart, quiet expensive shoes and her discreet leather handbag.

Discrete things or ideas are totally separate from and unconnected with each other. **Discrete** is a rather formal word.

Occupations are grouped into discrete categories.
The mind divides the continuity of the world around us into discrete units.

disinterested, uninterested

Someone who is **disinterested** is not personally involved in a situation and can act or think in a fair and unselfish way.

I am confident that you will give me a disinterested opinion.
I know personally of his disinterested help to unknown, ill and dying people.

Someone who is **uninterested** in something shows very little interest in it.

No one here is interested in religion, it's amazing how uninterested they are.
She seemed to be talking to herself, uninterested in whether Tim was there or not.

Some people also use **disinterested** to say that someone is bored or not interested in something. However, this use is often regarded as incorrect.

distinct, distinctive

Something that is **distinct,** or **distinct** from something else, can be recognized as different and separate from it, even though the two things might be similar in some way.

Each of his eight animals had a distinct personality.
This is not a cross between a cherry and a plum, but a distinct species.
The British Museum is now distinct from the British Library.

If something like a shape or a sound is **distinct,** you can see or hear it very clearly.

'You don't make yourself clear,' said Sticking, in his most distinct voice.

You use **distinctive** to describe things which have a special quality that makes them easy to recognize.

Mr Ross noted their distinctive Glasgow accents.
Jossi's appearance was distinctive. He was a powerful giant who stood over six feet tall.

distrust, mistrust

If you **distrust** someone, you are sure that you cannot trust them and are very suspicious of them.

You can't trust anyone. Now I even distrust Cynthia.
For the first time in his life he was inclined to distrust Hintza's judgement.

If you **mistrust** someone, you are doubtful about them and are not sure of their motives or whether you can trust them.

It is unfortunately necessary to mistrust men and treat them with extreme caution at all times.

Distrust and **mistrust** are also used as nouns. Note that **mistrust** is used more often as a noun than a verb.

They stood facing each other in the darkness, filled with mutual distrust.
He took a week because he knew the deep mistrust that all Africans had of doing things in haste.
She gazed on me with a sudden fear and mistrust.

doubt, suspect

If you **doubt** that something is true or possible, you are not convinced or do not believe that it is true or possible.

doubt

He felt so weak that he doubted whether he would be able to walk as far as the bedroom.
Nobody doubted his integrity and knowledge of countryside matters.
Jane never doubted for a moment that her first child would be a son.

If you **suspect** something is true, you think that it is probably true, especially when you are relying on your intuition or when someone is not prepared to tell you the truth. You do not use **doubt.**

I suspect he was already in New York.
I suspect that many of them could barely read or write.
I'd never seen anything like this before – and I suspected no one else had either.

doubtful, dubious, suspicious

If you are **doubtful** about a situation or possible event, you are not certain about it and you may feel pessimistic or unconvinced that it can happen or take place.

The man behind the desk seemed doubtful. 'I'll just check. I'm not sure if we have a vacancy.'
Do you feel insecure and doubtful about your ability to arrange a conference?
I was doubtful of success.

If you think a result or a possibility is **doubtful,** you think that it is unlikely or not certain to happen. If you think something like evidence is **doubtful,** you are not really convinced by it.

The commission's chances of success are doubtful.
It was doubtful he would ever see that person again.
The independent military force is of doubtful value in deterring an invasion.

If you are **dubious** about something such as a proposal, you are not sure whether or not it is the right thing to do.

'You could – but I'm not sure you ought.' Alison sounded very dubious.
The men in charge were a bit dubious about taking women on at all.

If you describe something as **dubious,** you think that it is not completely honest, safe, or reliable.

The economic logic was in fact highly dubious.

He made several calls on the most dubious of pretexts.
My prestige, if any, is based on my dubious abilities as a teacher of English.

If you are **suspicious** of a person, you do not trust them and think they may be lying or may have committed or be planning to commit a crime.

Residents in a block of flats became suspicious of a man who sat in his car outside the flats for long periods.
I am suspicious of the government's intentions.
He was so good in the language that Miss Lenaut had grown suspicious and had asked him if his parents spoke French.

If you describe something as **suspicious,** you mean that you do not trust it because it is probably bad, dangerous, or wrong.

He listened for any suspicious sounds.
He was seen to make a suspicious movement with his hand towards his pocket.
Let's just say she is missing from home in suspicious circumstances.

drop, fall

Both **drop** and **fall** are used to describe what happens when an object suddenly moves downwards from one place to another lower place without any support.

When something **drops,** it usually moves down in a fairly straight line without anything stopping it.

You could throw a stone and it would drop thousands of feet.

You can use **fall** with a similar meaning but not always in the same structures. **Fall** can only be used intransitively, that is it is not followed by an object. You cannot say that someone 'falls' something. You say that they **drop** something.

The yellow leaves were falling to the ground.
He bumped into a chair and dropped his cigar.

Things often **drop** or **fall** in an accident.

Plate after plate dropped from his nerveless fingers.
Trees are allowed to lie exactly where they fall.

If something moves downwards but not in a straight line, you use **fall** and not 'drop'. For example, you can say that a ball **fell** down some steps or that a tree **fell** across a river.

He tossed her the magazine. It fell to the floor at her feet.

drop

You can say that a person **drops** when they deliberately jump straight down from something. They usually move in a controlled way. For example, you can say that a burglar **drops** from a window to the ground when he leaves a building quietly and is trying not to disturb anybody. You can also say that people **drop** from aeroplanes using parachutes.

4,255 British paratroopers were dropping on French soil.

When someone **falls,** it is usually because of an accident, and they are unable to control their movement properly.

I fell in a bramble bush.
He stumbled into a corridor and fell.

● The words **drop** and **fall** can also be nouns. A **drop** is the height of something vertical, such as a cliff or wall, when you are imagining something or someone falling off it.

Sixteen hundred feet is a considerable drop.

A **fall** is what happens when someone falls.

I hadn't noticed how badly I had been bruised by the fall.

E

earn, win, gain

If you **earn** money, someone gives you money for the work you do for them.

A certain amount of the money you earn in any one year will be untaxed.
He earns two rupees a day collecting rags and scrap paper.

If you **earn** respect or a good or bad reputation, you get it by acting in a way that deserves it.

Benn had earned the reputation of being a formidable opponent.
...a system that would earn the hatred of the world: Apartheid.

If you **win** money, you get it as a prize in a competition or as a result of a bet.

He became the first man to win over £500,000 in a single season.
I am pleased to inform you that you have just won three hundred thousand pounds.

If you **win** something you want, such as respect or power, you succeed in getting it.

He soon won the respect of the civil servants.
He fell in love with her and tried to win her affection.

If you **gain** a reputation or power, you get it.

He had, however, gained an undeserved reputation as a magician very early in his career.
The Associated Television Corporation gained control of another of the big five television companies.

If you **gain** an advantage or benefit, you obtain it.

People earning in excess of £10,000 a year gained an average tax benefit of £480.

east, eastern, easterly

The **east** is the direction you look towards in the morning in order to see the sun rise. The **east** of a country or area is the part towards the east. You use **east, eastern,** and **easterly** to describe things that are in or come from the east.

You use **east** to describe a part of a place that is in the east, whether it is a large place like a country or a smaller place like a building. Note that **east** is often used to make a contrast with the west, north, and south: if a building has an '**east** wing', it probably also has a 'west wing'.

We flew over the east side of Lake Turkana.
...the relatively shallow waters of the east coast.
On a wall in the East Wing of our College, there hangs a picture.

Eastern means relating to the east and refers to a more general area than **east**.

...the countless fishing villages that dot the coasts of southern and eastern Africa.
...a little over half-way down the eastern coast of the South Island.
The trend spread well beyond eastern France.

You can also use **eastern** to describe things that come from the east or that are found there.

As she talked, her cultivated eastern accent started slipping.
The sun had not yet risen, but a line of pink on the eastern horizon told him that daybreak was near.

east

Winds that come from the east can be described as **east** or **easterly** winds.

I had trudged along the sea front in the teeth of the fierce east wind.
Many a day there was an icy easterly or northerly wind blowing off the sea.

You can also use **easterly** to describe directions and locations. If something moves in an **easterly** direction, it moves towards the east. Unlike **east** and **eastern, easterly** can be used with 'more' and 'most'.

The yacht was continuing in an easterly direction.
It reaches into the Atlantic in a direction more easterly than anything.
It is one of the most easterly Greek islands.

eatable, edible

Edible means that something is safe to eat and not poisonous.

The whole fish is edible.
Many seaweeds are edible.
...edible mushrooms.

You can use **eatable** or **edible** to say that something is good enough or tasty enough for a person to eat and enjoy.

To convert dried peas and beans into an eatable food they must first be soaked.
Chunks of uncooked potato are barely eatable.
The figs are edible and pleasantly tangy.
I thought rabbit the least edible of all the bush foods.

economy, economics, economic, economical

The **economy** of a country is the way money is organized in it and the way trade and industry are run.

The modern economy is propelled by a frenzy of greed.
Mass unemployment is always possible in a market economy.
New England's economy is still largely based on manufacturing.

Economics is the study of how economies are organized and work. Note that when **economics** has this meaning, it is used with a singular verb.

Economics is not an exact science.
Economics plays a central role in shaping the activities of the modern world.

Economy is careful use of money and resources so that there is no waste.

Unfortunately most chairs are designed for their looks or for economy but with little thought for the needs of the body.

Economic is the adjective that describes things relating to the economy of a country and economics. Note that when **economic** has this meaning, it always comes before a noun.

Economic conditions are more favourable.
...the economic theories of Ricardo.

If an activity is **economic,** it makes a profit or saves money. When **economic** has this meaning, it can go either in front of a noun or after a verb.

It is not always practical or economic to recover energy from organic matter.

Something that is **economical** does not cost a lot of money to operate or use.

This system was extremely economical because it ran on half-price electricity.

If a person is **economical,** they are careful not to waste money, effort, or time.

People are having to be as economical as possible.

edit, publish

The person who **edits** a book checks that there are no spelling mistakes and that it is clearly written.

Textbooks have to be written, edited, printed and distributed.
I am indebted to Mrs Maria Jepps, who checked and edited the entire work.

When a company **publishes** a book or magazine, it prints copies of it, which are then sent to shops to be sold.

One of the most influential books ever written about space travel was published by Viking Press in 1949.
Why a book by an Englishman, published in Britain, should be written in American I do not know.

Other words

A person who **edits** books is called an **editor.**

She's a very good editor and cuts much more energetically than I do.

edit

The **editor** of a newspaper or magazine is the person in charge of it.

Before joining ITN Sir Alistair had had a distinguished career as editor of The Economist magazine.

A **publisher** is a person or a company that publishes books, magazines, or newspapers.

The publishers of the book are Collins.

educate, bring up

Teachers, parents, and other people **educate** children and young people by teaching them the subjects and skills they require.

He was born in 1934 at Exeter and educated at Beckenham Grammar School.
Many more schools are needed to educate the young.

You can also say that parents **educate** their children by sending them to school.

He had paid out good money to educate Julie at a boarding school in Yorkshire.

When you are talking about parents looking after their children and helping them to develop physically and morally, you do not say that they 'educate' them, but that they **bring up** their children.

The way we choose to bring up children is vitally important. But where we bring them up also has a big effect on their lives.
She died soon after and I was brought up by an old friend of mother's called Lucy Nye.

Other words

Instead of saying that parents **educate** their children by sending them to school, you can say that they 'give them an **education**'.

elder, eldest, older, oldest, elderly

You use **elder** and **eldest** to say who was born before others in a family. For example, if you have an **elder** brother or sister, you have a brother or sister who was born before you. The **eldest** child in a family was born before the other children.

His mother had impressed upon him how hopeless he was compared to his elder brother.

Angela was very fond of her parents, though bitterly jealous of her elder sister.
They were pretty girls and I guessed that the eldest, Marianne, was no more than twenty.

You use **older** and **oldest** to say who was born first in any group of people, not just families.

One of the older boys had to be continually on watch for wild animals.
Some years ago I had the privilege of meeting the world's oldest man.

If you talk about '**older** people', you mean people who are no longer young.

The older people, like Miss Clare and Mrs Pringle, shake their heads sadly.

Older can be used to show differences in age, in comparisons using 'than'. 'Elder' cannot be used in this way.

Jemmy was at least five years older than I was.
She was a couple of years older than me.

If you describe someone as **elderly,** you mean that they are old. Some people consider **elderly** a more polite word than 'old'.

...a small, energetic, elderly man with a heavy moustache.

'The **elderly**' are **elderly** people.

...a psychiatrist who specialized in the care of the elderly.

electric, electrical

You use **electric** to describe particular machines or devices that use electricity.

Place all the chopped vegetables in an electric blender.
...an electric fire.

You also use **electric** to describe things that are directly involved in producing or conducting electricity.

Electric current does not flow through water, but through the impurities in water.
The electric wiring is dangerous.

You use **electrical** when you are talking in a more general way about machines, devices, or systems which use or produce electricity. **Electrical** is typically used in front of nouns such as 'equipment', 'appliance', and 'component'.

electric

Removal men won't disconnect any electrical or gas apparatus.
...electrical appliances such as dishwashers and washing machines.
...more attractive technologies for storing heat and electrical energy.

You also use **electrical** to talk about people or organizations connected with the production of electricity or electrical goods.

...a vast firm of consulting electrical engineers.
...the electrical and mechanical engineering industries.

embarrassed, embarrassing

If you are **embarrassed,** you feel nervous and upset about something that you have done or that has happened.

She was speaking in a very loud voice because she was so angry and Hugh looked at her in an embarrassed way.
She was a little embarrassed and did not know what to say.

Something that is **embarrassing** makes you feel embarrassed.

He said something that would be embarrassing for me to repeat.
Dubois's discovery helped to rescue Haeckel from an embarrassing situation.

emigrate, migrate

If you **emigrate,** you leave the country where you were born and go and live permanently in another. People often **emigrate** because they hope to find new opportunities or more freedom in another country.

He and Betty had been talking about the possibility of emigrating to Australia.
In 1973 he eventually emigrated and settled in Vienna.

You use **migrate** to talk about a large number of people leaving a country or an area temporarily. When people **migrate,** it is usually because they need money or work.

Millions have migrated to the cities because they could not survive in rural areas.
The men are leaving their wives to cultivate the home plot while they migrate in search of seasonal work.

You can also say that people **migrate** when they move home permanently because they believe living conditions will be better elsewhere.

The more prosperous middle-class inhabitants have increasingly migrated to the suburbs and the countryside.

When birds, animals, or fish **migrate,** they move at a particular time of year from one part of the world or a country to another, in order to breed or to find food.

Every spring they migrate towards the coast.

envelop, envelope

When one thing **envelops** another, it covers, surrounds, or encloses it completely. **Envelop** is a verb and is pronounced /ɪnˈveləp/.

Our heads were enveloped in smoke.
Deadly silence enveloped the War Room.

An **envelope** is the paper cover in which you send letters through the post. **Envelope** is a noun and is pronounced /ˈenvələʊp/ or /ˈɒnvələʊp/.

Enclosed is a stamped addressed envelope for your reply.
Tim, who usually received only bills through the post, looked at the envelope with surprise.

especially, specially

You use **especially** to emphasize one member or part of a group you have mentioned. You can replace **especially** by 'in particular'.

...the difficulty of the poor in advanced economies, especially the United States.

You can also use **especially** to emphasize one aspect, case, or circumstance where something that you are saying is true. You can replace **especially** by 'in particular'.

The true figures may be much higher, especially in rural areas.

You most often use **specially** to indicate that something is done for someone or for a special reason. It is often followed by 'for' or by a verb, usually the past participle.

I guessed that the mint had been put there specially for me.
What is a meal? It's food specially prepared to be appetizing.

Note that sometimes **especially** is used with this meaning when something is done or provided for a person.

...excellent clothes boutiques especially for the rich young female.

You can use **especially** or **specially** in front of an adjective and

especially

sometimes in front of a verb to mean 'more than usually'. Note that **specially** is more informal than **especially.**

It seemed especially illogical.
...a specially long and elaborate song.
I specially like her story about Norma Talmadge.

everyday, every day

You use **everyday,** spelled as one word, to describe normal life and the ordinary things that are part of it and which are not especially interesting or unusual. **Everyday** is an adjective which always comes in front of a noun.

We must return to everyday life, forget tragedies and love-affairs.
Children's language develops with everyday talk.
She was dressed in her everyday print frock.
In the rough, overcrowded conditions, injuries are an everyday occurrence.

If something happens **every day,** spelled as two words, it happens on seven days each week. **Every day** is an adverbial, rather than an adjective.

Lucy and I talk on the telephone every day.

You can also say that something happens **every day** when you mean that it happens very often.

Then there occurred one of those things that must happen every day in the world of big business.

except, except for, unless, besides

Except is normally followed by a noun group. You use **except** with a statement to introduce the only things, people, or ideas that your statement does not apply to. In the example below, the only thing that did not relax was the person's right hand.

All of his body relaxed except his right hand.

Except can also be followed by prepositional phrases and clauses of time, place, and manner.

The hot weather had made travelling impossible except in the cool of the morning before the sun rose.
We led almost completely separate existences, except when we came together to climb.

You use **except for** in front of a noun group when you are mentioning something that prevents a statement from being completely true.

The classrooms were silent, except for the busy scratching of pens on paper.
I had absolutely no friends except for Tom.

Unless is a conjunction and is followed by a clause. You use **unless** to introduce the circumstances in which something will not take place or is not true. In the first example below, the statement 'there was something wrong with Louise', would not be true if the speaker had made a mistake. Otherwise it would be true.

Unless I was mistaken, there was something wrong with Louise.
In the 1940s and 1950s, a woman was not properly dressed unless she wore gloves.
You must not give compliments unless you mean them.

You use **besides** to introduce further things in addition to those you are mentioning.

Soft fruit will give you, besides a lot of pleasure, a source of vitamins.

However, if you talk about 'the only person **besides** me', or 'the only thing **besides** that', you are referring to the only other person or thing in a particular situation or context.

He was now the only person besides Gertrude herself who regularly talked to Guy.

excited, exciting

If you are **excited,** you cannot relax, because you are looking forward to something very eagerly or because you are pleased about something that has happened.

He was very excited and talked non-stop as we drove through the lightening streets.
Of course I feel terribly honoured and excited by the way things have turned out.
He had been too excited to eat.

If something is **exciting,** it interests you and makes you feel full of ideas and enthusiasm.

We met people with interesting and exciting stories to tell.
She had had a very exciting career.

excuse

excuse, forgive

If you **excuse** someone or **excuse** their behaviour, you provide reasons or a justification for what they have done in order to make it seem less bad, especially when other people disapprove of it. **Excuse** is a verb and is pronounced /ɪkˈskjuːz/.

Can we excuse her by saying she was a victim of events?
He wrote humble letters in which he tried to excuse his actions.

If you **forgive** someone or **forgive** them for something that they have done, you decide not to punish them and not to continue feeling angry or upset.

Though she had eventually agreed to forgive him, the damage had been done.
Don't do it. You'll never forgive yourself.
I'll never forgive you for this – never.
Diaghilev asked me to change the ending. I refused, of course, and he never forgave me.

Occasionally, in fairly formal English, the meaning of the verb **excuse** can overlap with the meaning of **forgive**.

I could never excuse him for being so rude.

When **excuse** is used with a similar meaning to **forgive**, it can have two objects.

I excused him much of his prejudice because I liked him.

● **Excuse** can also be used as a noun. An **excuse** is a reason that you give in order to explain why something has been done, has not been done, or will not be done. Note that the noun is pronounced /ɪkˈskjuːs/.

That's a classic excuse for spending more than you earn.
It might be used as an excuse for evading our responsibilities.

exhausting, exhaustive

An **exhausting** experience or activity makes you very tired.

John and Dougal had had an exhausting day.
The argument is likely to prove long and exhausting.

An **exhaustive** search or study of something is thorough and complete.

These are findings we should not dismiss without exhaustive testing.
This list is by no means exhaustive.

Other words

If you are **exhausted,** you are very tired indeed.

At the end of the day I felt exhausted.

expect, wait for, look forward to

When you **expect** someone, you think that they are going to arrive. When you **expect** something, you think that it is going to happen or arrive.

I had sent a postcard saying I was coming so they were expecting me.
We are expecting rain.
I'll pay for it as soon as the money I'm expecting from Florence arrives.

When you **wait for** someone or something, you remain in the same place or delay doing something until they arrive or happen.

Whisky was served while we waited for Vorster.
We got off the plane and waited for our luggage.
They waited for orders to begin.

When you **look forward to** something that is going to happen or that you are going to experience, you feel happy because you think you will enjoy it.

I always looked forward to Charlene Mitchell's visits.
I'll bet you're looking forward to that hot Sicilian sun.

experience, experiment

If you **experience** something, or if you have an **experience,** something happens to you that has an effect on you.

...the very deep desperation that Jonathan must have been experiencing.
It was an experience each seemed to enjoy.
Their day of training had been a most trying experience for them.

An **experiment** is a scientific test that is done in order to discover something or to prove that a theory is true. Scientists do **experiments,** or, in more formal English, carry out **experiments.** They also **experiment** with things.

He frequently visited other labs to see which new experiments had been done.

experience

The first experiment were carried out by Dr Preston McLendon.
In his experiments high-altitude conditions were simulated.
He improved the efficiency of pumps, and experimented with
powering them by steam, water and gunpowder.

F

fairly, quite, rather

Fairly, quite, and **rather** are all used to say to what extent
something is true. For example, if you want to say how big
something is, you can say that it is **fairly** big, **quite** big, or
rather big.

If something is described as **fairly** big, it is at least as big as you
would expect or need it to be, but not as big as other things like
it. Note that when an adjective like 'big' comes before a noun, you
talk about 'a **fairly** big thing'.

There's a loaf of fairly fresh bread.
Her hair had been growing, but she had decided to keep it cut fairly
short.
I suppose we'd better get going fairly soon, hadn't we?
We live in a fairly rural area.

If something is described as **quite** big, it is usually bigger than
something that is described as **fairly** big, and bigger than most
other things like it. You can say that something is **quite** big when
you want to express surprise at how big it is. Note that when an
adjective like 'big' comes before a noun, you usually talk about
'**quite** a big thing' but you can also say 'a **quite** big thing'.

It was quite dark by now, and there was no moon.
The dog turned on her more than once and bit her quite severely.
It was quite a long climb up the white, chalky road to the cemetery.
She did so in a quite detached way.

If something is described as **rather** big, it is usually bigger than
something that is described as **quite** big. If you say something is
rather big, you are emphasizing how big it is, and you may even
be suggesting that it is too big. Note that when an adjective like
'big' comes before a noun, you can talk about either 'a **rather** big
thing' or '**rather** a big thing'. **Rather** can also be followed by
words like 'too' or 'more' and by comparative forms of adjectives.

Its apparent simplicity and reliability are rather deceptive.
She got rather angry with me when I tried to intervene.
He put an arm out and his father rather shakily took it as they began to walk.
They had a rather sad look.
I have had rather a sad life.
In the second year two rather more specialised subjects are chosen from a total of seven.

fantasy, imagination

A **fantasy** is a story or situation that someone creates in their mind which is different from what happens in normal life and which is usually pleasant or amusing.

Fantasies are quite usual in the normal child.
Every act of creation must be preceded by a fantasy.
She has her fantasy too, a hope that some day she will conceive a child to replace the one she gave away when she was sixteen.

Your **imagination** is the power your mind has to think of new ideas and situations.

In his imagination he took himself on a journey through the universe.
These plans reveal a complete failure of imagination.
You need a very good imagination to get to grips with these kinds of ideas.

farther, further

Both **farther** and **further** are used as the comparative form of 'far'. **Farther** and **further** can be both adjectives and adverbs.

Farther and **further** are both used to talk about distances and time.

Birds were able to find food by flying farther and farther.
He must have found a window open further along the balcony.
The domestication of animals stretches farther back in time than we had previously imagined.

Only **further** can be used to talk about the degree or extent of something. If you have **further** discussions, you have more discussions. If a situation is **further** worsened, a bad situation becomes worse.

It was agreed to call a further meeting on the 10th.
The price of energy has done further damage.

farther

The government itself announced further changes to the scheme.
The situation is likely to be further worsened by the expected population growth.
...aspects of advanced technology which complicate the world yet further.

Grammar

Note that **further** can also be a verb. If you **further** something, you help it to progress, be successful, or be achieved.

...a ploy by Morris to further his career.

female, feminine

You use **female** to describe women and things associated with women. You also use **female** to describe animals belonging to the sex that can give birth to babies or lay eggs, and things associated with them.

...the best female athletes.
...a very much smaller proportion of the female population.
...two horses, a wolf, three boars and three female deer.

You can also use **female** as a noun, but only when referring to animals.

He came upon a family of lions – a big male, a beautiful female, and two half grown cubs.

You use **feminine** to describe qualities and characteristics that society has traditionally associated with women rather than men. Often **feminine** has connotations of gentleness and passiveness.

She seemed to have plenty of feminine charm.
...a good, calm, reasonable and deeply feminine woman.
Feminine qualities are consistently invalidated, denigrated and suppressed.
...displays of every kind of feminine luxury from novelty jewellery to evening dresses.
Over the years, the ideals of feminine perfection change.

● Some languages divide nouns and adjectives into two classes, **feminine** and masculine, or into three classes, **feminine,** masculine, and neuter.

Other words

Feminism is the belief that women should have the same rights, power, and opportunities that men have.

The first two-thirds of the book is a discussion on feminism.

A **feminist** is a person who believes in and supports feminism.
Claudia thought of herself as a feminist.

few, a few

If you talk about **few** people or things, you mean not many people
or things. Often you are implying that there are not as many as
you would like or expect.

*He looked at natural phenomena in a way that few painters before
him had done.*
*There seemed to have been few places in Britain that Sarah had not
visited.*

You use **a few** to indicate that you are talking about a small
number of people or things. **A few** is often followed by a
measurement of time or distance.

A few youths were standing around and talking.
It would be interesting to ask her a few questions, wouldn't it?
*When she returned to the phone a few minutes later, she sounded
agitated.*

● **Few** and **a few** can also be used as pronouns.

Many are invited but few are chosen.
*Each volunteer spent one night a week in the cathedral. A few spent
two.*
But now, at least, the dull days for a few of us were over.

final, eventual, possible

You use **final** to describe the last thing or person in a series, or to
describe something that happens at the end of an event or series
of events.

The war in Europe was in its final few hours.
I quoted his final words of the interview.
*We had our last look at Africa as we took off for London on the
final stage of our journey.*

You use **eventual** to describe things that happen or are achieved
after a lot of delays or complications.

*The company's eventual collapse in 1971 in part stemmed from these
events.*
*He welcomed the Government's eventual decision in February to
hold a referendum.*
The eventual winner was Henrietta Murdoch.

final

You use **possible** to describe things that might happen or exist in the future, or people that might become something or do something. You cannot use 'eventual' in this way.

That's the time you especially need planning to minimise possible errors of judgement.
The possible danger lay in being seen in a hotel corridor or foyer.
You may have to draw yourself to your boss's attention as a possible candidate .

finally, eventually, possibly

When something happens after you have been waiting for it or expecting it for a long time, you can say that it **finally** happens.

Finally I went to bed.
The heat of the sun finally becomes too much for me and I shift my chair into the shade.
Davies was quiet for a long time. 'Yeah,' he finally said. 'This is bad.'

You can also use **finally** to say that something happens last in a series of events.

The mountains that ringed the horizon turned mauve, then purple, and finally black.

When something happens after a lot of delays or complications, you can say that it **eventually** happens.

Eventually they got through to the hospital.
You are going to tell us. Not now perhaps. But eventually.
I found Victoria Avenue eventually.

You can also use **eventually** to talk about what happens at the end of a set of events, often as a result of them.

The entire program will eventually cost them fifty billion rubles.
Eventually, they were forced to return to England.

You use **possibly** to talk about what might happen in the future. If you say something may **possibly** happen, you mean that although it may happen, you are not sure that it will. When **possibly** is used in this way it usually comes after the modals 'could', 'may', and 'might'. You cannot use 'eventually' in this way.

I took very good care to keep clear of any situation in which I might possibly meet him.

find, discover, find out

If you **find** someone or something, you see where they are or learn where they are, especially when you have been looking for them.

I want you to find him for me and bring him back.
They found the body in a dustbin.
When Mrs Oliver returned to the house, she found Miss Livingstone waiting for her.
It took him ten minutes to find the Encyclopaedia Britannica.

Discover is sometimes used instead of **find**. **Discover** is a rather formal word. It is used especially in formal investigations and scientific research. If, after a lot of research, you found a cure for the common cold, you would say that you had **discovered** the cure.

A great deal of research is being carried out to discover the benefits of regular exercise.
The two men were discovered dead.

You can also use **discover** when you find something by accident.

It is amazing to think that this well-known flower was discovered as recently as 1903.
Just before the war two hoards of treasure were discovered in England.

If you cannot see the thing you are looking for, you say that you cannot **find** it. You do not use 'discover' in this way.

I think I'm lost – I can't find the bridge.

If you **find, discover,** or **find out** that something is the case, you learn that it is the case.

The very young child finds that noise expresses best of all his power over his environment.
He was surprised and alarmed when he discovered the whole school knew about his efforts.
We found out that she was wrong.

In clauses beginning with 'when', 'before', or 'as soon as', you can omit the object after **find out.** You cannot do this with 'discover' or 'find'.

When mother finds out, she'll divorce you.
You want it to end before anyone finds out.
As soon as I found out, I jumped into the car.

find

If you succeed in obtaining some information which is difficult to obtain, you can say that you **discover** or **find out** what you want to know.

He has some reason for crying even if you cannot immediately discover what it is.
Have you found out who killed my husband?

You can also say that someone **finds out** facts that are easy to obtain.

I found out the train times.
I want to find out if the authorization for my visa has come through yet.

You do not say that you 'discover' facts that are easy to obtain.

find, found

If you **find** someone or something, you see where they are or learn where they are, especially when you have been looking for them. **Find** has an irregular past tense and past participle, **found.**

The mill will not be easy to find.
Somehow or other, he reached the Alps and found a remote village.
You might never have found me again.

There is also a verb **found,** which has a regular past tense and past participle, **founded.** If someone **founds** an organization, or an institution such as a school, they start it, often by paying for it.

The BBC was itself founded by men of vision and high-minded principle.
Only eight university institutions had been founded in the region.
There was talk about founding a professorship for political economy at Oxford.

floor, ground, grounds

The flat surface that you walk on in a building is called the **floor.**

The toilet was leaking and water was running all over the floor.
The kitchen was low and cool; white walls, pink brick floor.

The surface that you walk on when you are outside is called the **ground.**

The mist rising from the wet ground was getting heavier.
The cabin had burned to the ground.

The **grounds** of a building such as a school or a large house are the gardens or land that surround it.

These are private grounds and you are all trespassing.
Could Paul and Arnold have met in the hospital grounds in March?
Our bus carried us across the grounds of the Havana University.

● In British English, the **ground floor** of a building is the floor that is level or almost level with the ground outside. The **floor** above the **ground floor** is called the 'first **floor**'.

Their flat was on the ground floor at the back.
...on the first floor of the Museum.

In American English, the floor which is level with the ground outside is called the 'first **floor**' and the floor above it is the 'second **floor**'.

food, meal, dish

Food is what people and animals eat to keep them alive and to allow them to remain healthy. You can refer to a particular type of **food** as 'a food'.

Bring enough food and water for the trip.
Babies are meant to spend their first year getting hungry, demanding food, enjoying it.
Salmon was once a commonplace food in Scotland.

A **dish** is food specially prepared in a particular way. It may involve just one type of food, for example scrambled eggs, or it may involve several combined together, as in a stew, and it may be cooked or not cooked.

She could make a new dish without referring to any cookery book.
The vegetables are served as an accompaniment, not very often as a dish on their own.

A **meal** is an occasion when food is eaten, such as breakfast, lunch, or dinner. Several dishes may be served during a **meal**.

It's sensible to avoid sweets between meals.
On top of the normal work, you had to wash up after every meal of the day.

A **meal** is also the food that is eaten on one of these occasions.

...a simple meal of bread and cheese.
Most restaurants now include the tip in the price of the meal.

foot, feet

A **foot** is a unit for measuring length used in Britain and America. It is equal to 12 inches or 30.48 centimetres. When **foot** has this meaning, its usual plural is **feet.**

The pole is two or three feet away from the garage.
Climbing solo, he got to about twenty feet above the ground.

However, you can use **feet** or **foot** as the plural in front of words like 'high', 'tall', and 'long'.

The main dome was only twenty feet across.
...a great rough slab 20 feet high and 50 long.
As she was leaving, they asked her how tall she was. So I said, 'Five foot two.'

Note that you always use **foot** as the plural in front of another noun. For example, if a wall is six feet high, you refer to it as a six **foot** wall.

...a 5,000 foot limestone wall in the Dolomites.
...a 300 foot rope.

footpath, path, lane

A **footpath** or a **path** is a narrow strip of ground that people walk on to go from one place to another.

Then he left the churchyard and walked by a footpath that led out on to the cliff.
'Turn in here,' Lofquist said, pointing toward a footpath into the woods at their right.
From the harbour a narrow path runs around the foot of the cliffs.
On the side of the main road a narrow path zigzags up into the central hills.

A **path** is also a short strip of ground used by people to cross places like parks and gardens.

The track led to a farm. After that a path fringed with fennel and wild lavender led to some beehives.
A path strewn with tiny white stones led up to the first house.

A 'public **footpath**' is a path across private land which can be used by anyone, not just the landowner.

...the battle of Lord Rotherwick to win more than 1.5 million pounds as compensation for a new public footpath through the secluded woods of his estate.

A **lane** is a small road, especially in the country.

He trotted back along the lane admiring the autumn crocuses.
Boyd Stuart parked his car on a gravel patch just off the lane.

Lane is also sometimes used in the names of roads.

Back in Cannon Street, the next turning to the right is St. Swithin's Lane.

forbid, prevent

If you **forbid** someone to do something, or if you **forbid** an activity, you order that it must not be done. Someone may in fact do it despite what you say.

I forbid you to tell her.
Christopher was forbidden to see her.
I believe that parents should flatly forbid programmes that go in for violence.

If you **prevent** something, or if you **prevent** someone from doing something, you make it impossible for that thing to happen or to be done.

Measles can be prevented by immunization at 1 year of age.
She closed her eyes to prevent him looking into them.
My only idea was to prevent him from speaking.

forever, for ever

You use **forever** in front of the continuous form of a verb to mean 'very often'.

...the doctor who is forever winding up his watch.
Babbage was forever spotting trivial errors in their calculations.

You use **forever** in front of an adjective to talk about a quality or attitude someone or something always has.

The President remained forever grateful.

You use **forever** or **for ever** to say that something is or always will be the case.

I'll never leave you, I'll love you forever.
When the game is going well you feel you can go on playing forever.
I was quite certain she had left me for ever.
I just want to hide myself here for ever, and be safe and happy.

forever

Children sometimes use **for ever** in the phrase 'for ever and ever' to emphasize that something never stops.

'Daddy,' Libby said, 'does our blood keep going round inside for ever and ever?'

forget, leave behind

If you **forget** something such as your keys, you do not remember to take them with you when you go somewhere. If you **forget** to do something such as buy some milk, you do not remember to do it.

Take your raincoat. You forgot it before.
She had felt sick that morning in the village and had forgotten the bread and butter.

If you **leave** something **behind,** you do not bring it with you. You leave it where it is either because you decide not to take it or because you do not remember to take it.

We were worried when we found all that gear you left behind in the helicopter.
We cross the creek using a rope, which we leave behind.
Feeling in his pockets he found his wallet wasn't there; he must have left it behind at the inn.

former, late, deceased

You use **former** to describe someone who used to have a particular job or position, but who no longer has it. For example, the **former** president is someone who used to be the president, but is not any more. **Former** does not indicate whether the person is alive or dead now.

...former President Gerald Ford.
...Sir Ralph Verney, former chairman of the Nature Conservancy Council.

You use **late** when you are talking about someone who is dead. For example, the **late** president is someone who used to be president, but who is now dead. They need not have been president when they died.

My mother, although only a poor relation, nevertheless was related to the late Sir Perceval Large.
...Harold Ross, the late editor of The New Yorker.

A **deceased** person is one who has recently died. For example, the **deceased** president is someone who was president until they died a short time ago. **Deceased** is a rather formal word.

...Duke Amadeus IX, the sixteen-year-old son of the now deceased Duke Louis.
I felt grateful to the deceased Uncle James.

Grammar

Deceased is most commonly used as a noun. The **deceased** is a dead person, especially someone who has died very recently. It is a formal word, commonly used in legal contexts.

Did you know the deceased?

fragile, frail

Delicate things that are easily broken or damaged can be described as **fragile.**

She poured tea into cups as thin and fragile as magnolia petals.
...constructions built of fragile materials that simply fall apart after a short period of time.

Fragile is sometimes used to describe people. If someone feels **fragile,** they feel weak, for example because they are ill or because they have drunk too much alcohol.

He said that she had died of a broken heart. A lonely, incapable, fragile woman.
Burr looks pale and fragile today.

A **frail** person is weak and in poor health.

He saw that it was an old lady; she appeared small, demure, and frail.
Her head trembled on her frail neck.
He was the only person who had really noticed how little she ate, how thin and frail she was.

frightened, frightening

If you are **frightened,** you feel afraid or nervous.

I think he was truly frightened of me at times.
I was more frightened than I had ever been in my life because I knew that human lives were at stake.

Something that is **frightening** makes you feel frightened.

Do you ever have frightening dreams?
It was a strange, rather frightening place.

G

game, match

In some sports like football, rugby, or badminton, a competition between two teams or players can be called either a **match** or a **game**, but **match** is preferred as an official term.

...the game against Notts County.
...the atmosphere in the city on the day of a big match.

If you mention the name of the sport, it comes before the word **match**.

...a cricket match.
...a football match.

When you talk about **a game of** something, it does not usually involve professional players.

Don often came for a game of snooker.
He played in a game of cricket against a team from St Mary's.

In American football and baseball, a competition can only be called a **game**, not a **match**. If you mention the name of the sport, it comes before the word **game**.

You go to the baseball game for me and tell me who won.

● A **game** is also a part of a match in sports such as tennis and squash.

Becker leads by four games to one.

game, sport

Activities such as football, hockey, or athletics are called **sports**.

My favourite sport is football.

A **sport** such as football, rugby, or badminton, which involves two teams or players competing against each other, can also be called a **game**.

In a game like tennis, the score is kept by the umpire.

Activities such as athletics, skiing, and rowing are only referred to as **sports**. You do not called them 'games'.

In sports, he preferred fencing and rowing to traditional team games.

Sport, and not 'game', is used in formal situations, for example when referring to organizations which control sports.

...governing bodies of various sports should unite.
...the Sports Council.

Games is used in the names of some organized events in which competitions in several sports take place.

...the Olympic Games.

Games is also organized sports in schools.

I was hopeless at games at school.

gas, petrol

Gas is the name given to all air-like substances such as oxygen and hydrogen. Gas is most often used to refer to the substance that is burned in people's homes for heating and cooking.

The propellant gas in an aerosol does not simply disappear when you press the button.
She turned on the gas in the oven.

In American English, the liquid obtained from petroleum and used to power cars and other motor vehicles is called gas, or sometimes gasoline.

I'm sorry I'm late. I had to stop for gas, and the station was jammed.
Sometimes I pull in for gas when the tank is three-quarters full.

In British English, this liquid is called petrol.

The use of leaded petrol has resulted in gross contamination of the environment.
He pulled in at Keele for petrol.

gentle, polite

Someone who is gentle speaks or acts in a kind way without hurting people or damaging anything. For example, a good nurse is gentle with a patient.

...a gentle, sweet man.
... a boy with a gentle, sensitive nature.

You do not use gentle to talk about how well someone behaves: someone with good manners is polite.

I was very polite and called him 'Sir'.
One could always rely on him to be polite and do the right thing.

gentle

Other words

If someone is **gentle,** you can say that they behave **gently.** If someone is **polite,** you can say that they behave **politely.**

Dr Alexander asked gently, 'What hurts, Paul?'
'Sit down, please,' Claude said politely.

girl, daughter

A **girl** is a female child.

The little girl was wearing a white frilly dress.
...a girl of eleven.

Women up to the age of about thirty can also be referred to as **girls.** However, many women object to this and prefer to be referred to as 'women'.

At 17 he fell deeply in love with a girl of 24 and she with him.
We'd been invited to the wedding of a girl we knew.

You do not normally call someone's female child their 'girl'. You say that she is their **daughter.**

He looked up from the magazine and began thinking about his daughter.
Why do we go into such a rage when our daughter doesn't clean up her room?

gold, golden

Gold is a valuable yellow-coloured metal that is most commonly used to make jewellery.

A large gold ear-ring pierced his right ear.
Don't write hard because this pen has got a gold nib.

Gold can also be used as an adjective to describe something which is gold-coloured.

...a cap with gold braid all over it.
The islanders could see the sun glinting on the gold buttons of the officers' tunics.

Golden is also used to describe something which is gold-coloured.

The great banks of golden flowers smell of ripe peaches.
A soft wind blew through Kitty's golden hair.

Golden is also sometimes used to refer to something that is made of gold or covered with gold.

...local dignitaries in golden chains of office.

greatly, largely

You use **greatly** to emphasize the degree or extent of something. If you enjoy something **greatly,** you enjoy it very much; if you are **greatly** pleased, you are very pleased.

Most pilots said they greatly enjoyed flying.
The new policies could greatly help to develop India's agricultural potential.
The one thing as bad as a wrong decision is a decision that is greatly delayed.
I felt greatly honoured when I was asked to be godmother.

You use **largely** to emphasize that a statement is mostly but not completely true.

New England's economy is still largely based on manufacturing, farming and tourism.
At the moment he is largely unknown.

Largely is also used to introduce the main reason for something.

The tower's hilltop position must have been chosen largely for the pleasure of the view.
The British did not entirely believe what they were being told, largely because they did not want to.

grocer, greengrocer

A **grocer** sells food like flour, sugar, and tinned goods. A grocer's shop is called a **grocer's.**

I reached into my pocket and gave the nickel to the grocer.
I went over the cobbled road to the grocer's.

A **greengrocer** sells vegetables and fruit. A **greengrocer's** shop is called a **greengrocer's.**

Most greengrocers now sell green and red peppers, aubergines and artichokes.
On her way home she called at the greengrocer's, at the library, and at the chemist's.

grow, grow up

When children **grow,** they gradually become taller and stronger.

There's nothing in the world more fascinating than watching a child grow and develop.
They seem to think that the quicker the baby grows the healthier he is.

grow

As children **grow up,** they gradually develop into adults.

Perhaps when he grew up he would be allowed to do as he pleased.
The baby who doesn't get any love will grow up cold and
unresponsive.

H

hair, hairs

The mass of thin strands that grow on a person's head is called
hair. Hair also grows on other parts of the body. Note that **hair**
is an uncount noun when used with this meaning.

He asked me why I had dyed my hair.
He had finished combing his hair and was now inspecting the
result.
In most societies the fact that adult females have hair on their
bodies is taken for granted and even appreciated.

Individual strands of **hair** are called **hairs.**

...the sprinkling of grey hairs that had grown more noticeable with
each year.
She left trails of long grey hairs as she paced the house.

handbag, purse

A **handbag** is a small bag that women and some men carry and
use for holding things like keys, money, and small personal items.

Her aeroplane ticket to Chicago, dated tomorrow, was in her
handbag.
Slowly she reached into her handbag and took out her spectacles
and put them on.

In American English, a **handbag** is called a **purse.**

Kay took the letter out of her purse.
She took her large glossy black purse from the knob of the door.

In British English, a **purse** is a very small bag used mainly by
women for holding money, and is usually kept in a handbag.

She began hunting in her purse for some coins.
Mrs Hochstadt took Clarissa's purse away from her and counted
out the money for Clarissa's oranges.

116

handbag

In American English, this is called a **change purse** or a **money purse.**

...a pan of muffins on the kitchen table, next to it a change purse partly open, and a pair of steel rimmed glasses.
She showed me the empty inside of her money purse.

happy, happily, lucky, luckily

If you are **happy** you feel pleasure, often because something nice has happened.

I was happy to hear that you passed your exam.
I will make you happy, happier than you ever dreamed.

If you do something **happily,** you do it willingly and with feelings of pleasure.

After lunch, Flick and Angela went happily off with Karin to do some shopping.
We laughed and chatted happily together.

If you talk about someone's good fortune, you say that they are **lucky,** or that something **lucky** happens to them. You do not use 'happy' in this way.

There are some lucky children who rarely catch cold.
It was very lucky. The boy might have died.
Then, by a lucky coincidence, we had a visit from a friend.

You can add **luckily** to a statement to say that it is very fortunate that something happened, because otherwise something else might have happened which would have been unpleasant.

Luckily, in a day or two, I felt perfectly fit again.
Luckily for me and them, love did eventually grow and flourish.

hat, cap

You wear a **hat** on your head to protect it from the sun or the cold when you are outside. Most **hats** have a brim, a part that surrounds the bottom part and sticks out from it. However, some **hats,** for example some fashion **hats** for women, have no brim.

I hadn't brought a hat and sweat was soon trickling down from my head.
They bought the hat, a trilby, and then had coffee at the Mombasa Coffee House.
Giancarlo is adjusting a model's quilted satin hat.

117

hat

A **cap** is a type of hat made of soft fabric that fits closely over your head. **Caps** do not have a brim, but they often have a peak, a stiff part that sticks out over your forehead. **Caps** are usually worn by men and boys. They are often worn as part of a uniform, for example by some British schoolboys.

A massive police captain, gold braid on his cap, came up the steps.
He limped off down the shabby street, his cloth cap squarely on top of his head.
...cotton baseball caps (some with green celluloid visors) for glaring sun.

hear, listen to

When you **hear** sounds, your ears sense them and your brain reacts to them. You might pay attention to them or you might ignore them. You cannot stop yourself **hearing** something.

She could hear the birds, bursting with song, and see buds on the trees.
When I woke in the night, I could hear the cars and trucks still beating their way down the road.
Behind him, he heard the door to the room close softly.

When you **listen to** sounds or when you **listen to** someone, you pay attention to the sound or to what the person is saying. You can decide if you want to **listen to** something or not.

He told her about the play. She listened in silence.
She listened to the whole story of my visit to Brighton with her head bowed.
I was driving across Texas listening to a local radio station.

● If you have been to a musical performance, you do not usually say that you 'listened to' the music or 'listened to' the performer. You say that you **heard** them.

That was the first time I ever heard Jimi Hendrix.

height, depth

The **height** of a person or thing is their measurement from the bottom to the top. You measure the **height** of things that are above the ground or a particular surface, for example mountains or trees.

The man was of approximately the same height and build as himself.

... the height above sea level at which the measurement is taken.
Assistants had to build a platform to raise the camera to the
necessary height.
I had climbed to a height of 25,850 feet unaided by oxygen.

The **depth** of a thing is its measurement from the top to the
bottom. You measure the **depth** of things that are below the
ground or a particular surface, for example lakes or wells, or of
things that are hollow.

Hot water was successfully recovered from a depth of only 1600m.
The island is covered with a network of shallow lakes, none more
than a few yards in depth.
Place the terrine in a larger roasting tin with cold water to a depth
of 1 inch.

hire, rent, let

In British English, if you pay a sum of money in order to use
something for a short period of time, you can say that you **hire** it.
In American English, it is more common to say that you **rent** it.

He had been unable to hire another car because of the holiday
season.
He rented a car for the weekend.

If you make a series of payments in order to use something for a
long period, you say that you **rent** it.

The apartment he had rented was on the third floor.
He rented a colour TV soon after moving into his apartment in
Rummidge.

If you **rent** a house or room to someone, they pay you money to
be allowed to live in it.

Normally we live in Falminster but had rented our house there to a
visiting American professor and his family.
They had tried to make ends meet by renting the basement room to
a family of Italian refugees.

If you **let** a house or room to someone, they pay you money to be
allowed to live in it.

The people who have large houses would never dream of letting a
room to a school teacher.
The notice said: 'Room in private flat to let until end October.'

historic, historical

You use **historic** to say that something was important in history, or that it will be regarded as important in the future. For example, a **historic** building is a very old one where interesting things have happened.

...their historic struggle for emancipation.
We are seeing the birth pang of industrial democracy: this is an historic moment.
...a broad tree-lined, red-surfaced avenue bordered by St. James's Park and historic royal houses.

A **historical** event is a real event in the past which is part of history. You also use **historical** to describe things to do with history.

...actual historical events.
...autographs and manuscripts of historical interest.

Historical evidence is proof of things that actually happened in the past.

Historical evidence seems to support this conclusion.

Historical novels, plays, and films deal with real and imaginary events in the past.

It is as good a racy, romantic historical novel as one could hope to find.

Grammar

In formal English, the indefinite article 'an' is sometimes used before **historic** and **historical,** rather than 'a'.

history, story

History is the events of the past, either in the world as a whole or in particular countries, especially when they are seen as a process which leads up to the present.

In the whole of history, there had never been a situation quite like this.
Poverty, hunger, plagues, disease: they were the background of history right up to the end of the nineteenth century.

History is also the study of history.

Between 10 and 20 per cent thought history, art and handicraft and current affairs useless and boring.

If you write a **history** of a country or a subject, you write a book about what happened in that country or subject in the past.

She published a history of the Women's Institute movement of England and Wales.

A **story** is a description of a series of events that happened to a person or group of people. These events may really have happened, or they may be the product of someone's imagination.

It's a very long story about the mule I rode from West Point to Newburgh.
We had succeeded in selling the story of the expedition to the Daily Express.
She never read stories to me at night before I went to bed.

holiday, holidays

If you describe a single day as a **holiday,** it is a day on which nobody in a particular country is required to work, often because that day is a religious festival. In Britain these holidays are called 'bank holidays'.

This occurred at any time, and invariably before major public holidays.
It is always open 12 a.m. to 2 p.m., except Bank Holidays.

In British English, a **holiday** is also a period of time lasting more than two or three days that you spend away from home for pleasure. When you go away from home in this way, you say that you 'go on **holiday**'.

The remainder of that holiday passed without incident.
It was the warmest day of the holiday.
Remember to turn off the gas when you go on holiday.

When you spend a long period of time like this each year, you can also refer to it as your **holidays.**

Where are you going for your holidays?

The **holidays** are also the period of time when schools and colleges are closed.

I was staying with a school friend during the school holidays.
My mother took me and my two sisters for our summer holidays to Alt-Aussee, a village not far from Salzburg.

You can refer to a period of time away from work as **holiday.** You usually arrange with your employer when you can have this time. **Holiday** can be spent either at home or away from home.

The company offers a pension scheme and three weeks' paid holiday.

Other words

The usual American word for a longer period of time spent away from work or school, or for a period of time spent away from home enjoying yourself, is 'vacation'.

Harold used to take a vacation at that time.

At a British university, the 'vacation' is one of the periods of several weeks when the university is officially closed for teaching.

I've a lot of reading to do over the vacation.

homework, housework

Children at school do **homework** after their classes, usually at home in the evening. For example, **homework** may involve doing maths problems or writing essays.

What do you do if children ask for help with their homework?
He wouldn't do his chemistry homework.

Housework is the work that you do to keep your home clean and to look after the people living in it. It involves jobs like washing-up and cooking.

Boys can do as much bed-making, housework, and washing-up as their sisters.
She relied on him to do most of the housework.

Other words

Traditionally, **housework** was done by a 'housewife' who stayed at home to look after the house while her husband went out to work.

I was a housewife and mother of two small children.

house, home

A **house** is a building in which people live, usually the members of one family. **Houses** are separate from other buildings, or joined on one or both sides to other houses. When you refer to someone's **house,** you are not emphasizing any emotional attachment to it by the people who live in it; you are simply referring to the building.

I was furious and told him to get out of my house.

Helen invented a flimsy excuse to take her out of the house.
On Sunday morning Waddell came to Dick's house.

Your **home** is the place where you or your family live
permanently. Your **home** may be a flat or apartment or a house.
It may even be a tent or caravan. You are usually very fond of
your **home** and have warm feelings about it.

The Benns' home stood in a row of Victorian town houses.
Pensioners should be able to live an independent life in their own
homes.
Some couples, soon to marry, required new homes.
When my husband came home at five I stopped working.

Adjectives are often used before **home** to describe the way of life
of the people there or to talk about a particular kind of home.

Most children fear ghosts, especially children from religious homes.
The others were all brought up in working-class homes.
...a happy home.

● A **home** is also an institution where people with particular
needs are cared for.

...a children's home.
...an old people's home.
...a home for the mentally handicapped.

human, inhuman, humane, inhumane

You use human to describe anything to do with people. **Human**
is pronounced /hju:mən/.

There are hundreds of thousands of things that can go wrong with
the human body.
...human relationships.

If you describe a particular person or their behaviour as **human,**
you mean that they show certain qualities that are considered
typical of most people. These qualities include kindness and a
tendency to make mistakes.

For the first and only time in our dealings with one another he was
almost human.
If I have given offence, remember that my failure was simply
human and not for want of the spirit to do good.

If you describe a person or their behaviour as **inhuman,** you
mean that they do not have or respect decent human qualities,
and usually that they are very cruel.

human

How inhuman, I wonder, can the world become?
The violence of the gunmen, he thinks, is inhuman, barbaric,
simply impossible to justify.

You can also describe something as **inhuman** when you mean
that it is not human, or does not seem human, and is therefore
strange or frightening.

Their faces looked inhuman, covered with scarlet and black paint.

If you describe a particular person or their behaviour as
humane, you mean that they behave in a kind and thoughtful
way and avoid making people or animals suffer. **Humane** is
pronounced /hju:meɪn/.

They succeeded in turning humane, cultured upper-class liberals
into bomb-throwing terrorists.
...the humane treatment of psychiatric patients.

Something that is **inhumane** is cruel and causes unnecessary
suffering.

Prison conditions are, quite simply, uncivilized and inhumane.
They will be killed by trapping or poisoning, both of which are
extremely inhumane.

I

illegal, unlawful, illegitimate, illicit

Something that is **illegal** is against the law of a country and you
can be punished for it.

The Government aimed to eliminate unofficial strikes by making
them illegal.

Something that is **unlawful** is **illegal. Unlawful** is a formal
word. **Unlawful** is sometimes used to indicate that in different
circumstances an act may be lawful. For example, in Britain a
person may have a gun if they have a licence. If they do not have
a licence, you can say that they are in **unlawful** possession of a
gun.

It is difficult to think of a more blatant example of unlawful sex
discrimination.
They were charged with unlawful possession of explosive substances.
...a verdict of unlawful killing.

Unlawful is also used when considering religious laws which are not necessarily the same as the laws of a country. For example, a divorced person cannot marry again in the Roman Catholic church. Such a marriage could be called **unlawful** by the church, but it would not be considered **illegal** by the state.

If someone is **illegitimate,** their parents were not married at the time that they were born.

Ellen had three marriages, several love affairs and two illegitimate children.

Something that is **illegitimate** is not approved of by the law or by social customs, but it is not actually breaking any laws.

All parties regarded the treaty as illegitimate.
...the illegitimate gain of a considerable empire.

An **illicit** activity is not allowed by the law, or not allowed or approved of by the social customs of a country.

They were all prosecuted for illicit liquor selling.
They view pregnancy as a punishment for illicit sex.

Other words

Lawless is used to describe places, people, and actions that are violent and take no notice of the law. **Lawless** is a formal word.

...to provoke them into further lawless violence.
...the lawless days of the West.

imaginary, imaginative

Something that is **imaginary** is not real and only exists or happens in someone's imagination.

Many children develop fears of imaginary dangers.
She remembered how for years she had held imaginary conversations with the empty bed which had been Alan's.
...pictures of completely imaginary plants.

People who are **imaginative** are good at forming ideas of new and exciting things. The ideas themselves, or the things they produce with their imagination, can also be described as **imaginative**.

Her name as an excellent and imaginative dressmaker was getting widely known.
They were both unusually loving, caring as well as sensitive and imaginative people.
...an imaginative scheme.

immoral, amoral

If you describe someone or their actions as **immoral,** you believe that what they do is morally wrong.

They believe that it is immoral for Britain to rely for its defence on nuclear weapons.
...the evil ideas which lead him to kill, commit adultery, and do other immoral things.

If someone is **amoral,** they do not care whether what they do is morally right or wrong, or they do not understand what is morally right and wrong.

The huge global conglomerates are amoral beings. Their ethics are the minimum required for political survival.
...one of those amoral immature photojournalists who hop from trouble spot to trouble spot.

imply, infer

If you **imply** that something is the case, you suggest that it is the case without actually saying so.

Was it true, as Rose's barrister had implied, that he had married her simply for the money?
My father's employer implied that he would take me on.

If you **infer** that something is the case, you decide that it must be the case on the basis of what you know already, but without actually being told.

But after all, he was married, and, I had inferred, to a rather difficult sort of woman.
As a result of this simple statement, I could infer a lot about his former wives.

● Some English speakers use 'infer' with the same meaning as **imply,** but this is considered incorrect by careful speakers.

impractical, impracticable

An idea or a method that is **impractical** is not sensible or realistic and will not produce good results.

To expect automatic protection from the police is impractical.
It would be impractical to try out every single new idea.

Something that is **impracticable** is impossible to do. For example, an **impracticable** plan cannot be carried out.

It is increasingly impracticable to deal with all your money needs in cash.
The enforcement of the rules had proved impracticable.

include, consist of, comprise

If one thing **includes** another, it has that thing as one of its parts.

The course includes a substantial programme of laboratory work.
The fish has a mixed diet which includes fly larvae, freshwater shrimps, snails and vegetable matter.

You say that something **consists of** a number of things when you are mentioning all of its parts.

The building consists of two rooms divided by a partition of glass and wood.
Her demands were few – her diet consisted of bread and a handful of lentils.

You can also say that something **comprises** a number of things or people when you are mentioning all of its parts.

The committee comprised 14 MPs drawn from all parties.
The small convoy comprised a police squad car and two closed vans.

Some people say that something 'is comprised of' particular things, but this is generally thought to be incorrect.

indoors, indoor

Indoors is an adverb. If you go **indoors,** you go into a building. If something happens **indoors,** it happens inside a building.

Alexandra ran indoors and up the stairs to pack her bag.
She hated being indoors and dragged us from park to park.
Indoors, our mother was cooking pancakes.

Indoor is an adjective used in front of a noun. You use it to describe objects or activities that exist or happen inside a building.

...an indoor swimming pool.
Our indoor games are table tennis, chess, cards.
I propose that indoor football be forbidden.

inedible, uneatable

You use **inedible** to describe things such as berries or mushrooms that cannot be eaten because they are poisonous.

The berry of the wild plant is inedible.

inedible

You use **uneatable** and **inedible** to describe food that tastes so
unpleasant that you do not want to eat it.

'Did you have a good flight?'—'The food was uneatable.'
Was she the one who used to make that uneatable gingerbread?
Only twenty of these species are poisonous, but many hundreds are
inedible because of toughness, indigestibility, or taste.

inflammable, flammable, non-flammable

Both **inflammable** and **flammable** are used to describe materials
or chemicals that can easily catch fire and start burning.
Inflammable is more common.

The factory used and stored a huge quantity of inflammable and
explosive chemicals.
Don't pack anything dangerous or inflammable such as matches,
chemicals, or a battery gas lighter.
Napalm, the most common incendiary, is a highly flammable jelly
made from aviation fuel and certain chemicals.

Materials which do not catch fire easily are described as
non-flammable.

institute, institution

An **institute** is an organization set up to do a particular type of
work. **Institutes** are very often concerned with academic
research or medicine.

The work is being funded by the Institute of Political Science.
... a team of psychologists at the Institute of Psychiatry.

The building where such work is carried out is also called an
institute.

...standing outside the Institute for Contemporary Studies.

The word **institute** is also used in the titles of organizations for
particular professional groups such as accountants or surveyors.

... the council of the Institute of Chartered Accountants.

An **institution** is a large, important organization, for example a
college, hospital, or company.

Some institutions accommodate only full-time students.
We're not a charitable institution.
... the First National Bank of Boston, a proper and prosperous
institution.

Some organizations also have **Institution** in their name.

...*economist George Perry of the Brookings Institution.*

interested, interesting

If you are **interested** in something, you are keen to know or hear more about it or to spend time doing it.

Of all the group Clive was the most interested in animals.
Asked how he became interested in politics, he replied, 'I was born that way.'

If you find something **interesting,** it attracts your attention and you enjoy finding out about it or doing it.

It must be an awfully interesting job.
The interesting thing is that this is exactly the answer we got before.

its, it's

Its is a word like 'my', 'your', 'his', 'her', and 'their', which is used to show that something belongs to or relates to a thing, a place, an animal, or a child. The thing, place, animal, or child has already been mentioned or is known about by the listener or reader.

The refining of any grain further reduces its vitamins, proteins and roughage.
The trade union movement has undergone many changes in its long history.
He liked London for its exotic quality.
Suddenly the dog whined, tucked its tail between its legs and ran indoors.
She hoisted the child on her shoulder and started patting its back.

It's is the usual spoken form of 'it is' or 'it has'. 'It has' is only shortened to **it's** when 'has' is an auxiliary verb.

It's a beautiful day.
It's getting late.
It's been two years.
It's been very nice talking to you.

J

jealousy, jealous, envy, envious

If you feel **jealousy** or are **jealous,** you have feelings of resentment and bitterness because you think someone is trying to take away something that you feel belongs to you, for example a partner or a possession.

She was a very jealous woman.
He was jealous of his wife and suspected her of adultery.
He was very good at talking me out of things, suspicions, jealousies and so on.

If you **envy** someone, feel **envy,** or are **envious** of someone, you feel that you would like to have something that they have.

I envy him. He is never bored.
A man driven by greed or envy loses the power of seeing things as they really are.
Being a cook was regarded as a good job, and several people were envious of me when I was given that job.

Jealous can be used with the same meaning as **envious.**

I always felt that she was slightly jealous of Ellen's enormous fame.
I often felt jealous because David could go out when he wished.

job, work

A **job** is something that a person does regularly in order to earn money. If you want someone to employ you, you can say that you are looking for a **job.** Note that **job** is a count noun.

Leaving school and starting a full-time job is likely to be one of the biggest changes in your lifestyle.
A local banker offered Bill a job.

A **job** is also a particular task that you have to do, like cleaning or writing a letter.

If I didn't have all these notes to write I could get so many jobs done.

Your **work** is the job that you do regularly, especially if you are paid to do it. If you want someone to employ you, you can also say that you are looking for **work.** Note that **work** is an uncount noun.

I thought everyone would have a job and that I would find work easily.
Blind people also need more meaningful work than making baskets and brooms.

Work is also the various jobs that you have to do, especially things which you do not enjoy doing.

A housewife's work can take ten or twelve hours a day.

Grammar

Work is also used as a verb.

He was working in a bank.

journey, voyage, trip, excursion

A **journey** is the process of travelling from one place to another by land, air, or sea.

Zarin arranged transport and accommodation for the rest of the journey.
It was a journey of over 2,000 miles, and took nearly three days.
Driving made him tense, and long journeys affected his bad back.

If you **journey** to a place, you travel there. This is a literary use.

The nights became colder as they journeyed north.
We journeyed to Naples together.

A **voyage** is a very long journey from one place to another, usually by sea or in a spacecraft.

The harnessing of steam had made sea voyages quicker and more comfortable.
...the voyage to the moon in 1972.

If you **voyage** to a place, you travel there by sea. This is a literary use.

It was frustrating to live at the sea's edge and be unable to voyage upon it.
...the land which St Brendan and his companions reached after seven years of voyaging.

A **trip** is the process of travelling from one place to another, staying there, usually for a short time, and coming back again.

Morris decided to take a trip to London and stay overnight.
Jarl and Jytte were off to Milan on a business trip on the Monday.

journey

An **excursion** is a short journey, either as a tourist or to do a particular thing.

A small tourist office organizes excursions to the palace of Knossos. Sometimes we made a weekend excursion to the hippopotamus island in the river, above the rapids.

Other words

Note that **trip** has another meaning when used as a verb. If you **trip,** you knock your foot against something when you are walking so that you fall or nearly fall.

She tripped over a stone.

judicial, judicious

A country's **judicial** system is the way it organizes its courts and the administration of justice. If you talk about **judicial** procedures and **judicial** decisions, you are talking about the way the courts work and the decisions they take.

I would like to go through proper judicial procedures.
...the tradition of judicial independence for all Supreme Court judges.
...a judicial enquiry.

If someone acts in a **judicious** way, they show good judgment and careful thought. A **judicious** decision is a sensible one.

She is always ready to give judicious parental advice.
'It's not bad,' Kay said in a judicious voice.
If the policies are judicious and far-sighted, they can help a lot.

K

keep, guard

If you **keep** something, you have it and do not throw it away, give it away, or sell it. You may want to go on having it because you need it, are looking after it, or do not want to give it back to its owner.

...the few books and possessions I kept at the apartment.
I noticed he was keeping a carbon copy of the editorial and I asked him why.
Why didn't Daddy let me keep the ten dollars?

If you **guard** something, you protect it by being near it and not letting anyone else take it, harm it, or approach it.

Every door was guarded, and nobody could get in or out without a pass.
In Norse mythology the wolf-dog Garm guarded the entrance to the underworld.
One of our subsidiary companies was a security company, guarding factories and homes at night.

L

lamp, light

Lamps and **lights** are both devices for giving light and making places brighter.

A **lamp** can usually be moved around and gives light to a small area. You often find **lamps** on desks, beside beds, or over pictures or mirrors. Most **lamps** are powered by electricity, but they can also use oil or gas.

Bradshaw walked to his desk and flicked on the lamp.
She got up to adjust the shade of the standard lamp by her chair.
From his hand the paraffin lamp cast flickering splashes of light over the group.

When you talk about the **lights** in a house or building, you are usually referring to the main sources of electric light which are often attached to the ceiling.

Will you turn on the light, please, Hurtle?
He sat with the lights off and the curtains drawn back.

A **light** can also be anything that produces or reflects light, for example a traffic light or one of the lights on a car.

She began to run towards the lights of the main road.

lawyer, solicitor, barrister, attorney

In both British and American English, **lawyer** is a general term for a person who is qualified in law and is entitled to represent people in legal matters. American **lawyers** can both prepare cases and represent their clients in court.

'I have nothing to say,' I told him, 'until I see my lawyer.'

lawyer

...a witty speaker and the most successful criminal defence lawyer in Scotland.
I think you should talk this over with your lawyers in New York and your bankers.

In Britain, a **solicitor** prepares legal documents, for example wills and contracts, and prepares cases that are heard in court.
Solicitors can also represent their clients in certain courts, but not in the highest appeal courts.

My solicitor phoned, and told me that the police wanted to see me again.
Arrange for the seller to leave the keys with either the estate agent or the solicitor for you to pick up when you want to start moving in.

In the higher British courts, the arguments for each side are usually presented by **barristers.**

A solicitor will arrange at least one conference between the barrister and the defendant.
There is a right of challenge that a barrister can use to have seven members of the jury changed.

In the American legal system, an **attorney** is a person who is qualified in law and who represents someone else in legal matters.

No one wanted to accept the position of defense attorney.
Gordon's attorney had had long discussions with the police.
A Justice Department attorney had confirmed that the Watergate prosecutors were suspicious.

Other words

In Scotland, a **barrister** is usually called an 'advocate'.
He was a skilful and experienced advocate.

lay, lie

If you **lay** something somewhere, you put it there, often rather carefully. The other forms of **lay** are **lays, laying,** and **laid.**

Take the top sheet and lay it in the centre of the bed.
She laid her hand on his.
He laid the two objects on the table side by side.

To **lie** somewhere means to be there in a horizontal position, or to get into that position. The other forms of **lie** are **lies, lying, lay,** and **lain.** The past participle **lain** is rarely used.

The baby was lying on the table.

He made me lie on this couch.
Then he went into the cabin and lay on the bunk.

Lie is often followed by an indication of how somebody is lying.

I lay still on the bed, watching him.

To **lie** can also mean to say or write something which you know is untrue. When **lie** is used like this, its other forms are **lies, lying,** and **lied.**

Why should he lie to me?
Rudolph was sure that Thomas was lying.

Lie is also used as a noun. A **lie** is something that someone says or writes which they know is untrue.

He knew that all these statements were lies.
I have never told a lie to my pupils.

Grammar

Both **lay** and **lie** are often used in phrasal verbs.

Lay is often used with 'down' or 'out'. When you **lay** something **down,** you put it down on a surface.

Hilary laid down her soup spoon.

When you **lay** something **out,** you put it in a particular place, spread out and neatly arranged.

I watched him start to lay the papers out on the table in the conference room.

Lie is often used with 'down'. When you **lie down,** you move into a horizontal position, usually in order to rest or sleep.

What I really wanted was to lie down and go to sleep.

Other words

A **lie-down** is a short rest, usually in bed.

Have an aspirin, a cup of tea and a good lie-down.

learn, teach, study

When you **learn** something, you obtain knowledge or a skill as a result of studying or practising. You can **learn** a subject, **learn** about a subject, **learn** to do something, or **learn** how to do something.

Lots of Americans learn Spanish.
They can also learn about child care.

learn

He had never learnt to drive.
I learned how to fix radios in the Army.

If you **teach** a subject, you explain it to people so that they know about it or understand it. You do not say that you 'learn' someone something. Note that the object of **teach** can be either a person or a subject such as mathematics.

She taught Portuguese literature at Oxford.
I like teaching sixth-formers.

It is more common for **teach** to have two objects: you **teach** someone something. In the passive, someone is **taught** something.

Will you teach me this game?
She was taught embroidery by the nuns.

You can also **teach** someone about something, **teach** someone to do something, or **teach** someone how to do something.

In high school she was taught about equality.
He taught her to fish on Lake Taupo.
You should teach me how to listen to music properly.

You **study** a subject by reading books about it and often by following a special course at a university or college.

He had studied engineering at the University of Riga.
He won a scholarship to the Slade School, where he studied under Henry Tonks.
After supper, I went to my room and studied until midnight, and then I went to bed.

legal, lawful, legitimate

Legal is used to describe things that involve the law.

...the British legal system.
...legal advice.

If something such as an action is **legal,** it is not against the law and you cannot be punished for it under the law.

The decisions are all legally correct but as someone once said, 'Being legal doesn't make it right.'
They used their opportunity, skilfully combining both legal and underground methods.

If something is **lawful,** it is allowed by law or acceptable to the law. **Lawful** is a formal word.

All his activities had been perfectly lawful; he had only exercised his rights.
Their aim was to 'educate public opinion to demand, by every lawful means, the prohibition of hunting in Britain.'

If something is **legitimate,** it is correct or acceptable according to a law or rule. **Legitimate** can also mean that something is justified under the circumstances.

Both regimes claimed to be Korea's legitimate government.
Religious leaders have a legitimate reason to be concerned.

less, fewer

You use **less** in front of an uncount noun to say that one quantity is not as big as another, or that a quantity is not as big as it was before.

A shower uses less water than a bath.
She may even give him less attention.
Britain's industry is using less and less oil.

Less is also sometimes used in front of the plural form of count nouns. Some people object to this use. They say that you should use **fewer** instead.

They tend to eat fewer cooked meals and more sandwiches.
There were fewer people and a more relaxed atmosphere altogether.

You use '**less than**' in front of a noun group to say that an amount or measurement is below a particular point or level.

Half of all working women earned less than twenty pounds a week.
I travelled less than 3,000 miles.

'**Less than**' is sometimes used in front of a noun group referring to a number of people or things.

The whole of Switzerland has less than six million inhabitants.
The country's standing army consisted of less than a hundred soldiers.

Some people object to this use. They say that you should use '**fewer than**' in front of noun groups referring to a number of people or things.

He had never been in a class with fewer than forty children.
In 1900 there were fewer than one thousand university teachers.

less

Grammar

The superlative form of **less** is **least**. The superlative form of **few** is **fewest**.

Experiment to see which precautions work best and with least effort.
The champions in golf are the players who hit fewest bad shots.

library, bookshop

A **library** is a place where books are kept. People read the books there or borrow them to read at home. You can also study in a **library**. A **public library** also keeps newspapers, magazines, records, and similar items.

It is a beautifully produced book to borrow from the library.
...a new extension to the library.

A **library** is also a private collection of books or records.

He had recommended a book to her and had loaned it to her from his library.

A 'library' is not the place where you go to buy books. A shop that sells books is called a **bookshop** in British English and a **bookstore** in American English.

...a second-hand bookshop.
...the technique of perusing books in bookshops without actually buying them.

licence, license

The word **licence** is a noun in British English. **License** is a verb in British English, and a verb and noun in American English.

A **licence** or, in American English, a **license** is an official document that gives you permission to do, use, or own something. For example, in Britain, you need a **licence** to drive a car. In America, you need a **license**.

I disagree with the two pound licence to fish the Thames.
He could lose both his liquor and his hotel licence.
The black automobile bearing New York license plates stopped in front of the Adams' home.

An official body like a government or the police can **license** a person or an organization to do something. If someone **is licensed**, they have a **licence** for a particular activity. If a gun or a business **is licensed**, its owners have been given a **licence**.

Dogs should be more strictly licensed and controlled.
Their bars are licensed to sell alcohol.

little, a little

You use **little** to say there that there is not much of a thing, often when there is not as much as you would expect or not enough. For example, if you say that there is **little** time, you mean that there is not enough time to do a particular thing.

We had little chance of success.
John and I had very little money left.
It is clear that little progress was made.

You use **a little** simply to indicate that you are talking about a small quantity or amount of something. For example, if you say there is **a little** bit of cake left, you mean that there is some cake but that it is not very big. You are not saying whether you think there is enough.

'Have a drink. Scotch or Bourbon?'—'A little drop of Scotch would be very welcome.'
She lay awake a little while longer.
I had made a little progress.

● **Little** and **a little** can also be used as pronouns.

Little has changed.
Beat in the eggs, a little at a time.

little, few

You use **little** to say there that there is not much of a thing, often when there is not as much as you would expect or not enough. For example, if you say that there is **little** time, you mean that there is not enough time to do a particular thing. Note that you use **little** with uncount nouns.

There was little time for formalities.
She had little affection for him.
Gertrude paid little attention to him.

You use **few** to say that there are not many of a thing, often when there are not as many as you would expect. For example, you can say that there are **few** eggs, coins, or mistakes. Note that you use **few** with plural count nouns.

They were strange, lonely years, for my mother had few friends.
Forests are one of Europe's few major natural resources.
There were very few young people in the audience.

lose, loose

If you **have lost** something, you no longer have it and cannot find it. You may have forgotten where you put it, you may have thrown it away by accident, or someone may have taken it from you. **Lost** is the past participle and past tense of the irregular verb **lose.**

'Isn't it silly of me?' Mrs Bixby said. 'I've lost my pocketbook.'
You complain about losing the things, and you complain about my finding them.

Loose is usually an adjective. If something like a handle is **loose,** it is not properly fixed in place.

The loose boards on the landing were creaking.
My father took the butter-knife and prised loose a brick in the wall.

If you **loose** an animal, or let an animal **loose,** you release it from where it was kept.

The wolves were loosed late last night.
A youth had brought a pair of white rats into church and had let them loose on the floor during my sermon.

Other words

The verb **loosen** means to make something less tight or to undo it slightly.

With the aid of a screwdriver, loosen the two screws at each end.
He loosened his seat-belt.

love, like

If you **love** a person or a place, you feel a strong affection for them. For example, parents **love** their children and people who want to get married usually **love** each other.

Oh I love you, I love you with all my heart.
A boy loves his mother much more than he loves any little girl.
He loved his country above all else.

If you **like** someone, you enjoy their company. If you **like** something, it gives you pleasure. For example, you can say that you **like** your neighbours if they are friendly and helpful. Your favourite television programme is the one you **like** best.

I liked Brian, but we had never been close friends.
Tim and Daisy liked the place because it was quiet.

In conversation, people sometimes use **love** to emphasize that they enjoy or **like** something very much.

Children love noise and mud.
I love your new hairdo.

M

machine, motor, engine

A **machine** is a piece of equipment which uses electricity or some other form of power to perform a particular task.

...a washing machine.
He has even devised a simple machine for cutting the fibre up.

When a machine operates by electricity, you refer to the part of the machine that converts power into movement as the **motor**.

The washing machine is powered by an electric motor.
Efficiency improvements in electric motors could save more electricity than UK nuclear stations currently produce.

Larger machines are usually powered by petrol or diesel **engines**. For example, the part of a car that provides the power to make it move is usually called the **engine**.

The man went on working, or appearing to work, on the engine of the small car.
She turned her engine on, then her parking lights.
The aircraft's passengers were aware that they were operating with three engines instead of four.

You talk about the **engine** of a ship, but the **motor** of a small boat.

Black smoke belched from the engine into the cabin.
We patched leaks, overhauled the motor, and refitted her.

Some people refer to the engine in a car as the **motor**.

He started the motor of the car and drove off abruptly.

magazine, newspaper, paper, journal

Magazines, newspapers, papers, and **journals** all contain information and articles for people to read.

magazine

A **magazine** is published regularly, usually every week or every month. It is often concerned with a particular subject such as computing or cars, or written for particular readers, for example teenagers. It is usually illustrated with photographs and pictures, often in colour, and contains articles, advertisements, and sometimes stories. Some **magazines** deal with news, but present background detail and analysis rather than the latest information. Some **magazines** are read for entertainment as well as for information. Many magazines are printed on shiny paper.

She was sitting on the divan, quite at home, reading a film magazine.
He was about to launch a quarterly magazine devoted to religious studies.

A **newspaper** is published either every day from Monday to Saturday or every Sunday. Daily **newspapers** report the news of the previous twenty-four hours. Sunday **newspapers** report the news of the previous week. **Newspapers** are illustrated with photographs and include articles about the background to the news, articles of general interest, and advertisements.

Agostino sat at the little desk with the newspaper spread out in front of him at the sports page.
She read in the newspapers about increasing unemployment among teachers.

A **newspaper** is often called a **paper**.

I read about the riots in the papers.

A **journal** is designed to interest a particular group of readers, often a professional group. For example, people in universities read academic **journals,** and doctors read medical **journals**. A **journal** is often a very serious publication. It may appear weekly, monthly, or every few months. It contains articles about its subject matter. Some **journals** are illustrated; some contain advertisements.

...the British Medical Journal.
Does your union journal have articles on health and safety?
...the sort of scientific information normally published in learned journals.

magazine, shop, store

A **magazine** is a publication which often has articles on a particular subject, for example computing or cars, or is intended for particular readers, for example women.

He switched his attention back to the magazine and went on with his reading.
...boys playing ping-pong, sitting over chess boards, reading magazines.

A magazine is not a place where you buy things. You do your shopping in a **shop** or a **store.**

From a shop specializing in camping equipment he bought a pair of hiking boots.
...articles that nobody really needs, but which occupy the ground floors of all big stores.

magic, magical

Magic is a special power that occurs in children's stories and that some people believe exists. It is supposed to make apparently impossible things happen such as make people disappear or control events in nature.

Janoo-Bai was suspected of practising magic.
She was accused of inflicting bad fortune on them through evil magic.

You use the adjective **magic** in front of a noun to describe things that perform **magic** or that are believed to perform **magic.**

They raided the Isle of Annen to seize the magic cauldron from which only the brave and the true could eat.
The words were used as a magic charm to ward off fear.
Hecate was invoked in magic spells.

You can use **magical** in a similar way.

Iron was once thought to be a magical metal with supernatural powers.
It was believed that this magical essence would protect a man from possession by evil spirits.
...magical garments.

You also use **magical** to say that something involves magic or is produced by magic.

...magical processes.
Explanations are found for what seemed magical.

You can also use either **magic** or **magical** to describe things which have a mysterious, pleasant, and exciting quality.

The shrine is a magic place.

magic

...this strange magic brown-haired girl with long heavy sleepy eyelashes.
The Dordogne is a kind of magical, picture-book world.
Close up to that magical face, the lovely violet eyes, he lost his anger.

make, do

If you produce or construct an object or substance, you **make** it out of other materials. For example, you can **make** clothes to wear or **make** a meal or a drink.

Sheila makes all her own clothes.
The heat is enough to make perfect yoghurt overnight.
Then he came into the kitchen to make the coffee.
...the big companies that make women's face creams.
You can make petroleum out of coal.
I have made you a drink.

Another use of **make** is in expressions where it does not have a distinct meaning of its own, but where most of the meaning is in the noun which is the object of **make.** For example, if someone decides something, you can say that they **make** a decision.

You can use **make** with nouns referring to talking, sounds, and gestures, for example:

appeal	confession	gesture	remark
claim	distinction	noise	signal
comment	enquiry	point	sound
comparison	excuse	promise	speech
complaint	fuss	protest	suggestion

She made an angry gesture with her fist.
She made a remark about the weather.
May I make a suggestion?
He made the shortest speech I have ever heard.

You can use **make** with nouns referring to plans and attempts, for example:

appointment	change	effort	start
arrangement	choice	plan	
attempt	decision	progress	

I'd like to make an appointment to see one of the doctors this morning.
He made an attempt to calm down.
I think I made the wrong decision.
Daintry made one more effort to escape.

You can also use **make** with some other nouns, for example:

appearance	fortune	mess	phone call
contribution	impact	mistake	profit
debut	loss	note	recovery

She has made several television appearances recently.
He had made a terrible mistake.
The company made a profit of 113 per cent.
She made a very good recovery.

Do is used to say that someone performs an action, activity, or task. It is not normally used to say that someone produces something.

We did quite a lot of work yesterday.
Small children want to do a lot of things that get them dirty.

Do is often followed by an '-ing' form such as 'cooking' or 'shopping', and by other nouns referring to work and to jobs connected with the home.

I do the cooking and Brian does the cleaning.
I want to do a little shopping on the way to the hospital.
You never do any housework.

Here is a list of nouns which are often used with **do**:

business	dishes	ironing	washing-up
chores	duty	job	work
cleaning	exercise	research	
cooking	homework	shopping	
course	housework	washing	

You can also use **do** when you do not specify exactly what action you are referring to. You cannot use 'make' in this way.

What have you done?
You've done a lot to help us.
We'll see what can be done.

In conversation, **do** is often used to replace a more specific verb. For example, if you '**do** your teeth', you brush them, and if you '**do** the flowers', you arrange them.

She had done her hair for the party.
We have a man to do the garden.

Occasionally, **do** can replace 'make' in this way.

I have just done three hundred and fifty dresses.

● **Do** can also be used as an auxiliary, for example in questions and negative sentences.

make

Do you understand what I'm saying?
Does she still want to come?
We didn't have much money.

In some sentences, **do** may occur twice: once as an auxiliary and once as a main verb.

What did she do all day?
If this exercise hurts your back do not do it.

male, masculine

You use **male** to describe men and things associated with men. You also use **male** to describe animals belonging to the sex that cannot give birth to babies or lay eggs, and things associated with them.

A taciturn male companion stood next to her.
This style of male dress was established in the mid-nineteenth century.
...three large strong male camels.

You can also use **male** as a noun, but only when referring to animals.

The males establish a breeding territory.

You use **masculine** to describe qualities and characteristics that society associates with men rather than women.

...masculine notions that striving and achievement are for men only.
...what used to be called masculine assertiveness.
Boys are brainwashed into thinking that it's smart, trendy, masculine to smoke.
It must have something to do with masculine pride.

● Some languages divide nouns and adjectives into two classes, **masculine** and feminine, or into three classes, **masculine,** feminine, and neuter.

man, husband

A **man** is an adult male human being.

Larry was a handsome man in his early fifties.
He was visited by two men in the morning.

The person a woman is married to is normally called her **husband,** not her 'man'.

She and her husband were new people in the town.
She met her husband in 1942.

many, a lot of, a lot, much

Many, **a lot of**, **a lot**, and **much** are all used to talk about large numbers of people or things, or large quantities or amounts.

You use **many** or **a lot of** in front of a plural count noun to talk about a large number of people or things.

There must be many men who do not want to change these attitudes.
There were many complex problems to be solved.
A lot of people thought it was funny.
You've done them a lot of favours.

After 'too' and 'so', you have to use **many**.

She had been most afraid of living like her mother, too many children, too little money.
I had spent my entire life with so many books I wanted to read and no time to do it in.

You also use **many** in the phrase 'as **many** ... as'.

His ambition now is to win as many tournaments as he can.
I cannot claim to have talked to as many people as he does.

In spoken English, **many** often sounds formal in affirmative sentences in which it does not follow 'too' or 'so', or in which it is not part of the phrase 'as **many** ... as'. However, it does not sound formal in negative sentences, or in questions.

When you first go there, not many people talk to you.
How many times must I tell you?

In writing, **many** can be used as a pronoun to refer to a large number of people or things. This use of **many** is fairly formal. You do not normally use 'a lot' in this way.

In the Hong Kong camps alone, there are over 20,000 people. Many have been there for five or ten years and have nowhere to go back to.
Many were still lying where they had been injured.

When you want to talk about a large number of the people or things in a particular group, you can use **many of** or **a lot of** followed by a plural pronoun or by a plural noun group which begins with 'the', 'these', 'those', or a possessive.

A lot of them are married women.
Many of his books are still available.
...the great dream many of us had thirty years ago.
We had already heard a lot of these songs at least once.

many

You use **many** or **a lot** in front of a noun group beginning with 'more' to emphasize the difference in size between two groups of people or things, or between the same group of people or things at different times.

I know many more country people than I do town people.
There are many more training courses on offer.
There is still room for a lot more people.
There will be a lot more flights.

You use **much** or **a lot of** in front of an uncount noun to talk about a large quantity or amount of something. **Much** is not usually used like this in affirmative sentences, because it sounds very formal. However, it does not sound formal in negative sentences, or in questions.

I didn't seem to have much strength left in my hands.
Is this going to make much difference?
He's lost a lot of weight.

However, you have to use **much** after 'too' and 'so' and in the phrase 'as **much** ... as', even in affirmative sentences. **Much** does not sound formal when used in this way.

It gave the President too much power.
There's so much pain in the world.
It absorbs as much heat as possible.

Much or **a lot** can be used as a pronoun to refer to a large quantity or amount of something. This use of **much** sounds formal in affirmative sentences.

There wasn't much to do.
I suppose they learned a lot by doing it.
...a dog who has lived long, and experienced much.

When you want to talk about a large quantity or amount of a particular thing, you can use **much of** or **a lot of** followed by 'it', 'this', or 'that', or by a noun group which begins with 'the', 'this', 'that', or a possessive.

I still remember much of it in some detail.
A lot of this is shared accommodation.
One thousand years ago thick forests covered much of the UK.
Caroline devoted much of her life to education.

You use **much** or **a lot** in front of a noun group beginning with 'more' or 'less' to emphasize the difference between two quantities or amounts.

Children, whose bones are growing, need much more calcium than adults.
It has led to divorce and a life with much less time for her child.
He had gained a lot more sleep than the others.
You can stay on the island for a lot less money.

You use **much** or **a lot** in front of comparative adjectives and adverbs, and in front of adjectives and adverbs that are preceded by 'less', in order to emphasize the difference between two people or things.

She was much older than me.
Unfortunately the aim is a lot more limited than the experts realize.
Mrs Salt's statement should have been disclosed much earlier.
It is much less likely.

You use **very much** or **a lot** as an adverb to say that something is true to a great extent.

I enjoyed it very much.
You like Ralph a lot, don't you?

In clauses that do not have an object but which are followed by a 'that'-clause or a 'to'-infinitive, you can use **very much,** but not 'a lot', to add emphasis to a verb.

We very much hope he'll continue to be able to represent you.
He would like very much to write to Dennis himself.

You do not use 'much' without 'very' in affirmative sentences to say that something is true to a great extent. However, you can use it without 'very' in negative sentences.

The situation isn't likely to change much.
I didn't like him much.

You can use **much** in negative sentences and questions to mean 'often'. **A lot** can be used to mean 'often' in negative sentences, questions, and affirmative sentences.

She doesn't talk about them much.
Does he come here much?
They talk a lot about equality.

Grammar

When the subject of a sentence consists of **a lot of** followed by a plural noun group, the verb which follows is plural. When the subject consists of **a lot of** followed by an uncount noun group, the verb which follows is singular.

many

Quite a lot of people at work think I'm rather lucky to be your daughter.
A lot of the arable land was under-used and poorly tended.

You can use 'there are' or 'there were' in front of **a lot of** when it is followed by a plural noun group. You can use 'there is' or 'there was' in front of **a lot of** when it is followed by an uncount noun group.

There are a lot of companies whose profits are going to disappear if things remain the same.
There were a lot of people about.
There is a lot of corruption.
There was a lot of business to sort through.

Other words

In writing, you often use 'a great deal of' instead of **much** in front of an uncount noun group in affirmative sentences. Similarly, you often use 'a great number of' instead of **many** in front of a plural noun group in affirmative sentences. These phrases are slightly more formal than 'a lot of', but not as formal as **much** or **many**.

He said a great deal of information had been provided by the American authorities.
Among the horsemen were a great number of officers.

In conversation, you can use **lots of** instead of **a lot of,** and **lots** instead of **a lot.**

He has lots of friends.
I have lots to do.

memories, memoirs

Someone's **memories** are the things they remember about their past.

Some of his earliest memories are of camping in the Flint Hills with his parents.
He was full of memories, nostalgic for the past, hating change.
In the main, though, my memories of a London childhood are happy ones.

Someone's **memoirs** are a written account they give of their life, in the form of a book.

In the past, most former presidents retired to write their memoirs.
He was writing his memoirs of his career abroad.
They're making a movie of his war memoirs.

memory, souvenir

A **memory** is something that you remember from your past.

That sweet smell brought the memories flooding back.
Although he is now a wealthy man he cannot erase the memories of childhood.
...a memory of an old friend.

A **souvenir** is an object that you keep to remind you of something that has happened to you or of a place that you have visited. Tourists often buy **souvenirs** when they are on holiday.

The walls were filled with photos and souvenirs of the colonel's army days and his hunting expeditions.
You can shop for souvenirs – the black and brown coral jewellery is particularly fine.

meter, metre

A **meter** is a device that measures and records something, for example the amount of electricity or gas used in a home, or how much a passenger must pay a taxi driver.

To know how much electricity you use in a week, learn how to read your meter.
The taxi driver hadn't bothered to switch off his meter.

A parking **meter** is a device on a street into which you put money in order to be allowed to park your car for a period of time.

Occasionally, I just park at a meter, and walk around for a while.

A **metre** is a metric unit of length, equal to 100 centimetres or 39.37 inches.

At a cafe a hundred metres down the street he again used the phone.
The flames and smoke rose hundreds of metres into the sky.

Note that in American English 'metre' is spelled **meter**.

He poked his head into the cab to read the meter.
They are flying at five hundred meters over a high shallow valley.

middle, centre

The **middle** or **centre** of something is the part furthest away from its outer part.

You can talk about the **middle** of a two-dimensional shape or area. Usually you mean an approximate area rather than an exact point.

middle

We pull off into a little town that could be in the middle of Iowa.
In the middle of the lawn was a great cedar tree.

You can talk about the **centre** of an area or three-dimensional shape. Usually you mean an exact point rather than an approximate position. For example, in mathematics you talk about the **centre** of a circle, not the 'middle'.

...the centre of the cyclone.
Bake the buns in the centre of a very hot oven.

If you talk about the **centre** of a town or city, you mean the area where there are the most shops, offices, or places where people meet.

At the centre of the huge city rose a complex of skyscrapers.

The **middle** of a road or river is the part that is furthest from its sides or banks. You do not talk about the 'centre' of a road or river.

...white lines painted along the middle of the highway.
We managed to pull on to a sandbank in the middle of the river.

mistake, fault

If you make a **mistake**, you do the wrong thing. For example, you may make a wrong decision, produce the wrong answer in a calculation, buy something you do not really want, or call someone by the wrong name.

I'm afraid you've made a mistake. My name is Mary Taylor. Mrs Taylor.
In some elementary schools, even today, small children are punished for mistakes in addition or in spelling.
The World Bank has clearly learned from past mistakes.

A **fault** is a bad feature of a person's character or of the way they do something.

Ryden idolized his daughter so much that he could not see her faults.
'Thoughtless of me.'—'Thoughtlessness is hardly one of your faults.'
That was always one of my faults. I was always too intense.

If you say that something is someone's **fault**, you mean that they are responsible for something bad or wrong happening.

It's important guests should be well-fed. If they overeat it's their fault.
It was all Jack's fault.

You also use **fault** to refer to something wrong in a machine or structure.

The machine has developed a fault.
Computer faults are commonplace.

moral, morals, morale

Moral means relating to right and wrong behaviour. **Moral** values or **moral** issues involve your sense of what is right and wrong. **Moral** is pronounced /mɒrəl/.

It is our moral duty to stay.
This presented them with moral choices concerning the distribution and use of power and wealth.
...a whole system of moral behaviour which the young child was not ready for.

The **moral** of a story or of a situation is the lesson that you can learn from it about how you should or should not behave.

The moral is obvious; it is that great armaments lead inevitably to war.

A person's **morals** are the principles and values they use to decide the right and wrong way to behave.

Many of the early laws were concerned with the morals and education of children and women.
The parent of the problem child never thinks of challenging his own code of morals.

A person's **morale** is the confidence and optimism they have when they are dealing with an important, difficult, or dangerous situation. **Moral** is pronounced /mərɑːl/.

Rothermere's morale depended apparently on his immense success in making money.
There is nothing like winning to boost the morale of players.

Other words

Morality is the idea that some forms of behaviour are right and others are wrong. **Morality** is pronounced /məræləti/.

Sexual morality was enforced by the fear of illegitimacy.

more, most

More and **most** are used to make comparisons or to describe an increase in a quality such as size, amount, beauty, or intelligence.

more

The comparatives and superlatives of some adjectives and adverbs are formed by using **more** or **most** rather than by adding '-er' or '-est'.

You use **more** to compare one person or thing with another. It indicates that the first person or thing has a particular quality to a greater extent than the second person or thing.

Many parents are still more ambitious for their sons than their daughters.
Moist, cold air is more chilling than dry air of the same temperature.
The psychological effects are much more difficult to cope with.

You also use **more** to compare the extent to which a person or thing has a particular quality at two different times.

I saw Baschia every day and every day he seemed more tired.
Next time, I will chose more carefully.

You use **most** to compare one person or thing with other members of a set or group. It indicates that the person or thing that you mention has a particular quality to a greater extent than any of the others.

...his closest and most intimate friend.
I thought up two or three different excuses, including of course the most obvious one.
Britain's most famous aviation pioneer, Sir Thomas Sopwith.

Note that when you use **most** in front of an adjective, you are usually referring to one person or thing in a set or a group which has at least three members. In conversation, some people use **most** in front of an adjective when they are comparing just two things. For example, someone might say 'Which book did you find most interesting?' when talking about two books. You should avoid this in formal writing.

much, very

Much is an adverb, used to emphasize that something is true to a great extent. When used with a verb, it is usually found in negative sentences, questions, or after words such as 'very', 'so', 'as', and 'too'.

I don't feel the cold much.
Does he come here much?
I enjoyed it very much.
I hope very much that you will be coming on Saturday.

There is so much financial hardship.
They liked him almost as much as his money.

Much is also used with verbs in the passive, and with past
participles.

It had been much discussed with the group.
Well, good-bye and thanks, Mr Welch. Much obliged to you.
This led to frequent and much publicised threats of dismissal.

Much is also used to emphasize comparative and superlative
adjectives and adverbs.

Now I feel much more confident.
I thought that he was much the best speaker.
I'm treated so much better than Judy was.
This could be done very much more quickly.

Very is an adverb, used to emphasize an adjective or another
adverb.

You are going to become very rich and very powerful.
He greeted me with a very gentle voice.
She says you're very clever.
This highly automated plant operated very successfully.
Hanover was very badly damaged.

● Note that **very** is often used to emphasize **much**.

I very much doubt that.
At 67, Ford very much wants to stay active.
*I hoped very much that Miss Gray would stay with me at Fairacre
School.*
...a very much heightened susceptibility to infection.

N

narrow, thin

Something that is **narrow** has a very small distance between its
two sides, so that it is not very wide. You can describe roads as
narrow, as well as other spaces that people or things move along
or fit into.

*Tom drove the bike down the narrow back road behind the Boylan
estate.*
Watch the stairs, they're narrow.

narrow

The room was small, and had in it a narrow bed and a cupboard.

Something that is **thin** has a very small distance between its two opposite surfaces, so that it is not very thick. You can describe lines as **thin,** as well as things such as curtains or walls.

...a collarless shirt with a thin grey stripe.
I gave Aicha the thin silver chain I was wearing.
A long way off she saw Kate Ferreira, in her thin white embroidered linen dress.

People and parts of their bodies can also be described as **thin.**

He was a tall, thin man with a deeply lined forehead.
The fire warmed their thin legs.

nervous, irritated

If you are **nervous,** you are worried and tense, and may behave in a frightened way. You might be **nervous** if you have to take an examination or have to make a speech in public.

Colin's driving made her nervous.
It was the first time I had ever been in front of a TV camera, and I was so nervous I could barely keep the quaver out of my voice.
A funny little nervous half-smile appeared on Landy's mouth.

If you are **irritated,** you are annoyed by something which you cannot prevent or stop. You might be **irritated** if someone is making too much noise or if a machine keeps breaking down.

My father had called me twice, and he sounded irritated.
'How long have you been watching me?' the little man asked in an irritated voice.

no, none

You use **no** in front of nouns to mean 'not any' or 'not one'. For example, you might say that you have **no** time or **no** stamps.

Have I not just told you that I had no extra information?
There was no moon that night.
We saw no houses, no smoke, no footprints, no boats, no people.
He has given no reason for his decision.

You use **none** instead of a noun group that begins with 'no' to indicate that there are not any of the things or people that you have already mentioned.

*Occasionally a new star would appear in the sky where none had
been detected before.*
*I have answered every single question. My opponent has answered
none.*
Part-time assistance is a lot better than none at all.

none, neither

You use **none** to refer to three or more people or things when you
are making a negative statement that applies to all of them.

None could afford the books or food.
*The bomb exploded and knocked out a few men. Luckily, none were
killed.*

You can also use **none of** followed by a pronoun or noun group.

None of them had learned anything about the teaching of reading.
None of his black companions answered.

You use **neither** to refer to each of two people or things when you
are making a negative statement that applies to both of them.

Neither had close female friends at the university.
*She chose first one, then another, but neither was to her
satisfaction.*

You can also use **neither of** followed by a pronoun or noun
group.

Neither of them spoke again for a long while.
Neither of these extremes is desirable.

● You can also use **neither** immediately in front of a singular
count noun.

Militarily, neither side can win.

none, no-one, nobody

None means 'not a single thing of a particular kind' or 'not a
single member of a particular group'.

*This created a class of large landowners where none had existed
before.*
*They later went to work at regular jobs. But none rose to become a
good scholar or a fine artist.*

You can also use **none of** followed by a pronoun or noun group.

None of them spoke Sinhalese.
None of the clothes were any use, anyway.

157

none

No-one or **nobody** means 'not a single person'. You may be making a general statement or talking about a particular group of people. You do not have to mention the group of people. Note that there is no difference in meaning between **no-one** and **nobody**.

I knocked on the door. No-one answered, so I went in.
She's the sweetest girl, Jane, I swear no-one could help loving her.
That's a question nobody can answer.
The room looked so pretty when there was nobody in it.

north, northern, northerly

The **north** is the direction on your left when you are looking towards the direction where the sun rises. The **north** of a country or area is the part towards the north. You use **north, northern,** and **northerly** to describe things that are in or come from the north.

You use **north** to describe a part of a place that is in the north, whether it is a large place like a country or a smaller place like a building. Note that **north** is often used to make a contrast with the south, west, and east: the **north** side of a building is opposite the south side.

Male unemployment in the North Wales town of Flint now stands at 38 per cent.
...Molyvos – a charming hill village on the north coast.
How about making a film on the North Wall of the Eiger?

Northern means relating to the north and refers to a more general area than **north**.

I didn't know much about the geography of Northern California.
...the northern regions of the British Isles.
It is a tiny harbour on the northern coast of Cyprus.

You can also use **northern** to describe things that come from the north or that are found there.

There was no northern puritanism here in the Middle Ages.
He held her hand lovingly when they walked in the sunlight of the northern summer.
...Sunday evening in a small northern industrial town with the intermittent cold rain.

Winds that come from the north can be described as **north** or **northerly** winds.

There was a smell of snow on the north wind.
Heavy walls at the rear sheltered buildings from cold northerly winds.

You can also use **northerly** to describe directions and locations. If something moves in a **northerly** direction, it moves towards the north. Unlike 'north' and 'northern', **northerly** can be used with 'more' and 'most'.

...the wet, northerly slopes.
He recommended a more northerly course than usual to avoid strong headwinds.
We proceeded along a more northerly route.

notable, noticeable

If you describe something as **notable,** you mean that it is important, interesting, or remarkable. A **notable** writer, for example, is a good writer whose work is worth reading; a **notable** exception is an exception which is important. **Notable** is a fairly formal word.

One of the notable historians of the period is Adam Ulam.
Most of the foods we eat do contain small amounts of protein, notable exceptions being fat, sugar and alcohol.
The most notable quality of a convention is its sheer tedium.

Something that is **noticeable** is easy to hear, see, or recognize because it is so obvious.

The years had made a noticeable change in Muller – his hair was almost white now.
Effects such as pollution and ecological damage begin to become noticeable.
The teachers reported a noticeable increase in the amount of reading done by the pupils.

note, notice

Note and notice can be used as both nouns and verbs.

A **note** is a short message you write for someone else to read, or something you write down to help you remember something.

Wilt opened the note. 'I'm going away with Sally and Gaskell to think things over.'
She wrote the milkman a note.
Hercule Poirot, with a sheet of paper in front of him, was making notes.

note

A **notice** is a sign giving information or instructions which is put in a place where people can read it.

Billy caught sight of a printed notice propped up against the glass in one of the upper panes. It said BED AND BREAKFAST.
In the crypt of the eleventh century church, so notices and posters indicated, wine was being served.
She was staring at the notice that claimed 'A Woman's Right to Choose'.

If you **note** a fact, you become aware of it and keep it in your mind. You can mention it in order to point it out to others.

It was a surprising vanity in such a composed figure; Stuart noted it with interest.
Note that the report does not carry any form of official recommendation.
The committee also noted that this was not the first case of its kind.

If you **notice** something, you observe it at a particular moment. You might forget about it later.

He waited a moment and hoped she wouldn't notice he was out of breath.
I had noticed by the streetlight that his face was red and swollen.

notice, observe, pay attention

If you **notice** something, you become aware of it by seeing it or by using your other senses.

I noticed she was wearing a new dress.
I noticed a new tranquillity about him.
I have noticed that your father is not as friendly towards me as he used to be.

Observe can be used with the same meaning as **notice**. However, **observe** is a rather formal word.

Glancing cautiously about the room, she observed a threadbare rug and a few pieces of sadly shabby furniture.
The Count, I observed, had a mildly speculative expression on his face.

You also use **observe** to talk about watching someone or something deliberately and very carefully.

A half dozen spectators gathered on the outside to observe the proceedings.
He will stand well back in order to observe you from a distance.

If you **pay attention** to someone or something, you watch or listen with great concentration, especially in order not to miss anything.

For the first time he paid attention to the driver.
I was not paying attention to what was going on.

now, at present, presently

You can use both **now** and **at present** to talk about things as they are at the time when you mention them.

Now may refer to a period of time or to a particular moment.

She gradually built up energy and is now back to normal.
I'm feeling much better now.
I'm going home now.

At present refers to a period of time and may imply that the situation may change. **At present** is quite formal.

I don't want to get married at present.
At present there is a world energy shortage.

Presently means 'quite soon'. For example, if something is going to happen quite soon, you can say that it will happen **presently**. This use is slightly old-fashioned.

The Prince of Wales will be here presently.
I shall have more to say presently.

Presently is sometimes used in the same way as **at present**.

...Leningrad, presently a city of four million.
American and Japan are presently working on chips which will hold a million words.

Some speakers of English find this use of 'presently' unacceptable.

● You cannot use 'actually' to talk about things as they are at the time when you mention them. You use **now, at present,** or less commonly **presently**.

O

occasion, opportunity, chance, possibility

An **occasion** is a time when a particular event happens or a particular situation arises.

Several times as a child I was bullied by older boys. On one occasion, I was knocked unconscious.
I met him on only one occasion.
There are occasions when you must not refuse.

An **occasion** can also be the event itself, especially an important event such as a wedding or public ceremony.

In his shirtsleeves he felt he wasn't properly dressed for the occasion.
This garment is just special enough to be worn for casual evening occasions.

If you say you 'have **occasion** to do' something, or that an event is an '**occasion** for' something, you mean that people and circumstances make it possible. This is a rather formal use.

She had had little occasion to mix with the opposite sex.
The question remained whether Benn could succeed in making this crisis the occasion for fundamental change.

If you have the **opportunity** or the **chance** to do something, you can do it because people and circumstances make it possible. **Opportunity** is more formal than **chance**. Note that you do not say that you have the 'possibility' to do something.

You will have the opportunity to ask the athlete questions about his personal career.
New job opportunities have been found for women.
The cinema specialized in revivals, and this was a quite wonderful chance to see this unique masterpiece.
I didn't have a chance to say a word.

A **possibility** is something that might happen or be done, but that also might not happen or be done. You say that there is a **possibility,** that a **possibility** exists, or that something is a **possibility.**

There was just a possibility that they had taken the wrong road.
Only then did he permit his mind to consider the possibility of an accident.
The possibility exists for trade unionists to rebuild their confidence.

If only they had told me of this possibility, how much suffering I would have been saved!
They rang to say that Jeffrey might have typhoid, it was a possibility, but no one was to worry.

office, bureau

An **office** is a room, a set of rooms, or a whole building where people do professional work, for example administration or computing.

Dominic wants to see you in his office.
I was alone in the office when Mark Rutland came in.
...a massive programme for the insulation of houses, factories and offices.

Bureau is used, especially in the United States of America, in the names of organizations that deal with collecting or giving information.

She worked for the Bureau of Indian Affairs on a reservation in Arizona.
You can ask the Citizens' Advice Bureau if you need help with the letter.

In Britain, **bureau** is also used in the names of organizations that introduce people to each other. For example, an employment **bureau** is where employers can find temporary staff.

Freelance Work for Women Bureau was started by a married woman who needed a job.
...the first marriage bureau specifically aimed at young black professionals.

In American English, a **bureau** is also a branch of an organization which has its headquarters in a different city or country.

Luce was infuriated to hear from his Washington bureau what Marshall really thought.

● In British English, a **bureau** is also a writing desk with shelves and drawers, and a lid that opens to form the writing surface.

one, you, people

You use **one** or **you** to make a statement which is true of any individual person, rather than a particular person. **One** is more formal than **you**.

one

I was as certain as one could be without absolute proof.
I suppose one can't blame him.
...just as one acquires skill in golf or skiing or foreign languages.

In conversation, most people use **you**.

Now, a camel can kick you in any direction, within a radius of six feet.
If a child seems sick with a rash or if the rash is extensive, you should call the doctor right away.
A crisis can be a blessing in disguise if it makes you stop and take a long look at your life.

People is used to talk about men, women, and children in general, or about a particular group of them.

The amount of potatoes and bread people buy has dropped.
When people charter my boat, I don't ask questions about them.
Don't go on about it. People may get bored or embarrassed.

opposed, opposite

If you are **opposed** to something such as a new development, a policy, or a belief, you strongly disagree with it or disapprove of it.

Steve was uncompromisingly opposed to apartheid.
...the movements opposed to nuclear weapons.
I am opposed to capital punishment.

You also use **opposed** to describe ideas, systems, or philosophies that are very different from each other.

The dispute revealed two totally opposed concepts of the role of the public sector.
...two bitterly opposed schools of socialist thought.
...a style of power that was diametrically opposed to that of the Labour Party.

Opposed can only be used as an adjective or past participle.
Opposite can be used as a preposition, adverb, adjective, or noun.

You use the adjective **opposite** in front of a noun when you are mentioning one of two sides of something. So, for example, if you are on one side of something, the other side is the **opposite** side.

I was moved to a room on the opposite side of the corridor.
On the opposite side of the room a telephone rang.

Opposite has a similar meaning when it is used as a preposition or an adverb. If something is **opposite** you, it is on the other side of a space such as a room or a street, and it faces you.

We sat opposite each other.
The only other hotel of any size in London is opposite a railway station.
I was sent out to buy tea from the cafe opposite.

You also use **opposite** in front of a noun to describe things of the same type that are as different as possible in a particular way.

Little girls, on the other hand, get the opposite training.
I wanted to impress them but probably had the opposite effect.
Too much pressure would produce overheating, whereas too little would produce the opposite result.

You use the noun **opposite** if two things of the same type are completely different in a particular way.

Hell is the opposite of heaven.
She was so quiet and the very opposite of my dad.
In general, well-cooked food is nourishing food. And the opposite can be equally true.

opposite, in front of

You use **opposite** when you are mentioning one of two sides of something. If something is **opposite** you, it is on the other side of a space such as a room or a street, and it faces you.

She sank down on the sofa opposite him.
On the opposite side of the room, on the wall, hung an African mask.

If something is **in front of** you, it is ahead of you in the direction you are facing. It is usually relatively close to you, and may be facing in any direction.

A girl in front of her had been trying to post a parcel.
I jumped up and stalked over and stood in front of her.
A crowd had assembled in front of the courthouse.

outdoor, outdoors

Outdoor is an adjective and is always used in front of a noun. You use it to describe things that happen or exist in the open air rather than inside a building.

Could I still indulge in outdoor activities, like sailing and fell walking?

outdoor

Breakfast may be taken in the dining room or on an outdoor terrace.

Outdoors is an adverb and is usually used after a verb or to qualify a whole sentence. If something happens or exists **outdoors,** it happens in the open air rather than inside a building.

It was such a beautiful day, that I decided it would do him good to be outdoors.
The doctor tells the parents to let the child outdoors as soon as the cold is gone completely.
Outdoors, they are delighted to watch leaves and shadows. Indoors, they study their hands.

P

pants, shorts, trousers

In British English, **pants** are an item of underwear worn by men and women. They cover the part of your body above your legs and below your waist. Men's **pants** are also called 'underpants' and women's **pants** are sometimes referred to as 'knickers' or 'panties'.

He dried vigorously, then put on newly laundered pants and vest.
Instead of a bra and pants, for instance, I decided to take a bikini.

In American English, this item of underwear is usually called **shorts** or 'underpants' when it is for a man and 'panties' when it is for a woman.

In British English, a pair of **trousers** is a single piece of clothing that covers each of your legs in a long tube of fabric and that covers your hips.

He put the money in the left side of his trousers.
He wore brown corduroy trousers and a tartan shirt.

In American English, this piece of clothing is called **pants.**

Boon was already removing his shoes and socks and rolling up his pants.
He always wears the same thing: faded khaki pants, a shirt, a loosely fitting gray sweater.

In both British and American English, **shorts** are short trousers that leave your knees and part of your thighs bare.

I tucked my shirt into my shorts.

parcel, package, packet

A **parcel** is an object or group of objects wrapped in paper or a cardboard box. You often pack things in **parcels** when you want to send them by post.

She was always scribbling away at something, or weighing a parcel, or licking a stamp.
I waited for the postman today; I'd hoped he'd bring a new parcel of books.

A **package** is the same as a parcel. In American English, a **package** can be any size, but in British English **package** usually refers to a fairly small parcel.

The package from Hilary evidently contained a book.
He dug into the pocket of his jeans and pulled out a small package wrapped in tissue.
He went off and left a large package on the kitchen table for me to post.

A **packet** is usually a box made of thin cardboard, or a bag, envelope, or wrapper, in which a quantity of items or of a substance is sold.

...a packet of cigarettes.
...a cereal packet.
...soup out of a packet.

Sometimes a **packet** is a very small parcel that is usually flat.

I've got a packet for you – from somewhere abroad.
...a rather messy packet, in greaseproof paper, which presumably held his lunch.

particular, particularly, peculiar, peculiarly

You can use **particular** to indicate that you are talking about a special or individual case of something.

Let us consider a particular example in which this problem emerges vividly.
It is important to discuss a child's particular problems and interests.

particular

You can use **particularly** to indicate that something applies more to one person, thing, or situation than others.

It was hard for the children, particularly when they were ill.
Protests came against the severity of the sentences, particularly against the imprisonment of three Union officials.

You can also use **particular** or **particularly** to emphasize how great or intense something is. For example, if you have **particular** difficulty in doing something or find something **particularly** difficult, you find it very difficult.

These children need particular care in being shown how to tackle arithmetical problems.
He was proud to be host to so many people and was paying particular attention to Ellen.
She was looking particularly attractive today.

If you describe something as **peculiar,** you find it strange often in a way you do not like. You can also describe people as **peculiar** or say that they behave **peculiarly.**

He was wearing a peculiar suit.
Les had a most peculiar sense of humour.
Uncle Harold smiled at him peculiarly, blinking in the light.

You can also use **peculiar** and **peculiarly** to talk about something which is unique or characteristic in a pleasing way. This is a formal use.

Here Pimlico has its own peculiar flavour and atmosphere.
Pregnancy is a peculiarly important time in a woman's life.

pass, take, sit

If you **pass** a test or examination, you are successful in it.

To pass examinations you need to work effectively.
Your object is to learn facts and retain them long enough to pass the examination.

You do not use 'pass' to say that you do a test or examination. You say that you **take** or **sit** a test or examination.

Whatever examinations you intend to take in the future you need to be numerate and literate.
Pupils at the schools run by Trafford Council sat the exam in November.

pavement, sidewalk

A path with a hard surface by the side of a road where pedestrians can walk is called a **pavement** in British English and a **sidewalk** in American English.

The street lamps cast a dull yellowish glow on the pavement every few hundred yards.
He strolled out of the bar on to the pavement.
The sidewalk is narrow, only wide enough for one person.
We walk under shady trees on very neat sidewalks past neat houses.

Note that in American English, the **pavement** is the hard surface of a road, sidewalk, or area such as a playground.

Traunsteiner swerved the car back full onto the pavement.
The ribbon of pavement goes on more or less endlessly through broken country.

pay, buy

When you **pay** someone, **pay** them money, or **pay for** something, you give someone money for something that they are selling to you or for a service that they have done for you.

The two packing cases are taken out and set on the pavement.
Flecker pays the driver.
I've left you some money to pay the window cleaner.
In many cases people are forced to pay for their own medicines in full.

When you **pay** a bill or debt, you pay the amount of money that is owed.

He paid his bill and left.
We had been paying £50 a week for a single room in London.

If you **buy** something, you obtain it by paying money for it.

Gaskell's bought a bicycle. He says it's quicker and it keeps him fit.
You could use that money for buying beef from the butcher.

place, room

You use **place** to talk about areas or points where things are.

It's not easy to find a comfortable place to sit.
It's a good place for a serious talk.

You can refer to the position where something belongs as its **place**.

place

She put the book back in its place on the shelf.
Don't park your car in the wrong place.

A **place** at a table is an area for one person to use.

I found a vacant place for my meal at one of the tables in the dining hall.
Everyday 12 places are laid for dinner.

You do not use 'place' to talk about the space you need for doing something. If you want to say that there is enough empty space to do something or to fit something, you say that there is enough **room**.

There was plenty of room for Daisy's potted plants.
...the relief of being alone with enough room to stretch himself.

If you provide space for something by moving other things, you **make room** for it.

He pulled mail in from the side of the desk to make room for the books.

play, show

A **play** is a piece of writing with dialogue which actors are intended to speak. It usually has a story and it can be serious or amusing. **Plays** are performed in theatres, on the radio, or on television.

I never stopped quoting my own stories, plays and poems.
He often flew to Minneapolis to see plays at the Guthrie Theatre.
...the delicate subtlety of character that Chekhov's plays have.

A **show** is a performance that is intended to entertain an audience. Most **shows** involve music, and they often consist of a series of comedy sketches and scenes with singing and dancing. A musical is a **show,** and a **play** can also sometimes be called a **show.**

I have a couple of glasses of red wine in the pub after the show.
I had booked for the show by phone.

please, thank you, thanks

You say **please** when you are politely asking for something or asking someone to do something.

Can I have my hat back please?
Could you turn left at the next lights, please?
Please hurry up and get dressed, Morris.

You also use **please** when accepting an offer in a polite way.

'Shall I read to you?'—'Yes, please.'

You say **thank you** or **thanks** to show that you are grateful for something that someone has given you or done for you. **Thanks** is more informal than **thank you.**

Thank you for a delicious lunch.
'There's your receipt.'—'Thanks.'

You also say **thank you** or **thanks** when accepting an offer, because you are grateful for the offer.

'Would you like some more sherry?' I asked her. 'Well, just half a glass, Mr Desland, thank you.'
'Help yourself to sugar.'—'Thanks.'
'I'll ring you tomorrow morning.'—'OK, thanks very much.'

You say 'no, **thank you**' or 'no, **thanks**' when you are refusing an offer in a polite way.

'Would you like some coffee?'—'No, thank you.'
'Do you want a biscuit?'—'No, thanks.'

You can also refuse an offer by using **thank you** or **thanks** with a phrase such as 'I'm all right' or 'I'm fine'.

'Is the sun bothering you? Shall I pull the curtain?'—'No, no, I'm fine, thank you.'
'Do you want a lift?'—'No, it's all right, thanks. I don't mind walking.'

Note that you do not use 'Thank you' or 'Thanks' on its own to refuse an offer.

power, strength

If you say a person or an organization has **power,** you usually mean that they are able to control other people and their activities.

It gave the President too much power.
The military authorities are refusing to hand over power.

You do not usually say that someone who has well-developed muscles has 'power'. The word you use is **strength.**

He pulled with all his strength.
They wouldn't have had the strength to drag it back to the village.
This glancing blow would have felled most men, but Parker had exceptional strength.

power

Other words

Instead of talking about the **power** of a person or organization, you can say that they are **powerful**.

Until his illness, President Botha was by far the most powerful and popular figure in white South African politics.
They organize themselves in powerful and effective trade unions.

Instead of talking about someone's **strength,** you can say that they are **strong**.

She was small and frail-looking, but deceptively strong.
His strong arms were around me, pinning me down.

Powerful is sometimes used with a similar meaning to **strong**.

He had broad shoulders and powerful arms.
...a powerful man.

practical, practicable

You use **practical** to talk about what happens in real life rather than in theory. A **practical** example is one that might really happen. A **practical** difficulty is one that actually has to be dealt with.

Let's take a practical example of what one group of workers did.
They refuse to face any of the practical difficulties that would come from changing things.

Ideas, methods, and plans that are **practical** are realistic and produce good results or are likely to produce good results.

He may well be able to suggest practical ways round a financial difficulty.
How long will it be before nuclear fusion becomes practical?

Something that is **practicable** is capable of being carried out successfully. **Practicable** is a formal word.

It would be perfectly practicable for us to get married in England.
State intervention to aid private industry was both practicable and beneficial.

practice, practise

Practice is the regular training you do in order to improve your skill at a sport or at an activity such as music. **Practice** is a noun.

He fell over, narrowly missing a flowerbed. 'You need some more practice, my lad,' said Karin, picking him up.

She didn't show up for choir practice this morning.
A little practice will be needed to really benefit from this exercise.

If you **practise,** you do the training necessary to improve your skill at something. **Practise** is a verb.

Bob Charles did not become a great golfer overnight. He had to practise hard.
On his own Alec could be gently encouraged to practise his reading and writing.
Occasionally they would practise manoeuvring the bus round obstacles.

Note that in American English, the spelling 'practise' is not normally used. The verb is spelled **practice,** like the noun.

I practiced and learned the headstand.

present, actual

Present is used in front of a noun to indicate that you are talking about things as they are now, rather than how they used to be or will be in the future.

The present system has many failings.
Economic planning cannot succeed in present conditions.

You also use **present** in front of a noun to indicate that you are talking about the person who has a job, role, or title now, rather than someone who had it in the past or will have it in the future.

The present chairperson is a woman.
...Zanussi's new film about the present Pope.

You do not use 'actual' to describe things as they are now. You use **actual** to emphasize that the place, object, or person you are talking about is the real or genuine one.

The predicted results and the actual results are very different.
The interpretation bore no relation to the actual words spoken.

prevent, avoid, warn

If you **prevent** someone from doing something, you do not let them do it.

These laws specifically prevented workers from meeting or acting together.
He did nothing to prevent her from walking over to the desk.

prevent

If you **prevent** something, you do something to ensure that it does not happen.

...calls for urgent action to prevent a famine in Sudan.
There is little that can be done to prevent this kind of misuse of computer power.

If you **prevent** accidents or diseases, you stop them from happening. If you **avoid** accidents or diseases, you succeed in not having them or catching them.

She slept soundly tied to him by a length of cloth that prevented her from falling.
The human mind holds a great deal of power to prevent many diseases.
...a sound recommendation for avoiding cancer.

When you are talking about dangers and risks, you normally use **avoid**.

You must avoid the danger of writer's cramp and muscular tension.

You do not use 'prevent' when telling people about a danger or giving them some other important information. The word you use is **warn**. You can **warn** someone about a danger or **warn** them of a danger, or **warn** them that something is happening. You can also say that you **warn** someone to do something when you tell them to do it in order to avoid a danger.

I withdrew to the back seat, warning her about the hole in the floor.
I did warn you of possible failure.
The doctors had warned us that he was in a serious condition.
She had repeatedly warned me to stay away from the Black Forest.

price, prize

The **price** of something is the amount of money that you have to pay in order to buy it.

He wanted to know the price of the car.
He paid $500 for an Indian python which might bring four times that price in Japan or Europe.

A **prize** is something of value that is given to someone who has achieved something, for example winning a competition or passing an exam.

I entered one or two competitions and won prizes.
I was the clever one at school. I always got the prizes.

priceless, worthless

If you say that something such as jewellery or a work of art is **priceless,** you mean that it is extremely valuable and worth a great deal of money.

The place is crammed with priceless carvings and statuettes.
...the priceless collection of the Byzantine emperors.

If you say that something is **worthless,** you mean that it is of no value or use.

The promises made between Cochise and the government would be worthless.
The goods are often worthless by the time they arrive.

principle, principal

A **principle** is a rule that someone has to guide their behaviour, or a rule which explains how something works or is organized. **Principle** is a noun.

...a man of high principles.
This is the principle on which the common barometer operates.
...the 'one man, one vote' principle.

Principal means first in order of importance. For example, your **principal** reason for doing something is your main or most important reason. **Principal** is an adjective.

Burkitt's work centred around a search for a virus infection as the principal cause of this disease.
Chamberlain consulted his principal colleagues.

Principal can also be used as a noun. A **principal** is a person who runs a school or college.

They arranged with the principal of her school to take time off.
The Principal had begun to regret his criticisms of Liberal Studies.

proceed, precede

If you **proceed** to do something, you go on to do it after doing something else.

She proceeded to ask my name, address and age.
He was in a position to make a scandal, which he now proceeded to do.

If you **proceed** with a course of action you have started, you carry on with it.

proceed

I suggest we proceed with dinner.
It is necessary to examine this claim before we proceed any further.

If an activity **proceeds,** it continues as planned.

The development process can proceed more rapidly.
The council have now reopened the account and payment is proceeding normally.

You can also use **proceed** to talk about where someone goes or where something leads. For example, if you **proceed** to a place, you continue travelling till you reach it. If a road **proceeds** north, it leads north.

Leaving Soho Square, proceed westwards through Carlisle Street and Sheraton Street.
He knows nothing can happen till he arrives so he proceeds at a leisurely pace.
Along the top of the park the North Walk proceeds through grass and trees to the children's playground.

Note that **proceed** is a fairly formal word. It is used mostly in written English.

You use **precede** to talk about what comes or happens before another thing. If one event **precedes** another, it happens first. For example, the month of March **precedes** the month of April.

No one knows how many wooden bridges preceded the first stone bridge over the Thames.
...the special silence that precedes an airliner's landing.

If someone or something **precedes** you somewhere, they go there before you go, or they go in front of you.

I arranged that he should precede me to Scotland.
A cabbie precedes him up the stairs, loaded with bundles.

Note that **precede** is a formal word.

programme, program

A **programme** on the television or radio is a broadcast of something such as a film or documentary.

What is your favourite television programme, Gillian?

A research **programme** or a development **programme** is a plan for future research or development.

The party had failed to state how it would pay for its ambitious social programme.

He had not been able to prise any information about his own teaching programme from the university.

A **programme** is also a plan which gives details of actions or events that are to take place.

...their programmes of meetings, talks and exhibitions.

A theatre or concert **programme** is a booklet giving details of a performance.

Note that in American English the spelling **program** is used for the above meanings.

There's a good program on the Late Late Show. An old Bela Lugosi movie.
Citizens' response to conservation programs is enthusiastic.
'From what I understand,' he continued, 'your hosts plan an extensive program of entertainment.'
The program listed William Warfield as Porgy and Leontyne Price as Bess.

A computer **program** is a set of instructions that is used by a computer in order to perform a particular operation. Note that the British and American spellings are the same.

Recently, for example, I decided to write a program for a microprocessor using machine code.
I couldn't see how one could get a good chess-playing program onto a cheap computer so soon.

prove, test

If you **prove** a fact, you show by logic or demonstration that it is definitely true. For example, you can **prove** that someone is guilty by producing evidence.

He is going to have to prove his innocence.
Even the lowest ranking civil servant is required to pass tests proving competence.
He was able to prove that he was an American.

You do not use 'prove' to talk about trying something out to see if it works or is effective. The word you use is **test**.

He stood up and tested his leg by walking round and round the cave.
A number of new techniques were tested.

Other words

The noun related to **prove** is **proof** .

What proof have you that this is true?

Q

quite, quiet

You use **quite** to emphasize adjectives and adverbs. For example, if you are **quite** sure about something, you are completely sure about it. **Quite** is pronounced /kwaɪt/.

I used to go out alone. Quite alone.
Please make yourself quite comfortable and call for anything you like.

You also use **quite** in front of adjectives, adverbs, and verbs to indicate that something is the case to a fairly great extent but not to a very great extent. For example, if something moves **quite** slowly, it moves rather slowly.

Fortunately they found it quite amusing.
Once she even got Lynn to admit that Martin was quite a nice boy.
They roamed the streets, played football, lived quite easily without us.
I quite enjoy looking round museums.

Someone or something that is **quiet** makes very little noise. A **quiet** place is one where there is very little noise. **Quiet** is pronounced /kwaɪət/.

Everyone is quiet. No one is talking.
Everything became very quiet and the full focus of attention fell on Ann.
She went into the church. It was quiet, and smelled of incense.

R

raise, rise, arise

You use **raise, rise,** and **arise** to talk about moving upwards.

If you **raise** something, you move it so that it is in a higher position. **Raise** is a regular transitive verb. The past tense and past participle are **raised.**

He began to raise a massive fist.
Raise the legs, trying to lift the thighs off the floor.
Hooper raised his camera and pressed the button.

If something **rises,** it moves upwards. For example, if smoke **rises,** it moves up towards the sky. **Rise** is an irregular intransitive verb. The past tense is **rose** and the past participle is **risen.**

In the distance he could see the smoke from his bonfire rising up in a white column.
Clouds of birds rose from the tree-tops.

If you **rise,** you get out of bed or you stand up after sitting, kneeling, or lying down. This is a formal use.

She could not have told you at what time she had risen that morning or how she made her way to the station.
When he saw us arrive, he attempted to rise but couldn't quite make it.
Ash had bowed, knelt and risen in imitation of the other worshippers.

Arise can also be used to say that someone gets out of bed or that they stand up after sitting, kneeling, or lying down. When **arise** is used like this, it is very old-fashioned or literary. **Arise** is an irregular intransitive verb. The past tense is **arose** and the past participle is **arisen.**

I arose at six.
He arose to greet her.

● **Raise** and **rise** can also be used as nouns. A **rise** is an increase in an amount or quantity.

...price rises.
...the rise in crime.

In British English, a **rise** is also an increase in someone's wages or salary.

He went to ask for a rise.

In American English, this is called a **raise.**

He thought about asking his boss for a raise.

relation, relative

Your **relations** or your **relatives** are the people who belong to your family, especially your cousins, aunts, uncles, and grandparents.

...people visiting family and relations in the two settlements.
...letters to Papa, relatives and friends.
I was a distant relation of her first husband.

relation

You use the words 'close' and 'near' with **relative** to describe those members of your family most directly related to you, for example your parents, brothers, or sisters.

Sometimes two or three close relatives are admitted.
The current immigration policy favours those who already have close relatives in the country.
Those with information need to ensure that the nearest relatives are told before any lists are issued to the press and media.

You use **relation** but not 'relative' in questions such as 'Are you any **relation** to Carole?' or 'Are you a **relation** of Carole's?'. You can use 'No **relation**' if you want to say that you are not related to a person with the same name as yours.

Are you any relation to the Nicolson whose wife wrote 'Heritage'?
'Barrett, like the poet?'—'Yes,' I said. 'No relation.'
Mr Mugabe (no relation of Robert Mugabe) spent ten years in exile in the United States.

Other words

People who are **related** belong to the same family.

...four people closely related to each other.

relations, relationship

When you talk about the **relations** between people or groups of people, you mean the ways in which they are in contact with each other and the way in which they behave to each other when they are in contact. Phrases such as 'human relations', 'industrial relations', and 'race relations' refer to relations between individuals, between management and workers, and between races. **Relations** is a plural noun.

One of his weaknesses was human relations. He seemed unable to communicate well with most people.
He identified the need for an enquiry into industrial relations in the car industry.
All these recent provocations are designed to disturb the good relations between Cuba and Ecuador.
His personal relations with Callaghan were far more cordial than they had ever been.

When you talk about the **relationship** between two people or groups of people, you mean the way that they feel and act towards each other.

She and my father always had a nice, warm relationship.

...the atmosphere of informality in the relationship between staff and pupils.
The intensity of her relationship with Mary dated from that time.

remark, notice

If you **remark** that something is the case, you say what you think about a particular subject or what you have observed about it. What you say may be an opinion or a statement of fact.

All day people had remarked that I looked well.
But as the journalist himself remarked, clothes alone cannot disguise anyone.
'A fine autumn morning, Mr Castle,' Mr Halliday remarked.

If you **notice** that something is the case, you become aware of it. You may say something about it, or you may not.

The first thing you noticed about him was his eyes.
I noticed a stranger leaning over the gate, watching us with interest.
She stood back so that they would not notice her.

remember, remind

If you **remember** something such as a name or a fact, you are able to bring it back into your mind in order to think about it.

He remembers everything that happened in the afternoon.
When I phoned I could not remember any of the girls' names.

If you **remember** to do something, you do the thing you intended to do without forgetting or being told to do it.

He remembered to turn the gas off.
Do remember to leave time and energy to put all your tools away.

If someone **reminds** you of a fact or event or **reminds** you about it, they say something which causes you to think about it.

I decided this was the moment to remind the lads of their responsibilities.
And then, thank God, Yvette reminded me about the food.

If someone **reminds** you to do something, they tell you to do something which you already know you are supposed to do.

She also reminded me to be careful.
She reminded me to wear the visitor's badge at all times.

rest, remains

You use **the rest** to talk about all the parts of a thing or all the members of a group apart from those that have already been mentioned. You can also use **the rest of** followed by a noun group.

Only a quarter were able to function as normal whilst the rest had suffered damage.
He spent the rest of his life in prison.
We drove the rest of the way in silence.
I don't know why you don't come and live here like the rest of us.

You use **the remains** to talk about what is left of something when most of it has been taken away or destroyed. You can also use **the remains of** followed by a noun group.

A piece of skull has been found among the remains uncovered at the site.
Exposed by excavation are the massive remains of heated rooms, Turkish baths and swimming pools.
The door splintered and left the remains of the lock dangling from the frame.

rest, stay, stop

When you **rest,** you do not do anything active for a period of time, especially after working or travelling.

Chris is all for exploring, but I'm so tired I just want to rest.
They walked for two hours, then they rested, then they walked for another two hours.
He sits under a tree and rests.

When you **stay** somewhere, you continue to be in a place without leaving it.

Daniel wanted to stay and hear the music that was starting up again.
People have been warned to stay indoors.
But now I felt it would be impossible for me to stay in Germany any longer.

If you **stay** at a hotel or at someone's house, you live there for a period as a guest or visitor.

My mother never asked where I would be staying in New York.
Guy and Gertrude had stayed at the castle once.

If you **stop** something that you are doing, you no longer do it. For example, if you **stop** when you are walking or driving, you no longer move.

He followed them for a few yards, and then stopped.
The van crept forward a little then stopped again.
She wept for a time and Mr Craft looked at her sternly until she stopped.

If you **stop** in a town or at a place, you spend a short time there before going on somewhere else.

We then sailed to Stockholm, stopping long enough to hear a performance of the Marriage of Figaro.
They'd ride for hours on end, stopping at some little pub for lunch.

restless, restive

If you are **restless,** you find it difficult to keep still and relax, often because you are bored and want to start doing something else.

After a flight she is restless, can't sit down, can't sleep.
A baby that is getting too little to eat will be restless and cry a good deal.

If you are **restive,** you are impatient or disobedient because you are bored or dissatisfied, and are likely to become rebellious if there is no change.

Allen grew restive because his music was interrupted.
The crew, who disliked the new Captain, were restive and mutinous.

retire, resign

When someone **retires,** they leave their regular employment and stop working, often because they have reached the age when they can get a pension. In Britain, men can get a state pension at sixty-five, and women at sixty. However, some people continue to work for longer, and others **retire** early.

Two-thirds of head teachers retire before the age of sixty.
Viscount Whitelaw has been speaking about his decision to retire from full-time politics.

If you **resign** from your job, you say that you do not want to continue doing it and you leave it. You can **resign** from your job at any age, and often you start another job soon afterwards.

retire

All he had to do was threaten to resign and he'd have got
promotion like a shot.
He had to resign from the council after the scandal.

● When professional sportsmen and women stop playing sport as
their profession, you can say that they **retire** from the sport, even
if they are fairly young.

Alvin Kallicharran is to retire from first-class cricket at the end of
his contract with Warwickshire this year.

review, revue

A **review** of something such as a film or a book is a discussion of
it by a critic who gives an opinion about its quality. A **review**
can be an article in a newspaper or magazines or part of a radio
or TV programme.

I collected £10 from an actor in the cast who had bet on good
reviews for the play.
I held an exhibition of my own paintings at Cambridge. The critical
reviews were memorable.
...a collection of his television reviews.

A **review** can also be a magazine, or occasionally a programme
on television or radio, which deals with intellectual subjects,
especially literature and the arts, and in which critics express
their opinions. Some of these magazines have **Review** in their
titles.

He made occasional contributions to the arts sections of the weekly
reviews.
...The New York Review of Books.
In an article in the Jewish Quarterly Review he found the
information he was looking for.

A **review** can also be a study by experts of how something is done
or managed. It is usually carried out in order to recommend
changes and improvements.

He initiated a comprehensive review of industrial policy.
Nevertheless the review concluded against all the alternatives.
On 1 April he announced a full public review of the project.

A **revue** is an amusing entertainment produced in a theatre, with
songs, dances, and comic sketches. **Revues** are often satirical.

...a four-man stage revue called Beyond the Fringe.
He had just finished writing a revue for Cochran called On With the
Dance.

reward, award, prize

A **reward** is something that you are given for doing something which people approve of. For example, an employer might give a worker some extra money as a **reward** for being efficient, or parents might give a child a toy as a **reward** for being good.

He had given me a day off – a reward I accepted with suspicious gratitude.
There were never any rewards for being good at games.

A **reward** is also a sum of money offered to anyone who can give information about stolen property or about someone who is wanted by the police.

Hurst announced a reward of £50,000 for information.

A satisfying experience can also be considered a **reward**.

But the walk brought its reward: a splendid view.

An **award** is a certificate or medal that is given by an organization such as a university or council.

...a new award, the diploma of Higher Education.
Food and service fully warrant the Egon Ronay award as Hotel of the Year.

When an award is given in recognition for an outstanding achievement, it may be referred to as a **prize**.

We are sometimes asked why it is right to give a prize for tennis, but wrong to give one for geography.
...the Nobel Prize for Peace.

A **prize** is also something that you are given for winning a competition or a game.

Prizes include free holidays.
I entered two competitions and won prizes.

● Both **reward** and **award** can also be used as verbs. If you **reward** someone, you give them a reward. Note that **reward** is often used in the passive.

Work hard and you will be rewarded.
They rewarded the winners with gifts of fruit and flowers.

If you **award** something such as a prize or certificate to someone, you give it to them. Note that **award** may be followed by two objects. It is often used in the passive.

Five campaign medals were awarded to those who fought in the Free French Forces.

reward

Sinha awarded contracts to favoured firms.
The British Government awarded him a grant of £1500.
Jennifer was awarded her degree on Wednesday.

road, street

Both **roads** and **streets** are routes used by people on foot and in vehicles to get from one place to another. Both **road** and **street** can be used in names.

Roads are found in the country, in villages, and in towns and cities. **Roads** sometimes have buildings on each side.

Miss Clare was waiting outside her gate, just before the road bends to Beech Green.
Villages are short of schools, health clinics, roads – and so they are short of jobs for teachers, nurses, engineers.
...Windsor Road.

All the routes in a country can be called its **roads** when you talk about them all together, even those that have **'Street'** in their names.

In 1976 there were 14.5 million cars and taxis on the country's roads.
The ancient ruins were accessible by road.

Streets are found in towns and cities, and have buildings on each side.

...the tacky, unimaginative shop fronts that lined the main street.
They went into the café across the street.

Routes that have **'Street'** in their name are usually in the centre of a town or city.

I left the office in Pine Street and started toward Broadway.
...the little eighteenth-century houses along Palace Street.

The 'High Street' is the main street in a town, where all the most important shops are located.

On the east side of the High Street, opposite the Cathedral, is London Bridge Station.
...Wapping High Street.

All the routes in a town or city can be called its **streets** when you talk about them all together, even those that have **'Road'** in their names.

*In Oxford the rain had cleared the streets, and only buses and cars
splashed through them.*
The two men walked slowly down the street.

● When writing addresses, you often abbreviate **'Road'** to 'Rd',
and **'Street'** to 'St'.

row, quarrel, fight, argument

When people disagree and argue with each other, you can say that
they have a **row**, a **quarrel**, a **fight,** or an **argument**.

A **row** is a disagreement between angry people who know each
other well. A **row** usually involves a lot of shouting. **Row** is an
informal word.

They had not spoken since the row on Saturday.
We had big rows, he got very angry and violent with me.
*There was one hell of a row when they came on and found the
double bass wrecked.*

A **quarrel** is a disagreement between angry people, usually
between people who know each other. A **quarrel** can continue
over a long period of time.

*If he were to continue it would only lead to another quarrel and
more tears.*
*It was the first prolonged quarrel between Churchill and
Beaverbrook.*

A **fight** is a disagreement between angry people. They may know
each other or they may not. It can involve physical violence, but
it does not always do so. Using the word **fight** for a disagreement
which does not involve violence is more common in American
English and in informal British English.

A vicious fight appeared to be going on.
*She doesn't like this guy I'm going out with. We get into terrible
fights.*

An **argument** is a disagreement between people who may know
each other or who may not. People are sometimes reasonable
during an **argument,** but they can become angry.

*Immediately an argument broke out about the wisdom of the
decision.*
During the two days' visit, we had quite a few friendly arguments.
*I'm sorry about this but there's nothing I can do right now. Any
argument will just worsen things.*

Grammar

Row, quarrel, and **fight** are also used as verbs with the same meanings. The verb related to **argument** is **argue**.

rule, regulation, law

Rules, regulations, and **laws** tell people what they are allowed to do and what they must not do in particular places and particular circumstances.

Regulations are made by an official organization or authority and are written down. They are intended to control the way people behave or how things are done. For example, the army's **regulations** say what a soldier's duties are and the things a soldier must not do. Planning **regulations** control the construction of new buildings and the sort of buildings which are acceptable in particular places.

I asked my secretary to get copies of all the relevant prison regulations.
This regulation does not apply to graduate students.
The Council points out that planning regulations have been altered to favour developers.

If you are speaking or writing less formally, you can use **rule** instead of 'regulation'.

There are strict rules governing the killing and cooking of kangaroo.
One important rule is that the au pair's working day should last no more than five hours.

You use **rule** when talking about games such as chess.

...the rules of chess.
You don't need to know the rules of the game to enjoy it.

Rules do not have to be written down. They can be an informal agreement about how something should be done.

Rules about bedtime are made by vote.
He lives as someone in another 'pretend' family, with its own rules about washing and mealtimes.

Laws are made by governments and rulers. They are written down and apply to all the people in a country. They say what is and what is not a crime and how citizens are required to act in their dealings with each other.

We shall need more stringent laws against pollution.
Health and safety laws are enforced by inspectors.

Certain sports also call their rules **laws.**

...the Rugby Union's laws.

S

sack, bag, pocket

A **sack** is a large container made from rough cloth or very strong paper, used for carrying or storing things such as coal, grain, or potatoes.

...a large hessian sack containing oranges, lemons, potatoes, garlic, onions, and coconuts.
My sack had about sixty birds inside it.

Similar containers made of plastic and often used for rubbish are sometimes also called **sacks.**

...a garbage sack which is supplied as part of the system.

A **bag** is a container of any size made of fairly soft material, for example paper, plastic, leather, or cloth, and used for carrying things such as shopping or tools, or for storing things such as rubbish or clothes.

Tony pulled out a bottle of wine and a corkscrew from his bag.
He poured all the oranges out of the bag back into the box.
He puts them in plastic garbage bags and locks the bags in the garage.
She came back with the white plastic bag containing the dress.

A **pocket** in a piece of clothing is an opening in which you can put small things, for example a handkerchief or money.

He reached into his breast pocket again and extracted a bundle of five-pound notes.
The visitor got the car keys from his pocket and gave them to him.

A **pocket** in something such as a briefcase or handbag is a compartment in which you can put things like credit cards or documents.

Both my cases had elasticized linen pockets in the lids.

safety

safety, security

You use **safety** to talk generally about being protected from harm
or danger. If you are worried about someone's **safety,** you are
worried that they might have an accident or be attacked. If you
are worried about the **safety** of a ladder, you are worried that it
might cause an accident. If you are worried about the **safety** of a
drug, you are worried that it might have bad side effects.

I was more concerned for his safety than I was for my own.
*We need to clearly establish the employers' responsibility for health
and safety at work.*
*Professor Goldberg, Chairman of the Committee on Safety of
Medicines, stated: 'No drug is completely safe.'*

You use **security** to talk about the precautions that are taken to
protect someone or something from attack or something from
being stolen. For example, if you are worried about the **security**
of your property, you are worried that someone might attack it or
steal it.

*You may want travellers cheques which have the advantage of
considerable security against theft.*
The Queen's visit has been marked by tight security.

The **security** of a country is the measures it takes to prevent
attacks and spying.

*He argued that security depended upon disarmament and the
co-operation of free people.*
*He was still regarded by the U.S. Government as a possible threat to
national security.*

salary, wages

If you are employed, your employer pays you a **salary** or **wages**
for doing your job.

A **salary** is the amount of money that someone is paid each year,
although they actually get a certain amount each month. In the
past, it was only people with professional or non-manual jobs who
received **salaries.** A person's **salary** is usually paid directly into
their bank account or paid to them by cheque.

*In a good year, a top executive's bonus can outstrip his annual
salary.*
*The state provides 85 per cent of teachers' salaries and certain
standard equipment.*

Wages are usually paid once a week. In the past, manual and non-skilled workers received **wages**. Nowadays they may receive either **wages** or a **salary.** A person's **wages** may be paid to them in cash or by cheque, or the money may be paid directly into their bank account.

My husband was head horseman at Round Wood Farm and when we married his wages were 13 shillings a week.
They hated working underground, but the wages seemed high to them.

salute, greet, welcome

When a soldier **salutes** an officer or gives a **salute,** he or she makes a formal sign of respect. The most common form of **salute** is to raise the right hand so that the fingers touch the forehead with the palm facing down or away from the face. It is normally only members of the armed forces and organizations such as the police who **salute** each other.

A large uniformed police sergeant recognized him at once and saluted.
Then Major Franks from Washington's staff entered and saluted me.
'Yes, sir,' said Pitman, giving the major an exemplary salute.

When people **greet** each other, they say something like 'Hello' or 'Good morning' or make a gesture such as waving or shaking hands.

She limped down the stone steps to greet Harry with a kiss on both cheeks.
The principal guests were greeted on arrival by the Lord Mayor of London.

When you **welcome** someone, you show that you are glad to see them when they arrive.

As the king arrived he was welcomed at the door by the prince.
At the airport we were welcomed by Caledonian Airways and shown to the first-class cabin.

You can also use the word **welcome** to welcome someone, but this often sounds rather formal.

Welcome to Peking.

Grammar

The noun related to **greet** is **greeting.**
She didn't acknowledge Ginny's greeting.

salute

The adjective related to **welcome** is **welcome,** not 'welcomed'.

I was a welcome visitor in both camps.

satisfactory, satisfying

If something is **satisfactory,** it is as good as it needs to be. Note that **satisfactory** often follows an adverb. For instance, if you say that something is 'very satisfactory' or 'highly satisfactory', you mean that it is very good and that you are pleased about it.

I find this method very satisfactory.
It produces highly satisfactory results in the hands of competent teachers.
Do you want to stay, then? Will the room be satisfactory for you?
There is no satisfactory, scientific explanation.

If something is **satisfying,** it gives you a feeling of pleasure and fulfilment.

It had been a busy but satisfying day for Tom Hagen.
Linda cut the cotton with a satisfying snip of the scissors.
The school wants to respect your child and to offer him a satisfying social and intellectual experience.

say, tell

If you **say** something, you use your voice to produce words. **Say** is usually used with a report clause or a quote.

Janet says it's urgent.
'Come round this side of me,' said Daniel.

If you want to mention the person being spoken to, you can do this after the preposition 'to'.

'Sam,' said Mr Hearst to the news editor.
I said to him, 'I'd never do anything like that.'

You can use **say** with a question when you are quoting the exact words that were used.

'How are you doing?' Bobby said.

Note that you do not say that someone 'says' a question. You say that they 'ask' a question.

Jill began to ask Fred a lot of questions about his childhood.

Note that **say** is usually only used with an object if the object is a very general word such as 'something', 'anything', or 'nothing'.

I must have said something wrong.
The man nodded but said nothing.

If a notice or a book **says** something, that is what is written on it or in it.

There was a notice saying 'Corps Diplomatique'.

If someone **tells** you something, they give you information in words.You usually use **tell** rather than 'say' when you are mentioning the person being spoken to as well as the speaker. **Tell** is used with an object which refers to the person who is being spoken to, and a report clause or a quote.

We told them we were going to visit relatives.
I told him I'd be right back.
'I'll go with him to get the crowbars,' Miss Corrie told Sam.

Tell may be followed by two objects, one of which refers to the person being spoken to and one which refers to the words used. Sometimes when the information has already been given or suggested, only the person being spoken to is mentioned.

He told her his name.
Mr Jumperwala told her some amusing anecdotes about the English aristocracy.
Didn't they tell you?

You can use **tell** with an object and 'about' to refer to the topic being discussed.

Matt was just telling us about a shark he caught.
My aunt wrote and told me all about it.

You use **tell** with an object and a 'to'-infinitive when reporting an order or instruction.

He told her to sit on the bed.
She told me to be careful.

You can also use **tell** and a quote to give the same information. For example, the first example above would be 'Sit on the bed,' he told her.

There are a few nouns which can be used as the object of **tell** without an object referring to the person being spoken to. These include 'truth', 'lie' and 'story'.

I don't know whether you're telling the truth or not.
He was telling another fishing story.

say

● It is not usual to give someone's exact words, except in written narrative.

'Just a moment!' Mr Foster said suddenly.
'You'll have to come back some other day,' she told him.

scarce, rare

You say that something is **scarce** when there is not much of it, especially when people need it and cannot get it.

Reasonably priced accommodation in Britain is scarce.
At this time supplies of oil did become scarce and prices rose.
Heavy metals can sometimes be recycled, conserving scarce natural resources and solving a potentially serious pollution problem.

You say that something is **rare** when it is not common and is therefore considered to be interesting and valuable.

Today the plant is rare in its natural habitat.
I sheltered in a rare patch of shade under some trees.
I suffer from a rare eye disease.

scarcely, rarely

You use **scarcely** rather like a negative, to say that something is only just true or only just the case. For example, if you say that something has **scarcely** changed, you mean that it has changed very little; if you say that you have **scarcely** any money, you mean that you have very little money.

The leaves have scarcely been changed at all by cultivation.
There is scarcely anything to eat.
So much had gone wrong that he could scarcely believe his good luck.

If something **rarely** happens, it does not happen very often.

Ginny was in Vermont and rarely came to Hullsport any more if she could avoid it.
He rarely had more than fifty dollars in his pocket.
There are some lucky children who rarely catch cold.

Other words

'Barely' and 'hardly' have a similar meaning to **scarcely,** but do not mean the same as 'rarely'.

He was so drunk that he could barely stand.
I was beginning to like Sam, though I hardly knew him.

scene, scenery

You can refer to something that you see as a **scene** of a particular kind. You may be anywhere, and may be looking at pleasant or unpleasant things.

I looked out on a depressing scene; the streetlamps were highlighting the puddles.
...a scene of domestic tranquillity.

You refer to attractive countryside surrounding you as **scenery**. Note that **scenery** is an uncount noun.

He had time to admire the scenery.
The scenery was a mix of olive groves and farmland.

school, college, university

A **school** is where children are taught. Most children in Britain start **school** between the ages of four and five and leave between the ages of sixteen and eighteen. A **primary school** teaches children up to the age of about eleven; after that they go to a **secondary school**. In some areas there are **middle schools**, which teach children between the ages of about eight and twelve.

We greeted each other and I made enquiries about Betty's new school in Caxley.
Stanley asked Sylvia politely how Paul was getting on at school.
...what a child should know when he leaves the primary school.
Much emphasis is often placed on preparation for transfer to secondary school.

A **college** teaches students who have left secondary school and who want to specialize in a particular subject or area of study, especially those who want to study technical subjects or to do a particular job.

She was offered a lectureship at the Runcorn College of Further Education and she accepted it.
Wendy went to Brighton High School and then on to Art College.
Gerald Brooke was a young and idealistic lecturer at a London technical college.

A **university** teaches students who have left secondary school and who want to study any of a wide range of subjects. A **university** has the right to award degrees, for example Bachelor of Arts (BA) and Doctor of Philosophy (PhD), and has facilities for research.

school

His brother was a professor of mathematics at one of the northern universities.
Graduates will normally carry out their research and be supervised in the University.
...the Wolfson Research Laboratories, housed on the Birmingham University campus.

● Some colleges and university departments have **School** as part of their name. Note that in both cases the word **school** must be accompanied by a modifying adjective or a qualifying phrase.

...the Medical School and the adjacent Medical Centre.
...the Columbia University Graduate School of Business.
She took a part-time teaching post in a well-known London art school.

In American English, a university or college is often called a **school.**

He dropped out of school after a year.
He put himself through school, studied law.

● Some American universities use **College** as part of their name.

...Joan Shapiro, Professor of Social Work at Smith College.

Some of the older British universities are made up of **colleges.**

...the Mullard Space Science Laboratory at University College, London.

Some British secondary schools, especially some of those which charge fees, have **College** as part of their name.

It was run by a man who had been deputy headmaster at Dulwich College.

sea, ocean

The **sea** is the salty water that covers about three-quarters of the earth's surface. Sometimes the sea is referred to as **the seas,** especially in literary English.

The underlying belief has been that since the sea is so big no harm can come to it. Unfortunately this is not true.
So she shaded her eyes and looked out to sea.
They had fun fishing in the river, throwing stones into the sea, baking spuds over a log fire.
Much of his income, however, came from lobster fishing in the treacherous seas around Handa.

A **sea** is a large separate area of this salty water, usually partly surrounded by land. It normally has a name which includes the word **Sea**. Some **seas** can be entirely surrounded by land.

...natural gas, discovered in large quantities beneath the North Sea.
...semi-enclosed water bodies such as the Mediterranean and the Baltic Sea.
Sewage waste poured into rivers and seas.
They got as far as Persia, via Volga and the Caspian Sea.

An **ocean** is one of the five very large areas of salty water on the earth's surface: the Atlantic Ocean, the Pacific Ocean, the Indian Ocean, the Arctic Ocean, and the Antarctic Ocean.

Within about 1,000 miles of the equator the upper layers of the ocean are about 35 degrees Fahrenheit warmer than the deeper waters.
My family have been traders and merchants in the Indian Ocean for centuries.

In literary language you can refer to the sea as the **ocean** or the **oceans.**

This creature lies in the depths of the ocean.
The wind was the same wind that blew in China, blowing across oceans, valleys, and mountain ranges.

search, search for, seek, look for

If you **search** somewhere, **search for** something, **seek** something, or **look for** something, you try to find something.

If you **search** a place, or if you **search for** something in a place, you examine the place very thoroughly, making an effort to find something, usually by touching and moving things.

Ginny searched the bookcases, finally locating the bird book.
The cop searched the front of the car and told my father to open the trunk.
He searched in the glove compartment and found an airline timetable.
He searched through a drawer for a carving knife and fork.
He can't just have disappeared. I mean, you've searched for him?

You can also **search for** something such as an answer or information.

The people searched and searched for facts about their ancestors.
...searching for ways to end the dispute.

search

You usually **seek** something such as an answer or information rather than an object. You can also **seek** something such as a new job or a place to live. **Seek** is often used in writing, but you do not normally use it in conversation.

If an injury does occur, then it is advisable to seek a good diagnosis and treatment as soon as possible.
Sources of energy were sought in nature : wind, sun, water, steam, coal.
A good student seeks knowledge fairly and impartially.
They had to get special permission to go to any specific area to seek work.

If you **look for** an object, you try to find it. You often **look for** things you have lost or that you want. Sometimes you simply use your eyes without touching anything.

She was mumbling, looking for her shoes.
We were even thinking of looking for a cottage in the Peak District.

You can also **look for** something such as a solution or a job.

Britain is looking for a peaceful, diplomatic solution.
They came to look for work in the rich, developing south.

see, watch, look at, regard

When you **see** someone or something, you notice them with your eyes. You may examine them closely or you may pay very little attention to them.

He saw Karen standing rather meekly in the doorway.
I poked my head out of the tent to see a sky, velvet black, studded with stars.
He's got a paper hat stuck over his eyes and he can't see a thing.

When you go to the theatre or cinema, you say that you **see** a play or film. You do not use 'look at' or 'watch'.

I saw 'Dear Brutus' on its first night in 1917.
We saw Greta Garbo in 'Queen Christina'.

When you **watch** someone or something, you notice what is happening with your eyes, paying a lot of attention. Often what you are watching is moving or is about to move.

From the window he watched Louison cycle down the broad path that led towards the gates.
It was terrible. My every move was being watched.

Outdoors, they are delighted to watch leaves and shadows.
He watched and listened. There was no movement and no sound.

Both **see** and **watch** are used when you are talking about television or sport.

You say that someone **watches** television, but that they **watch** or **see** a particular programme.

He spends several hours watching television.
She went home to watch 'Alien'.
I saw it on television after the news.

Similarly, you say that someone **watches** a sport such as football, but that they **watch** or **see** a particular match.

More people are watching cricket than ever before.
I'd sooner go out with a gun than watch a football match.
...those of us who saw England's defeat at Wrexham.

If you **look at** someone or something, you deliberately direct your eyes so that you can see what they are like or what is happening. The person or thing may or may not be moving as you **look at** them.

He looked at her across the table, chewing his parsnips slowly.
Henri! Everyone is looking at you!
At 2, 3 and 4 months, they enjoy looking at bright-coloured things and things that move.

You do not use **regard** to talk about noticing things with your eyes. You use **regard** to talk about how you think of them with your mind. If you **regard** something as important, you think it is important.

Some women in this situation regard the journey to work as their only time in the day for relaxation.
I've never tried to resist what I regarded as inevitable.
We regard such visits as important.

sensible, sensitive

A **sensible** person makes good decisions and judgements and avoids risks, dangers, or problems. The decisions or judgements are based on reason rather than emotion.

She was far too sensible to believe these ridiculous lies.
He told her to be brave and sensible.
Of course, sensible precautions have to be taken.
It's sensible to avoid sweets between meals.

sensible

You can also describe clothes as **sensible** if they are practical and strong rather than fashionable and attractive.

She invariably wore 'sensible' clothes and plain shoes.
She wears a sweater, casual slacks and sensible shoes.

A **sensitive** person is easily upset or offended by other people's remarks or behaviour.

This may make a sensitive child tense and apprehensive.
There are sensitive children who are upset by fairy stories.

If you are **sensitive** to a particular thing such as criticism, you are easily upset or offended by it.

He's very sensitive to criticism.
...if you are sensitive to unintended slights.

You can also say that you are **sensitive** about something, if it worries or upsets you.

You really must stop being so sensitive about your accent.
Some parents are sensitive about advice from their children's teachers.

If you are **sensitive** to people's feelings or problems, you show understanding and awareness of them.

We're trying to make people more sensitive to the difficulties faced by working mothers.
...the protection and support of sensitive, perceptive parents.

Sensitive skin reacts badly to chemicals.

One person in five is sensitive to biological washing powder.

serial, series

You use both **serial** and **series** to talk about a set of programmes for radio or television or a set of pieces of writing printed in different editions of a magazine or newspaper.

A **serial** is a fictional story which is divided into parts. For example, a novel can be divided into parts and shown on television as a **serial**.

The novel has recently been dramatized as a television serial.
Many of Dickens' novels were published in serial form.

A **series** is a set of related programmes or pieces of writing. A **series** may be fictional, but each part is a complete story in itself. Many **series** are not fictional: for example a wildlife **series** on television is a set of programmes about nature. Note that the plural of **series** is also **series.**

...the 1960s TV puppet series 'Thunderbirds'.
...a comedy series.

serviette, towel

In British English, a **serviette** is a square of cloth or paper that you use to protect your clothes while you are eating, and sometimes to wipe your fingers and mouth.

He drew caricatures on the serviettes just as he had in Viennese cafés.

The piece of cloth that you use for drying yourself after washing is called a **towel.**

My hair is wrapped up in a towel, because I'd just washed it when you rang.
I've hung up a towel behind the bathroom door for you, if you want a wash.

shadow, shade

A **shadow** is a dark shape on a surface which is caused by a person or object that prevents light from reaching the surface. The dark shape on the surface is similar to the outline of the person or object.

The lamps cast my shadow along the street as I went my way alone.
The heavy shadow of a jet from Midway airport crossed the room.
The elm trees in the corner of the playground cast comforting cool shadows.

Shadow or an area of **shadow** is an area covered by the shadow of something. If something is **in shadow,** it is in an area that is covered by the shadow of something.

A mulberry tree threw a black patch of shadow above the place.
A slim figure in khaki moved through the shadow.
It was in shadow, but its shape and markings were plain enough.

The **shade** is an area which is dark and cool because the sunlight cannot reach it. **Shade** can cover a large area and be caused by the **shadows** of many different things.

...a nicely built stone house set in the shade.
The two men lay back in deckchairs in the shade of a fine copper beech tree.
I sheltered in a rare patch of shade under some trees.

ship, boat

Vessels that travel over water can be called **ships** or **boats**.

A **ship** is normally large and used either by the navy or for transporting passengers or goods by sea.

There were other ships in port and an oil tanker was creeping towards a storage wharf.
This is a cruise ship and I was taken on as a steward at the last minute.
During the following centuries, large areas were cleared to build the powerful ships of the British Navy.

Any vessel that travels over water can be described as a **boat,** but small ones that sail in rivers or that are used for leisure can only be called **boats.**

John took me down the river in the old boat.
He walked along the wooden pier and climbed down the short ladder into the boat.

In conversation, large passenger ships such as ferries, are also often called **boats.**

She was getting off at Hamburg to take the boat to Stockholm.
The shipping line operating the boat, the Sobral Santos, had not released the list of passengers.

shirt, blouse

Shirts and **blouses** are pieces of clothing that are worn on the upper part of the body. They are made of light materials such as cotton or polyester and they usually have a collar, sleeves, and buttons down the front.

Shirts are usually worn by men, and they are often worn with a tie. Most **shirts** have buttons up to the neck, but some casual **shirts** are open at the neck.

He had shaved and he had on not merely a white shirt but a clean one, with a collar and necktie.
He wore a dark blue shirt and cotton trousers and his sleeves were rolled up.

Blouses are only worn by women and are not worn with a tie. Sometimes they have buttons up to the neck, but many are meant to be worn open at the neck.

The efficient-looking dark suit only partly conceals a bright blouse.

She's so silly! She wears a big floppy bow on her blouse.
...the high-collared school blouse.

shorts, underpants, pants

Shorts are short trousers worn by men and women. They cover the tops of your legs and your hips. Some **shorts** are long enough to cover your legs almost down to your knees.

She took a pencil from the hip pocket of her shorts.
The second man wore a striped shirt and grey shorts.

In American English, **shorts** can also be a piece of underwear worn by men and boys. They cover the part of the body above the legs and below the waist. In British English they are called **underpants** or **pants**.

Your dad was in his underclothes – bright blue shorts and singlet.
She came in and picked up the underpants and vest that the child had peeled off.
He took off his shorts and pants and stood there naked.

sick, nauseous, vomit, ill

To **be sick** means to bring up food through your mouth from your stomach.

She was in a ship. She was going to be sick.
He was being violently sick.

To **feel sick** means to feel that you want to be sick.

Flying always makes me feel sick.

American speakers say they **feel nauseous** rather than 'feel sick'. They use the verb **vomit** instead of 'be sick'. **Feel nauseous** and **vomit** are also used in more formal British English.

I felt dizzy and nauseous.
She was stricken with pain and began to vomit.

If someone has a disease or a problem with their health, you can describe them as **ill** or **sick**.

I'm too ill to see anyone.
My boy's sick. Measles.

Most British speakers do not use **ill** in front of a noun unless they are also using an adverb such as 'very', 'seriously', or 'terminally'.

sick

We had two still very ill men on our hands.
It was a drug given to severely mentally ill people.

Some American speakers use **ill** on its own in front of a noun.
...one of our ill sisters

You can use **sick** in front of a noun.
I'd say he's a sick man.

snake, serpent

Snake is the normal word for the long, thin reptile that has scales on its skin and no legs. There are many different types of **snake**, for example vipers, cobras, and pythons.

No poisonous snake attacks, it merely defends itself.
Small snakes need feeding only once or twice a week.

In literary or old-fashioned English, snakes are sometimes called **serpents**.

The familiar tale of Adam and Eve, the forbidden fruit and the serpent is one of the key myths of European civilisation.
...a creature with the head of a lion, the body of a goat and the tail of a serpent.

someone, somebody, anyone, anybody

Note that **someone** means the same as **somebody** and **anyone** means the same as **anybody**.

You use **someone** or **somebody** to refer to a person without saying who you mean.

He had to see someone.
Just then somebody opened a door.

You use **anyone** or **anybody** to talk about people in general, or about each person of a particular kind.

He took longer than anybody else.
It must surely have been obvious to anyone with a spark of common sense.
...anyone who has a genuine concern for human beings.

You also use **anyone** or **anybody** in questions, clauses beginning with 'if' or 'unless', and in negative clauses with words like 'not', 'never', and 'hardly'.

Do you ever see anybody from the Club here?

If anyone wants me just say I've gone to the dentist's.
I don't want to see anyone.
Hardly anyone now seriously accepts this once-popular view.

You can use **someone** or **somebody** in questions if you expect the
answer to be 'yes', and in clauses beginning with 'if' and 'unless'
when you want to make a possibility seem more realistic.

Did someone pay you not to tell what you knew?
If someone hits you, you hit back immediately.
How can we tell if someone is lying?

● **Someone** and **somebody** do not have plural forms. If you want
to refer to a group of people without saying who you mean, you
say 'some people'.

Some people attempted to dash across the bridge.
The law may be held to be unsatisfactory by some people.

● You use 'any one' to emphasize that you are referring to only
one of something. You do not use 'anyone'.

That was more money than he had seen at any one time in all his
twenty-one years.

something, anything

You use **something** when you are referring to a particular thing
without saying exactly what it is.

There's something I have to tell you!
A security man in plain clothes who was eating something asked for
my papers.

You use **anything** to talk about a thing or event which might
exist or happen, or about each thing or event of a particular kind.

What can I do? I'll do anything.
Do go and help yourself to anything.
You can say and do anything you want and I can't fire you.

You also use **anything** in questions and in clauses beginning with
'if' or 'unless'.

Had anything happened? Was there some good news?
If you can find out anything, we'll be most grateful.

You also use **anything** in negative clauses with words like 'not'
and 'never'.

I don't know anything really.
He never seemed to do anything at all.

something

He had no idea anything like this was going to happen.

Note that you cannot use 'anything' with 'not' as the subject of a clause. The word you should use is 'nothing'.

She shook the bottle over the glass; nothing came out.

You can use **something** in questions if you expect the answer to be 'yes', and in clauses beginning with 'if' and 'unless' when you want to make a possibility seem more realistic.

Isn't there something we could play sitting down?
If I need a dollar or two to buy something I have to ask my wife for money.

sometimes, sometime

You use **sometimes** to say that something happens on certain occasions, rather than all the time.

'Do you hear from your sister?'—'Sometimes.'
Sometimes I wish I was back in Africa.

You can also use **sometimes** to say that something happens in certain cases, but not in every case.

Sometimes they just come for a term, sometimes six months.
Sometimes, people do not begin to examine their marriages until they see the divorce advancing upon them.

Sometime means at a vague or unspecified time in the future or past.

Can I come and see you sometime?
He saw Frieda Maloney sometime last week.

When it is used in this way, **sometime** is often written as two words.

He died some time last year.

You also use **sometime** in front of a title or name of a job to indicate the position or job that someone had at an unspecified time in the past.

...Sir Alfred Munnings, sometime President of the Royal Adademy.

somewhere, anywhere

If you talk about being or going **somewhere,** you are talking about a particular place, but you do not or cannot say exactly where it is.

He's somewhere up there by the bridge.
One always assumes that a track will lead somewhere.

If you talk about being or going **anywhere,** you are talking about any place in general, or any part of a particular place.

But if you really want me, I will come to you always, anywhere.
I was ready to go anywhere at all in the world where it rained more.

You also use **anywhere** in questions, clauses beginning with 'if' or 'unless', and in negative clauses with words like 'not', 'never', 'hardly', and 'seldom'.

Is there anywhere on the island you haven't been?
If that bull gets anywhere near my place, I'll kill it.
I have never been anywhere so desolate.
His parents seldom stayed anywhere more than a few months.

You can use **somewhere** in questions if you expect the answer to be 'yes', or in clauses beginning with 'if' and 'unless' when you want to make a possibility seem more realistic.

Shall we go and eat somewhere?
Have I seen you somewhere before?
...if Pegler is somewhere within the sound of these words.

sound, noise

A **sound** is something that you hear.

A few moments later Bonasera recognized the sound of a heavy ambulance coming through the narrow driveway.
The computer also lacks the ability to discriminate between speech and other sounds.

A **noise** is a sound that you hear, especially when it has no meaning or when it is unpleasant.

There was a sudden noise of distant explosions.
I looked at Anne – cheerfully eating her soup with sucking noises.

Sound and **noise** can both be use without 'a' or 'the'. **Sound** is the general term for what you hear as a result of vibrations coming though the air, or sometimes through water or solid materials.

The storm of sound beat at them.

You can use **noise** to refer to a lot of unpleasant noises.

For nearly forty years now, I have lived with children's noise.

207

south, southern, southerly

The **south** is the direction on your right when you are looking towards the direction where the sun rises. The **south** of a country or area is the part towards the south. You use **south, southern,** and **southerly** to describe things that are in or come from the south.

You use **south** to describe a part of a place that is in the south, whether it is a large place like a country or a smaller place like a building. Note that **south** is often used to make a contrast with the north, west, and east: the **south** side of a building is opposite the north side.

After a brief visit to the U.S., he returned to South America.
The south side of the church is elaborate.
In the west and along the south coast rocky shores and cliffs predominate.

Southern means relating to the south and refers to a more general area than 'south'.

The Thames is the great divide of southern England.
...the Oaxaca Valley in the southern highlands of Mexico.
He had arranged for him to be transferred to another town on the southern coast of Sicily.

You can also use **southern** to describe things that come from the south or that are found there.

A male voice with a thick southern accent answered. 'Hello. I'm a friend of Will's.'
His face was very tanned, as though he had been lying on a southern beach for months.

Winds that come from the south can be described as **south** or **southerly** winds.

The bigger islands gave some shelter from the south wind.
...a yard-wide belt of seaweed and kelp pushed ashore by the southerly breeze.

You can also use **southerly** to describe directions and locations. If something moves in a **southerly** direction, it moves towards the south. Unlike 'south' and 'southern', **southerly** can be used with 'more' and 'most'.

...Crete, the most southerly and largest of all the Greek islands.
Hooper stood at a southerly window.

speak, talk

When you **speak** or **talk,** you use your voice to produce words. Sometimes you can use both **speak** and **talk** without changing the sense very much, as in the following examples.

Johnny had been speaking almost in a whisper.
Uncle Sam went on talking, in his low, throaty voice.

You usually use **speak** when one person is addressing another, and the second person is listening rather than joining in. For example, a politician **speaks** to an audience. If you **speak** to someone about something that worries or annoys you, you say what you think is wrong.

It was Harold's turn to speak.
He never spoke at meetings but just stared at the other directors.
It was essential that I speak to Smithy.
Several parents had spoken to me expressing their grave concern.

You usually use **talk** when two or more people are having a conversation or discussion. For example, when people have a meal together, they **talk** to each other. If you **talk** to someone about something that worries or annoys you, you discuss it with them and expect them to express their point of view. Note that in American English you can also **talk** with someone.

A family of five were finishing lunch and talking loudly.
She said that she would like to meet me because Patricia had talked about me.
If you are really serious, Davis, I'll talk to Watson.
Have you talked with the doctor yet?

● If you **speak** a language, you know that language and can use it.

You speak such excellent French!
Peter was one of the few members of his team to speak good English.
He made friends with Korean labourers who spoke some English but wanted to learn more.

● During an actual conversation, you can **talk** or **speak** in a language, or **talk** or **speak** the language. Note that **speak** is slightly more formal.

Sitting Bull was to talk in the Sioux language; an interpreter was to translate.
They spoke in Yiddish in case the line was being tapped.
There were a lot of people on the boat talking French.
Then it dawned on me that they were speaking Spanish.

speech, conversation

Speech is the ability to speak, the act of speaking, or the way someone speaks.

Speech is controlled on one side of the brain.
They communicated, if they communicated, without speech.
The older he grew the more incomprehensible became his speech.

If two or more people have a **conversation,** they talk to each other in an informal way for a while. **Conversation** is the activity of having conversations.

The girl next to me tried to start a conversation.
The conversations were mostly about the heat.
Bal and his friends were too deeply engrossed in conversation to mind anything.

speech, talk, lecture

If you make a **speech,** you speak to an audience, usually in a formal way, and say things that you have already prepared; often you write down your text in advance and read it out. You usually speak about a situation or problem that concerns the audience. For example, people make amusing **speeches** at weddings, and politicians make **speeches** to express their views and policies.

The vicar made a speech wishing Miss Gray much happiness.
The opening sessions in the training course were welcoming speeches.
He worked on Wilson's policy speeches, particularly the speech on Labour's economic policy.

If you give a **talk,** you speak to an audience in an informal way. You normally prepare what you are going to say, but you do not always have a written text to read. In a **talk** you normally give people information, for example about your experiences or a subject you know well.

They are planning a series of hour-long talks by such speakers as the former Archbishop Donald Coggan and Delia Smith.
He achieved sudden notoriety by his weekly talks on BBC radio under the title 'People and Things'.

If you give a **lecture,** you speak in a fairly formal way to an audience, especially to a group of students, about an academic subject. **Lectures** are one of the main ways of teaching in universities.

I came to England in the autumn of 1935 to give two lectures at Bedford College.
Adam had been going to lectures on philosophy.
When I began my university course, the first lecture was given by the Professor of English literature.

spend, pass

If you do something from the beginning to the end of a period of time, you can say that you **spend** that amount of time doing it.

She woke early, meaning to spend all day writing.
At the end of last term I spent three days cleaning our flat.

You can also say that you **spend** time in a place, if you are there from the beginning to the end of that period of time.

We found a hotel where we could spend the night.
He spent most of his time in the library.

If you do something to occupy yourself while you are waiting for something, you say that you do it to '**pass** the time'.

He had brought a book along to pass the time.
'How am I going to pass the time here?' he wondered.

You can say that time **has passed** in order to express the idea that a period of time has finished.

The first few days passed.
The time seems to have passed so quickly.

square, place

A **square** is a flat open area surrounded by buildings in a town or city. Many such areas have **Square** in their names.

There was a policeman on the other side of the square.
He loved his house in the square at Delft and painted it continually.
...a mass procession from Marble Arch to Trafalgar Square.

Place is used as part of the name of a square or short street in a town, especially one where the houses are all of a similar type.

Inspector Cook began by describing his visit to 2 Blackburn Place.

stand, bear, tolerate, support

If you cannot **stand** someone or something, you find them so annoying or irritating that you do not want to be involved with

stand

them in any way. If you cannot **stand** a situation, that situation is too difficult and upsetting for you and you no longer wish to be involved in it. Note that **stand** is usually used in a negative context, or in a question. It comes after a modal such as 'can' or after another auxiliary such as 'do'.

I listened to his engine howling until I couldn't stand it any longer.
I don't think I can stand being in the house with him for another minute.
If it weren't for the children I couldn't stand living.
How do you stand the diet?

Bear is used in a similar way to **stand**.

I couldn't bear staying in the same town as that man.
I can't bear him!

If you **tolerate** something, you allow it or accept it, even though you do not agree with it or approve of it. You normally use the word **tolerate** when you are talking about someone who has some degree of authority or choice.

Why is it that parents, who are otherwise kind, tolerate cruel schools for their children?
All healthy societies can tolerate dissent.
This is the last occasion on which I can tolerate Macleod's gross neglect and carelessness.

You do not use 'support' to talk about what you can accept or allow. If you **support** someone or something, you give them your help and you want them to succeed. For example, if you **support** a political party, you vote for it. If you **support** a charity, you give money to it.

I travelled around the country appealing to people to support me and all political prisoners.
He was sure the men would support their unions.
In addition to the training of teachers, the University supports a Research Centre for the Education of the Visually Handicapped.

stationary, stationery

These words look similar and are both pronounced /ˈsteɪʃənəri/. However, their meanings are completely different.

Something that is **stationary** is not moving.

He made for a stationary lorry, got in and drove off.
The boats were nearly stationary in the water.

She could stop horses at will and keep them stationary for as long as she liked.

Stationery is all the various things you use for writing, such as paper, pens, envelopes, and ink.

They are Britain's biggest book publisher: diaries, stationery, textbooks, as well as major fiction and non-fiction titles.
...a short letter on prison stationery.

statistics, statistical

Statistics are figures which give factual information about the world or about an area, for example the number of dogs in a town, the average age of doctors, or the percentage of pupils who pass an exam.

There are no statistics showing any appreciable improvement in rural income levels.
Statistics never prove anything.
World expenditure on education exceeded defence and military budgets, a statistic which most people find very surprising.

Statistics is also the branch of mathematics which studies these figures and interprets them. When it has this meaning, **statistics** is an uncount noun, and takes a singular verb.

Social science courses commonly require elementary mathematics or statistics.
Modern mathematics courses tend to begin with set theory and the basis of statistics.
Statistics has never been taught here before.

Statistical is the adjective describing things related to **statistics**.

Little statistical work has been done on fads and fashions.
The paper also made statistical breakdowns regarding the number of dog owners.

Other words

Instead of saying that two things are have a **statistical** relationship, you can say that they are **statistically** related.

'But this is a rare case,' said Merkin, 'too rare to be statistically important.'

steal, rob

If someone **steals** something, they take it without intending to give it back.

steal

He tried to steal a caravan from a caravan site.
Armed raiders disguised as postmen stole 50 bags of mail.
My car was stolen on Friday evening.

The object of **steal** is the thing that is taken. For example, someone might **steal** money, food, or a car.

I slipped into the kitchen and stole some of the coins.
At first Jed was only ordered to steal small sums of money from his parents.

If someone takes something that belongs to you without intending to give it back, you can say that they **rob** you of it. **Rob** is not usually used in conversation, but it is often used in stories and newspaper reports. It usually implies that the crime is very serious, and often that it is violent.

The two men were robbed of more than £700.
...a film about unemployed teenagers joining forces to rob a factory of stainless steel sink units.

The object of **rob** is the person or place that something is taken from. For example, criminals **rob** people or places like banks.

One night they planned to rob an old widow.
Use your organization to rob a few banks.

Other words

A person who **steals** is called a 'thief'. The plural of 'thief' is 'thieves'. The act of stealing is called 'theft'.

...jewel thieves.
Police believe the thefts may be the work of one gang.

A person who **robs** someone is called a 'robber', and 'robbery' is the crime of taking money or property, often by using threats or force.

The robber knocked out a warden before stripping the portraits from their frames.
The robbery occurred at the Gardener Museum.

A thief who **steals** from someone's pocket is a 'pickpocket'.

They were prey to pickpockets and other criminals.

Someone who **steals** things from shops is a 'shoplifter'.

...the technology used in department stores to discourage shoplifters.

Someone who **steals** from houses and other buildings, can be called a 'burglar'. Note that, in British English, you say that they

'burgle' a house; in American English, you say that they
'burglarize' a house.

Burglars yesterday ransacked the offices of the Deputy Minister.
They worry that their house may be burgled while they are away.
Her home had been burglarized.

steps, stairs, staircase

Steps, stairs, and **staircases** are all used to climb up or down a
slope and are made up of a series of flat surfaces raised up on the
slope, one above the other.

A **step** is a single one of these raised surfaces. **Steps** are usually
outdoors, for example in front of a building. However, you
occasionally refer to **steps** indoors, especially when they are not
carpeted or do not connect two floors of a building.

She raced up the steps and into the cottage.
Back in Villiers Street there are steps leading up to the footway over
Hungerford Bridge.
...the short corridor that leads to the children's rooms, and the steps
that lead down to his basement study.
We halted at the bottom of a flight of steps leading onto the stage.

Stairs connect different floors inside a building and are often
covered in carpet.

They went up the stairs and into the flat.
He went out into the hall and stood at the foot of the stairs calling
for her to come down.
I climbed the stairs to our bedroom.

A **staircase** is a set of stairs considered as a structure, which
usually includes a rail or bannister at the side. **Staircases** are
usually inside buildings.

There were odd creaks from the staircase and inexplicable sounds
from the upper floor.
They went into a large, dark, marble-floored hall, with a big
staircase winding up from it.
Ahead of me the main corridor ended in a narrow twisting
staircase.

still, yet, already

If you say that something is **still** happening or is **still** true, you
mean that it has been happening or it has been true since some

still

time in the past, and that it continues to happen or be true. **Still** is often used to add emphasis, or to suggest that something is surprising.

She was still looking at me.
There are still plenty of horses round here.
An hour passed, two, and still she slept on.

You use **yet** in negative sentences and in questions. If you say that something has not happened **yet,** you mean that it has not happened at the time you speak. **Yet** is often used to add emphasis, or to suggest that it is surprising that something has not happened, or that it is likely to happen later.

Why should I die? I'm not eighty yet.
The troops could not yet see the misty shores of Normandy.
It isn't dark yet.

If you ask if something has happened **yet,** you want to know if it has happened at the time you speak. In British English, you use the present perfect tense for these questions.

Have you told her about her father yet?
Have you done that yet?

In American English, you can also use the past simple tense for these questions. For example, some Americans say 'Did he do it **yet?**' rather than 'Has he done it **yet?**'.

If you say that something has **already** happened, you mean that it has happened before the time at which you are speaking. **Already** is often used to add emphasis or to suggest that it is surprising that something has happened, or that you expected it to happen later.

The field beyond the orchard had already been sown with barley.
He had shaved already before dinner, but now he went over his chin a second time.
Lessep and Maury were already eating.

store, shop

Places where goods are sold are usually called **shops** in British English.

We're going to take the typewriter back to the shop.
Later in the morning, at lunch-time, she would go out to the shops.
Natural brown rice is obtainable from health food shops.

Large shops which sell a special type of goods are sometimes called **stores.**

All insecticides should be available from big stores, ironmongers or some do-it-yourself shops.
Wait to buy linen until the summer or winter sales, then go to stores with a good reputation.
...a furniture store.

A very large shop which has separate departments selling many different types of goods is called a **department store.**

...the famous London department store, Harrods.

In American English, places where goods are sold are normally called **stores.**

She came out of the store and sat down on the bench.
The clerks in the store raced to help us.
The next day he went down to a fancy stationery store on Market Street and bought himself a thirty-dollar fountain pen.

● **Shop** is also used as a verb. When people **shop,** they go to shops and buy things. However, it is more common to say that someone **goes shopping,** rather than that they 'shop'.

I usually shop on Saturdays.
They went shopping after lunch.

Other words

A **chain store** is a department store or supermarket that is part of a large number of similar shops in different towns, all of which are owned by the same person or company.

storey, story

A floor or level of a building is called a **storey** in British English and a **story** in American English.

So we start building a hotel and get the first storey finished.
It is a large late Georgian house, painted white, with four storeys, a basement, a back and front garden.
The paneled partitions can fold back to make one room of the whole story.
The house was four stories high and had at least thirty rooms.

In both British and American English, a **story** is a description of real or imaginary events.

He could be most witty, though, when telling stories about some of his famous colleagues.

storey

*The teacher then read a story about a young boy who had fallen
down and hurt himself.*

strange, foreign

Strange means odd, unfamiliar, or unexpected.

I had a strange dream about you and me last night.
Her husband had become strange and distant.

A **strange** person is a person that you do not know or have never
met or seen.

I realized it wasn't right to talk to a strange girl.
I don't like strange people coming into my house.

You do not use 'strange' to describe people or things that come
from a country which is not your own. You use **foreign**.

The United States had 68,000 foreign doctors in 1972.
We can give you sterling in exchange for most foreign notes.

stranger, foreigner

A **stranger** is someone that you do not know or have never met
or seen.

Her mother didn't trust strangers.
Antonio was a total stranger to all of us.

A **stranger** is also a person who does not know a place very well.

*The tourist's wife said to Harvey, 'What time do the stores close
downtown?' Harvey said, 'I'm a stranger here.'*

If you want to say that someone comes from another country and
not from your own, you do not call them a 'stranger'. You say
they are a **foreigner**.

*...that vague uneasiness that comes with hearing a newly-arrived
foreigner speak your language as well as his own.*
...a foreigner reading out of a phrase book.
In August there are over one million foreigners in France.

study, studio

A **study** is a room in a house that is used for reading, writing,
and studying.

*I pulled down a dull-looking book from an upper shelf in my
father's study.*

They exchanged good nights and he rapped on the door opposite Washington's study.

A **studio** is a room where an artist works, for example a painter or a photographer.

When I was at Moore's studio I was still a student.
In 1863 Edma and Berthe went to the studio of the famous landscape painter Corot.

A **studio** is also a room where radio or television programmes are recorded, music is recorded, or films are made.

...the big recording studio in Maida Vale.

A **studio** or **studio flat** is a small flat, with one or possibly two rooms.

I lived at that time in a studio flat near to Olympia.

subway, underpass

A **subway** is a passage that is used by pedestrians to go underneath a road.

There is a covered route to it from South Kensington Station by that weird subway with its grimy glazed tiles and naked electric light bulbs.

An **underpass** is either a passage for pedestrians or a road for vehicles that goes underneath a road or railway line.

...the lethal exhaust gases from the underpass beneath.
...a railroad underpass.

● In American English, **the subway** is a railway system in which electric trains travel below the ground in tunnels.

suit, suite

A **suit** is a set of clothes consisting of a jacket and a matching pair of trousers for a man, or a jacket and a matching skirt or pair of trousers for a woman. **Suit** is pronounced /su:t/.

Stein had changed into a sober, dark, woollen suit.
...the woman in the sensible grey wool suit and the frilly pink blouse.

A **suite** is a set of matching furniture used in a particular room, for example a bedroom or living room. A 'three-piece **suite**' is a set of two matching armchairs with a sofa. **Suite** is pronounced /swi:t/.

suit

...a three-piece suite for the lounge.
They went into the large living room with its red suite.
...a new bedroom suite.

A **suite** is also a set of connected rooms, especially in a hotel.

The hotel manager threw open the door of the suite.
We arrived in the penthouse suite at 7.15.

surprised, surprising

When something unexpected or unusual happens, you can say that you are **surprised**.

Those who expected this outcome were surprised.
I'm surprised at your behaviour.
I'm surprised it's this cold.

Something that is **surprising** makes you feel surprised.

At first it seems surprising that they have so few links with their counterparts in western countries.
Today there is nothing surprising about finding a woman holding down a successful job in high finance.

suspenders, braces

In British English, **suspenders** are the fastenings used by women to hold up stockings.

She kicked out a leg and unfastened her suspenders.

In American English, **suspenders** are the straps men wear over their shoulders to hold up their trousers. In British English, these are called **braces**.

The dealers sat hunched over their computers in their white shirts and red suspenders.
'Right,' said Donald, removing his coat to reveal red braces.

sympathetic, friendly

If you have a problem and someone is **sympathetic** or shows a **sympathetic** attitude, they show you that they care and would like to help.

It is youth today who are most sympathetic towards the elderly.
My boyfriend was very sympathetic and it did make me feel better.
He looked sympathetic and squeezed her arm affectionately.
I sought to preserve a sympathetic attitude to the culture of which they were a part.

A person who is **friendly** or has a **friendly** attitude is kind and pleasant and behaves the way a friend would behave.

...his wife, a friendly woman who offered me cakes and tea.
The woman had been friendly to Lyn.
...a pleasant, friendly smile.
Posy gave her a friendly hit with a newspaper.

You do not usually use 'sympathetic' to describe someone that you like. However, people occasionally refer to someone in a novel or play who is easy to like as a **sympathetic** character.

As there were no sympathetic characters in real life, there were none in my book.
Realistic and sympathetic elderly characters are seldom viewed on the television.

You are more likely to show that you like a real person by describing them as 'nice' or 'likeable'.

T

tall, high

You use both **tall** and **high** to describe things that measure a lot from bottom to top.

You use **tall** when you are talking about people.

He was tall and very thin, with narrow shoulders.
...a tall handsome man.

Other things, for example trees and buildings, can be described as **tall** if they are fairly narrow in relation to their height.

A faint breeze off the river stirred the tall elephant grass.
He looked round at the tall, narrow-fronted buildings on each side of the road.
With his left hand, he raised a tall glass of lemon tea to his face.

You can also give an actual measurement, by placing the measurement before **tall**.

Its chimneys are 600 feet tall.
Charles was about 5 feet 4 inches tall.

tall

You use **high** to describe things which measure a larger distance than usual from the bottom to the top.

She lives in the high mountains of northern Japan.
He saw them sitting on high stools at the semicircular bar.
...the high walls of the prison.

You can also specify an actual height, by placing a measurement before **high**.

...fences three metres high.
...a low mud wall about 10 centimetres high.

Note that **high** can also be used as an adverb.

The water rose dangerously high.
I threw the shell high up into the air.

taste, taste of

If you **taste** some food or drink, you eat or drink a small amount of it in order to try its flavour.

He tasted his cold soup. It was not quite chilled enough.
I have tasted the pie - it is quite excellent.

When you eat or drink something, you can describe the flavour by saying how it **tastes**. **Taste** can be followed either by an adjective such as 'sweet' or 'salty' which gives information about the flavour, or by an adjective such as 'delicious' or 'revolting' which gives your opinion about the flavour.

Strain or sieve it and add enough sugar to keep it from tasting sour.
The tears tasted salty, like sea water.
'I don't know what it is,' he said, 'but it tastes wonderful.'

If food or drink **tastes** like something, its flavour is similar to that thing.

She ate a bit of meat which tasted like chicken.
The bananas were small and tasted like soap.

You say that food or drink **tastes of** something if it definitely has the flavour of that thing. For example, soup made with fish **tastes of** fish.

With greasy fingers we ate the pie which tasted of cinnamon.
The tea tasted faintly of bitter almonds.
The usually sweet water from our pump turned brown and tasted of nails.

tax, duty, fine

A **tax** is an amount of money that you pay to the government so that it can pay for public services. You usually pay part of your income as **tax,** and companies pay part of their profits as **tax.** The price of many things that you buy also includes some **tax.**

A cut in taxes will mean a cut in government spending.
We do not propose to increase income tax.
You'll find each item has two prices. These are before and after tax is added.

A **duty** is a special tax that you pay on goods such as alcoholic drinks, cigarettes, and petrol, or that you pay when you import goods into a country.

This year's budget rises in excise duties on drink, tobacco and petrol also added two per cent to retail prices.
Britain hopes to persuade Japan to lower existing import duties on whisky.
You are allowed to bring into the UK certain goods without incurring duty.
This year's budget rises in excise duties on drink, tobacco and petrol also added two per cent to retail prices.

A **fine** is an amount of money that someone has to pay if they are found guilty of an offence or a crime.

They could get $22,000 in fines and 32 years in jail.
Some large fines have been imposed on employers exposing workers to asbestos.
Men were sent to prison for not paying the fines.

teach, instruct, educate

If you **teach** someone, you explain a subject to them as teachers do in school, or show them how to do a particular task like cooking or driving.

He couldn't read at eighteen; his wife had to teach him.
It is often grandmothers who teach children to cook, sew or knit.
I had taught in ordinary schools for many years.

If you **instruct** someone in a subject or skill, you give them information that they have to learn, so that they know how to do something in the approved way.

Reg Renn instructs the trainees at the college's motor vehicle unit.
The magistrate instructed me in the procedure of the court.

teach

If you **instruct** someone to do something, you tell them to do it.

The judge instructed them to keep silent about his decision.
I have been instructed to give you this.
You can instruct your bank to pay your bills by standing order.

If you **educate** someone, you teach them over a long period of
time, so that they gain knowledge and experience in several
subjects.

The more affluent the society, the better it educates its members.
John Tyndall was born in 1934 at Exeter and educated at
Beckenham Grammar School.

teacher, lecturer, tutor, professor

Anyone who teaches can be called a **teacher**. However, if you say
that someone is a **teacher,** you usually mean that they are a
schoolteacher and work in a primary or secondary school.

My mother, a primary school teacher herself, had already taught
me how to read.
Good teachers never underestimate the ability of children to learn.

In Britain, a **lecturer** is someone who teaches at a university or
college.

David is now a lecturer in mathematics at London University.
A lecturer gave a talk on the tsetse fly.

A **tutor** in a British university teaches small groups of students,
and is also responsible for giving individual students help and
advice.

The Head of a Department may appoint a member of his staff as
tutor to individual students.
His tutors in English and History give him quite favourable reports.

A private **tutor** teaches individual pupils, usually to help them in
subjects which they find difficult at school.

Ken had made progress with his home tutor.

In Britain, a **professor** is the most senior teacher in a university
department. In American and Canadian universities and colleges,
all of the senior teaching staff are called **professors**. Note that
Professor is also used as a title with a person's name.

...James Challis, Professor of Astronomy at Cambridge.
And everybody seems to have money these days. Except college
professors.
...the research being carried out by Professor Butler and his team.

terrified, terrifying

If you are **terrified,** you feel extremely frightened.

The girl was obviously terrified and wanted nothing so much as to get back to her seat.
You're terrified of thunderstorms.

Something that is **terrifying** makes you feel terrified.

Chicago was terrifying with its noise and confusion and buildings that seemed to reach the sky.
She was shaking with fatigue and reaction after the terrifying encounter with the tiger.

testament, will

If one thing is a **testament** to another thing, it is a sign that shows that the other thing really is the case. **Testament** is a formal word.

All six of them reflected their personalities in manner and dress: a testament to the liberating effect of lack of uniform.
It is a testament to the power of the forestry lobby that the study was followed up immediately.

A **will** is a legal document in which someone gives their instructions about who should receive their money and possessions when they die.

I'm not bothering to make a Will – everything will go to my wife and children.
He's not a young man. Has he made a will?

A person's **last will and testament** is their **will. Last will and testament** is a legal term which is normally used as the formal title of a **will.**

It's probably her last will and testament.

theatre, cinema

A **theatre** is a building with a stage where plays, musicals, and similar entertainments are performed. The spelling **theater** is used in American English.

You must see the new play at the Park Theatre.
The thundering applause of the audience went rolling through the theatre.
He told her about a Boston theater fire when he was young.

theatre

In British English, a **cinema** is a building where films are shown. In American English, this building is usually called a **movie theater** or a **theater**.

Wajda's Man of Iron seems to be playing at every cinema in Warsaw.
After lunch we went to the cinema.
An Albany movie theater lost the sound to the last ten minutes of Godfather III.
We managed, finally, to get a third-rate theater in New York to play the film.

Other words

When British people go to see a film, they say that they are going to the **cinema** or to the 'pictures'. American speakers talk about going to the 'movies'.

Everyone has gone to the cinema.
She went twice a week to the pictures.
Some friends and I were driving home from the movies.

thief, robber, burglar

Anyone who steals something can be called a **thief**.

I once saw a thief snatch a watch from a stall in Ibadan market.
You came sneaking up like a thief and stole Timmy's glasses!

A **robber** uses violence and threats to steal money or something valuable from places such as banks, shops, or trains.

Bank clerks were shot in different towns as they tried to resist the robbers.
The train robbers were given sentences ranging up to 30 years.

A **burglar** breaks into houses and other buildings and steals things.

You should see my place, that's really well protected against burglars.
There was a scullery window open and the burglar may have shot the dog.

though, although

Both **though** and **although** are used in subordinate clauses to introduce a fact which is not expected or that is contrasted with another fact. **Though** is not used in very formal English.

Though he was noisy and rather boastful, I got to like him.
It was certainly not paper, though it looked very much like it.
Karin, although she said she was hungry, declined food or drink.
The bazaar is much the same, although there are some rather smart new shops.

You can use 'even **though**' to emphasize a surprising fact.

She wore a fur coat, even though it was a very hot day.
He began to sweat, even though it was cold on the station.

You can use 'as **though**' to describe a situation by giving a comparison or a possible explanation.

I began to look at Monty as though he was a total stranger.
The furniture looked as though it had come out of somebody's attic.

Though can also be used to mean 'however'. This is a fairly informal use.

At weekends, though, the atmosphere changes.
He was dressed neatly, though.

tie, cravat

A **tie** is a long thin, strip of cloth that is worn under a shirt collar and tied at the front, so that it hangs down the front of your shirt.

Stein got to his feet, pulled off his tie and loosened his shirt collar.
When my tie was straight I went through into the living-room.

A **cravat** is a wide strip of cloth that a man wears wrapped around his neck and tucked inside the open collar of his shirt.

...his polka-dotted cravat and short-sleeved jacket.
She adjusted a scarf, worn like a cravat inside the collar of her green tweed coat.

tights, stockings

Tights and **stockings** are worn by women to cover their legs. They are normally made of nylon or a similar thin material, but may be made of a thicker material such as wool.

Tights are a single piece of clothing that covers the legs and goes up as far as the waist.

She picked out an old skirt and a pair of tights.
She discovered how difficult it was to finding matching tights for her dress.

tights

Stockings are two separate pieces of clothing; each one covers a leg as far up as the thigh. They are held up either by suspenders or by an elastic part at the top.

She pulled her stockings on, snapping the elastic a couple of times.
...a woman in a flowered skirt and black stockings and shoes.

tired, tiring

If you are **tired,** you have little energy and want to rest.

'I can't carry any more wood,' said Eric. 'I'm tired.'
Do you mind if I sit down? I'm feeling very tired.
Slowly Murdo went down the mountainside, feeling very tired and cold.

A task or a journey that is **tiring** makes you feel tired.

The nervous tension from caring for a new baby is tiring.
You could, of course, drive down, I imagine - and I know that can be tiring.

tiresome, tiring

A person or thing that is **tiresome** makes you feel annoyed, irritated, or bored.

...some rather tiresome questions.
He was drumming on his knee in a way which his solicitor found peculiarly tiresome.
Mrs Partridge spoke patiently, as to a tiresome child.

A task or a journey that is **tiring** makes you feel tired.

Our mother said we should have an early night after such a tiring day.
I tried to remember that I had made a long and tiring journey.

toilet, lavatory, loo, WC, bathroom

In English, there is a wide range of words that refer to the bowl used by people when they want to get rid of waste from their bodies. The same words are used to refer to the room that contains the bowl.

The most widely used words in ordinary English are **toilet** and **lavatory**. **Lavatory** is slightly more formal.

He asked to go to the toilet.
To a child, the toilet is the most interesting room in any house.

*'Have you been to the lavatory?', said my wife as we set off for
Buckingham Palace.*
The lavatories are through that door over there.

In conversation, many British speakers use the word **loo**.

*The houses on the estate were clean, centrally heated, with indoor
loos.*
He absolutely refused (and still does) to clean the loo.

The term **WC** is used mainly in writing when referring to a toilet
as a facility, for example in advertisements for houses or hotels.
WC stands for 'water closet'.

*All rooms have an en-suite bathroom with WC, wash-basin and
bath or shower.*
...one cold water tap outside; outside WC leaks.

A **bathroom** is a room with a bath, washbasin, and often a toilet,
but many speakers, especially Americans, talk about going to the
bathroom to refer to going to the **toilet**.

One of the girls left to go to the bathroom.
The kids had to go to the bathroom - you know how it is with kids.

Other words

In some public buildings, the toilets are called the 'cloakrooms'.

*We went along together to the cloakroom, where there were still two
or three girls powdering their noses.*
...the Staff Cloakroom.

town, city

Towns and **cities** are areas covered in streets where people live
and work, and where there are shops, offices, factories, schools,
and places for entertainment.

Usually **towns** are smaller than **cities,** but a large number of
people may live there.

Fraserburgh is a bustling fishing town.
'You know McCarthy?'—'In this town, everybody knows everybody.'
They aimed to attract industry to the new towns.

Cities are usually large. Officially, a **city** has a charter which
gives it certain privileges. This charter is given by the monarch
in Britain, and in America by the state. Most British **cities** have a
cathedral.

town

*Life in a smaller community may suit you better than that in a
large city.*
*...the millions who have migrated to the cities because they could not
survive on the land.*

tree, shrub, bush

Trees, shrubs, and **bushes** are all types of large plant.

A **tree** has a long woody stem called a trunk. Branches with
leaves on them come out of the trunk. Oaks and beeches are
examples of **trees.**

Every tree for miles had been knocked down for firewood.
The rough bark of the trees was wet and shiny.
A blackbird was singing in the ash tree.

A **shrub** or **bush** is a large plant rather like a small tree, without
a trunk, but with a group of branches growing from near the
ground. They do not usually grow as high as trees, but some can
grow to several metres. Roses and rhododendrons are examples of
shrubs or **bushes.**

When people are talking about these plants in a technical way, for
example in horticulture, they tend to use the word **shrub** rather
than 'bush'.

*Desert rocks, flowers, grasses, trees, shrubs, and cacti are arranged
here to show that yards without lawns can be attractive.*
This two foot tall shrub likes hot, arid climates.
The guelder rose is a handsome shrub.
...a small evergreeen shrub from the Mediterranean.

Bush is a more general word, used when people are not
concerned about the technical details, but more with the general
effect. Note that you can put **bush** after the name of a plant, as in
'rose **bush**', but you cannot do this with 'shrub'.

*The afternoon sun was low above the gorse bushes and the wind
was rising.*
...a clean-swept yard which had some flowering bushes in it.
He flung himself down under a bush to rest.
I peered through the bushes.

U

under, underneath, below, beneath

If something is **under, underneath, below,** or **beneath** another thing, it is in a lower position than the other thing.

You use **under** or **underneath** when you can imagine a straight vertical line joining the two things, or when one thing covers the other.

Did you put some newspapers under that clock?
We squeezed under the wire and into the garden.
The space under the bed was suffocating.
To help you with this, put a cushion underneath you.
Now the spider's underneath your dress.

Below is usually used to say that one thing is at a much lower level than another.

She would ring later to get the phone number in the call box below their flat.
Below the house the beach is long and shelving.
Down below in the valley the chimneys were smoking.

Beneath has a similar meaning to **under** or **below,** but it is used mainly in writing.

...the warm and sluggish river flowing past the Embankment beneath his window.
They searched everywhere, in the cupboards, under the carpets, beneath floorboards and mattresses, even in the bathroom and kitchen.
Far beneath them, the trees of the forest sighed in the breeze.

underground, tube, subway, metro

In British English, a railway system in which electric trains travel below the ground in tunnels is usually called an **underground** or **underground system**. People using a particular underground system usually refer to it as 'the **Underground**'. When you are talking about the system in a different city, you put the name of the city in front of the word **underground**; for example, 'the Stockholm **underground**'.

They travelled a little way together on the Underground.

underground

If you have a lot of luggage it will be difficult to travel by bus or underground.
...the Berlin underground.

In London, the **underground** also has an informal name, the **Tube.**

When I come by Tube it takes about an hour.
Our car was stolen from a Tube station car park.
It was still raining, but I walked to the tube instead of spending money on a taxi.

In American English, a railway system like this is not called the 'underground'. It is called the **subway.**

They had acted as consultants for the original New York subway at the start of the century.
She couldn't find a taxi so she took the Eighth Avenue subway uptown.

In some other cities, especially Paris, the underground railway is called the **metro.**

I travelled south on the Metro.
...the Moscow metro system.

● In both British and American English, a **subway** is also a path for pedestrians under a busy road.

unsocial, unsociable, anti-social

You use **unsocial** mainly in the phrase '**unsocial** hours', which are times outside normal working hours during which employees are paid extra for working. For example, people who work at night work '**unsocial** hours'.

There were also special provisions for those who worked unsocial hours.
The nurses say they stand to lose up to forty pounds a week in payments for unsocial hours.

Someone who feels **unsociable** does not want to talk to other people and tries to avoid meeting them.

They poured her a shandy, which she forced down, not wishing to appear unsociable.
'Can I get you anything? You're not feeling sick?'—'No, just unsociable.'

Someone who is **anti-social** behaves in a way that annoys and causes trouble for other people.

Her teacher says that Peggy seems very unhappy and anti-social.
The poor boy continued to be anti-social, dishonest, hateful, and full of anxiety.
...outbreaks of violent or anti-social behaviour.
Youngsters between 16 and 20, without higher education, were inclined towards anti-social activities.

Anti-social is also used with a similar meaning to **unsociable.**

They both were proud and shy and anti-social.
Some have blamed the régime for making them more aggressive and anti-social.

V

valuable, invaluable, valueless

If something such as jewellery is **valuable,** it is worth a lot of money.

This collection is the biggest and most valuable assembly of works of art ever given to the nation by an individual.
She collected vintage cars and built up a valuable stamp collection.

If something such as help or advice is **valuable,** it is very useful.

After-school play centres are valuable for all children.
He could give me valuable information.

Invaluable is not the opposite of 'valuable'. If you say that someone or something is **invaluable,** you mean that they are extremely good and useful.

The training they receive is considered invaluable experience for a career in finance.
Their evidence could be invaluable in proving that the accident was caused by negligence.

If you say that something is **valueless,** you mean that it is not useful, effective, or worth anything.

...involvement in valueless activities.
He knew an advertising campaign, however inspired, was valueless without the muscle of an organization behind it.
...the government's sudden decision to declare half the banknotes in the country valueless.

van, lorry, truck

A **van** is a vehicle that is used for carrying goods on roads. It has a roof, and no windows in the compartment where the goods are kept. Some **vans** are about the same length as a car. Others can be about a metre longer.

Mind the patch of mud near the shed; the baker's van got stuck in that last night.
Delivery vans could hardly get through the traffic.

A **lorry** is also used for carrying goods on roads. It is larger than a **van,** and much larger than a car.

Convoy after convoy of giant lorries thunders along the roads.
I almost hit the timber lorry before I even realised it was there.

In American English, a vehicle like this is called a **truck.**

Huge articulated trucks constantly arrive with thousands of turkeys.
He had a fleet of freight hauling trucks that made him a fortune.

vest, waistcoat

In British English, a **vest** is a piece of underwear that you wear on the top half of your body, under a shirt, blouse, or dress, in order to keep warm. It is called an 'undershirt' in American English.

He wore only a vest over his white pyjama trousers.
She came in and picked up the underpants and vest that the child had peeled off.

In American English, a **vest** is a piece of clothing worn over a shirt. It has no sleeves, fits closely to the body, and is normally worn by men, often under a jacket.

He was dressed as always in a black suit with vest, and high-topped black shoes.
...black jeans, a leather vest and, of course, a cowboy hat.

This piece of clothing is called a **waistcoat** in British English.

Grandison Whiting folded his hands across his waistcoat, just above his watch-chain.
The man noted the appointment in his tiny diary and replaced it in his waistcoat pocket.

W

want, wish

If you **want** something, you feel a need for it or a desire to have it.

He could have a lawyer if he wanted one.
If you want the job, it's yours.
The boy here wants a canary.
...ties and shirts that nobody wants.

You can also use a 'to'-infinitive after **want**. You can say that you **want** to do something, that you **want** someone to do something, or that you **want** something to happen.

I want to get out of here.
He dropped his wallet and I want to give it to him.
He wanted actors to perform his plays as though they were musical scores.
I do not want the garden to go jungly.

You use **wish** with a 'to'-infinitive with the same meaning as **want**. However, this is a formal use.

She said that she wished to consult him about her future.
He did not have to answer questions if he did not wish to.
I felt I was hearing everything that Mozart wished me to hear.
She added that she wouldn't wish him to be an artist unless he were a great one.

In stories, people sometimes say that they **wish** for something when they **want** it. Sometimes they are talking about their secret desires.

So your husband wishes for a son.
Whatever they wished for, they asked for, and it was brought.
He was afraid, because he had so often wished for his father's death.

Wish is normally followed by a 'that'-clause. If you **wish** that something was the case, you would like it to be the case, although you know it is unlikely or impossible.

I wish I could offer a magic solution to your problem.
I wish I lived near London.
He wished he had phoned for a cab.

235

wedding, marriage

A **wedding** is a ceremony in which a man and a woman become each other's husband and wife. A **wedding** usually includes a meal or other celebration that takes place after the ceremony.

What remained was to announce their engagement and fix the date of the wedding.
Even though it wasn't a formal wedding we'd very much like to give you a present.

This ceremony can also be called a **marriage**.

I remember the day of my marriage.
...the Archbishop of Canterbury's sermon at the royal marriage.

A **marriage** is also the relationship between a husband and wife.

It has been a happy marriage.
She feels no conflict at all between marriage and career.

west, western, westerly

The **west** is the direction you look towards in the evening in order to see the sun set. The **west** of a country or area is the part towards the west. You use **west, western,** and **westerly** to describe things that are in or come from the west.

You use **west** to describe a part of a place that is in the west, whether it is a large place like a country or a smaller place like a building. Note that **west** is often used to make a contrast with the east, north, and south: the **west** face of a mountain is opposite the east face.

They had established themselves almost everywhere in West Africa.
The only way it could be reached was by a dangerous and gruelling climb up the west face of the mountain.
This seaweed is often abundant on the middle and lower shore, especially on the West coast.

Western means relating to the west and refers to a more general area than 'west'.

He commanded a tank troop at Anzio while Dixon was an R.A.F. corporal in western Scotland.
On the western side was the precipice known as the Frog's Head.
...a location off the western coastline of the mainland of Scotland.

You can also use **western** to describe things that come from the west or that are found there.

*Down from the Arctic Seas the fish will move into the western
waters of Britain and Ireland.
The sun is setting over the western hills.*

Winds that come from the west can be described as **west** or
westerly winds.

*Mother said the west wind was bad for the nerves.
During the night a warm westerly wind blew across the downs.*

You can also use **westerly** to describe directions and locations. If
something moves in a **westerly** direction, it moves towards the
west. Unlike 'west' and 'western', **westerly** can be used with
'more' and 'most'.

*In order to avoid a storm, we flew over the east side of Lake
Turkana rather than take the more normal westerly route.
The mountainside facing the harbour has a westerly outlook.
We were standing on the most westerly point of England.*

whole, all

Whole is used to describe something that is being considered as a
complete, single thing, rather than being considered to be made
up of a set of individual parts. As an adjective, **whole** is preceded
by a determiner such as 'the' or 'this' or by a possessive such as
'my' or 'her', and followed by a singular noun.

*'Why do I have to go?'—'The whole class is going.'
The response was so great that a whole page had to be given over to
readers' letters.
Koch applied his whole weight to the brake pedal.*

The whole of is also followed by a singular noun.

*...throughout the whole of the industrialized world.
The whole of the right-hand side of his suit was black with blood.*

Like **whole, all** can be used to talk about something that is being
considered as a complete, single thing. **All** and **all of** are followed
by a determiner such as 'the' or 'this', or a possessive such as
'my' or 'your' and a singular noun. They cannot be followed by 'a'
or 'an'.

*A point of gold appeared above the sea and at once all the sky
lightened.
That means you'll lose all your investment.
A few minutes later Louison was pedalling down the drive with all
the force his frightened legs could muster.
I want to thank the people of New York for all their help.*

whole

All and **all of** are also used to talk about a complete set of separate parts considered together. **All** and **all of** are followed by a determiner such as 'the' or 'these', or a possessive such as 'your' or 'their' and a plural noun. **All** can also be followed by a plural noun on its own.

Page wanted all of the people to be there.
All of the defendants were proved guilty.
Few children nowadays have all these advantages in their own home.
All airlines kept uniformed representatives at airport post offices.

Note that in front of plural nouns **whole** has a different meaning from **all**. It is used to give emphasis. For example, if you say '**All** the streets are deserted', you mean that every street is deserted. If you say '**Whole** streets are deserted', you mean that some streets are completely deserted.

willing, wilful

If you are **willing** to do something, you will do it if someone asks you to.

She may be willing to do the washing herself for an extra charge.
The store manager was more than willing to help.

You describe someone as **willing** when they are eager and enthusiastic in the things they do, rather than being forced to do them.

There will be no shortage of willing volunteers.
He was a willing participant in my plays.

A **wilful** person is obstinate and determined to get what he or she wants.

She was a wilful child.

A **wilful** attitude or **wilful** behaviour is very deliberate, and is often intended to hurt someone.

I have rarely encountered such a spirit of wilful independence.
A public enquiry later cleared him of wilful misconduct.

woman, wife

A **woman** is an adult female human being.

...a tall, dark-eyed woman in a simple brown dress.
There were men and women working in the fields.

The person a man is married to is normally called his **wife,** not his 'woman'.

His wife and children were hungry.
He has now arrived back in Geneva, where he's expected to be reunited with his wife and daughter.

wood, woods, forest

A **wood** is a large area of trees growing close to each other.

It was cool and dark inside the wood.
At last we entered the cool beech wood through which the Squire's drive twisted.
I told her I had heard her talking in the wood.

If you talk about a particular **wood,** you can also call it 'the **woods**'.

I have to search the woods for hazel branches.
...a brisk walk through the nearby woods.
We rushed out of the woods and down the hill.

A **forest** is an extremely large area of trees. **Forests** are usually a long way from towns and cities.

They had their picnic in a clearing in the forest.
This would destroy the Amazon forest, believed to provide a quarter of the world's oxygen supply.

woolly, woollen

Woolly clothes look as if they are made from wool. They may really be made from wool or they may be made from a material that looks like wool.

Woolly scarves, thick coats and wellingtons decked the lobby.
She was very shy, and kept twisting the belt of her long droopy woolly cardigan.

Woollen clothes are actually made from wool or from a mixture of wool and artificial fibres.

Tim had run over to fetch a woollen jersey as the weather had grown colder.
He bought a pair of hiking boots, long woollen socks, denim trousers, check woollen shirt and a haversack.

worried, worrying

If you are **worried,** you are unhappy because you keep thinking about a problem or about something unpleasant that might happen.

She was worried about finding a job when she graduated.
I called after him, worried that I might have sounded ungrateful.
I began to feel worried.

Something that is **worrying** makes you feel worried.

For a few parents it remains a worrying question, no matter how much experience they've had.
He's had a worrying time at the office.

worth, value

If something is **worth** an amount of money, that is the amount you would get for it if you sold it.

The lens alone was worth about £100.
Two chairs like that must be worth at least a thousand pounds up in London.

In formal or literary English, you can talk about the **worth** of a person, meaning their usefulness, or importance.

...true knowledge of the other's worth and a profound awareness of their individual existence.
This job has robbed me of all worth.

You can also use **value** to talk about how useful or important a person is. **Value** is also used with things such as qualities and plans.

She is beautiful, but my concerns are of her true value as my son's wife. Is she a strong, hard worker?
Everyone realizes the value of sincerity.
Their task was to ensure that no information of positive military value to the enemy was sent out.

When you talk about the **value of** something that you can own such as a house or car, you mean the amount of money that someone will pay for it. You do not talk about the 'worth' of something that someone owns.

What would you say is the value of this property today?
They paid 28 percent above market value for it.
The value of the horse is now in excess of £500,000.

Index

If the word you are looking for is the first word in an entry, it appears on its own in **bold**. If it is not the first word in an entry, it is followed by the symbol ⇨ and the word which does come first.

Note that some words occur in more than one entry. For example, *actual* occurs once in the entry where *actual* is the first word in the heading, and once in the entry where *present* is the first word in the heading. *After* also occurs twice, but in both entries it is the first word in the heading. It is therefore listed in the index with the note: (2 entries).

arise ⇨ **raise**
arrive
arrogant
artist
artiste ⇨ **artist**
as ⇨ **because**
ashamed
ask for
asleep
assent
assignation ⇨ **assignment**
assignment
assist
assurance
assure
at last ⇨ **after all**
at present ⇨ **now**
attend ⇨ **assist**
attorney ⇨ **lawyer**
avenge
avoid
avoid ⇨ **prevent**
award ⇨ **reward**
away ⇨ **apart**
baby
back (2 entries)
backwards ⇨ **back** (1st entry)
bag
bag ⇨ **sack**
baggage ⇨ **bag**
bar
barrister ⇨ **lawyer**
base
basement ⇨ **cave**
basis ⇨ **base**
bath
bathe ⇨ **bath**
bathroom ⇨ **toilet**
be able to ⇨ **can**
beach ⇨ **coast**
bear ⇨ **stand**
because
become
become of ⇨ **become**
before
before ⇨ **ago**
begin
behind ⇨ **after** (2nd entry)
believe

believe in ⇨ **believe**
below ⇨ **under**
beneath ⇨ **under**
beside
besides ⇨ **beside**
besides ⇨ **except**
between
big
bill ⇨ **account**
birthday ⇨ **anniversary**
blame
blouse ⇨ **shirt**
boat ⇨ **ship**
bonnet
bookshop ⇨ **library**
border
bored
boring ⇨ **bored**
borrow
both ⇨ **all**
bought ⇨ **brought**
boundary ⇨ **border**
box
braces ⇨ **suspenders**
brand
bread
breath
breathe ⇨ **breath**
briefly
bring
bring up ⇨ **educate**
British
brought
bureau ⇨ **office**
burglar ⇨ **thief**
bus
bush ⇨ **tree**
buy ⇨ **pay**
by
café
cafeteria ⇨ **café**
can
canal
cancel
cap ⇨ **hat**
capability ⇨ **ability**
capability ⇨ **capacity**
capable ⇨ **able**
capacity

capacity ⇨ **ability**
carefree
careful ⇨ **carefree**
careless ⇨ **carefree**
carpet
carry (2 entries)
carton ⇨ **box**
cave
cavern ⇨ **cave**
cellar ⇨ **cave**
centre ⇨ **middle**
certainly
chance ⇨ **occasion**
channel ⇨ **canal**
chapel ⇨ **church**
characterize ⇨ **describe**
charge ⇨ **accuse**
check ⇨ **cheque**
cheque
child ⇨ **baby**
childish
childlike ⇨ **childish**
chips
choose
church
cinema ⇨ **theatre**
city ⇨ **town**
civic
civil ⇨ **civic**
civilian ⇨ **civic**
claim (2 entries)
classic
classical ⇨ **classic**
classics ⇨ **classic**
cloth
clothes ⇨ **cloth**
clothing ⇨ **cloth**
coach ⇨ **bus**
coast
coat
college ⇨ **school**
comic
comical ⇨ **comic**
commence ⇨ **begin**
comment
competition ⇨ **contest**
complement
compliment ⇨ **complement**
comprehend

comprehensive
comprise ⇨ **include**
confess ⇨ **admit**
confused
confusing ⇨ **confused**
conscience
conscientious ⇨ **conscious**
conscious
consciousness ⇨ **conscience**
consent ⇨ **assent**
consist of ⇨ **include**
constant ⇨ **continual**
contest
continual
continuous ⇨ **continual**
control
conversation
⇨ **speech** (1st entry)
cost
costs ⇨ **cost**
could ⇨ **can**
country (2 entries)
countryside
⇨ **country** (1st entry)
couple
crate ⇨ **box**
cravat ⇨ **tie**
crisps ⇨ **chips**
cry (2 entries)
cure
cushion
custom
damp
daughter ⇨ **girl**
dead
deceased ⇨ **former**
deceitful ⇨ **deceptive**
deceiving ⇨ **deceptive**
deceptive
declare ⇨ **announce**
delay ⇨ **cancel**
delighted
delightful ⇨ **delighted**
demand ⇨ **ask for**
demand ⇨ **claim** (1st entry)
deny
dependant ⇨ **dependent**
dependent
depth ⇨ **height**

243

describe
detract
diary ⇨ agenda
died ⇨ dead
dinner
disappointed
disappointing ⇨ disappointed
discover ⇨ find (1st entry)
discreet
discrete ⇨ discreet
dish ⇨ food
disinterested
dispute ⇨ argument
distinct
distinctive ⇨ distinct
distract ⇨ detract
distrust
disturb ⇨ detract
do ⇨ make
doubt
doubtful
drop
dubious ⇨ doubtful
duty ⇨ tax
each ⇨ all
earn
east
easterly ⇨ east
eastern ⇨ east
eatable
economic ⇨ economy
economical ⇨ economy
economics ⇨ economy
economy
edible ⇨ eatable
edit
educate
educate ⇨ teach
effect ⇨ affect
elder
elderly ⇨ elder
eldest ⇨ elder
elect ⇨ choose
electric
electrical ⇨ electric
embarrassed
embarrassed ⇨ ashamed
embarrassing ⇨ embarrassed
emend ⇨ amend

emigrate
engine ⇨ machine
English ⇨ British
ensure ⇨ assure
envelop
envelope ⇨ envelop
envious ⇨ jealousy
envy ⇨ jealousy
especially
evade ⇨ avoid
eventual ⇨ final
eventually ⇨ finally
ever ⇨ always
every ⇨ all
everyday
every day ⇨ everyday
except
except for ⇨ except
excited
exciting ⇨ excited
excursion ⇨ journey
excuse
excuse oneself ⇨ apologize
exhausting
exhaustive ⇨ exhausting
expect
experience
experiment ⇨ experience
fairly
fall ⇨ drop
fantasy
farther
fault ⇨ blame
fault ⇨ mistake
feet ⇨ foot
female
feminine ⇨ female
few
few ⇨ little (2nd entry)
fewer ⇨ less
fight ⇨ row
final
finally
finally ⇨ after all
find (2 entries)
find out ⇨ find (1st entry)
fine ⇨ tax
flammable ⇨ inflammable
floor

food
foot
footpath
for ⇨ ago
for ⇨ because
forbid
foreign ⇨ strange
foreigner ⇨ stranger
forest ⇨ wood
forever
for ever ⇨ forever
forget
forgive ⇨ excuse
former
found ⇨ find (2nd entry)
fragile
frail ⇨ fragile
french fries ⇨ chips
friendly ⇨ sympathetic
frightened
frightening ⇨ frightened
from ⇨ by
frontier ⇨ border
further ⇨ farther
fury ⇨ anger
gain ⇨ earn
game (2 entries)
gas
gentle
girl
gold
golden ⇨ gold
great ⇨ big
greatly
greengrocer ⇨ grocer
greet ⇨ salute
grocer
ground ⇨ floor
grounds ⇨ floor
grow
grow up ⇨ grow
guard ⇨ keep
habit ⇨ custom
hair
hairs ⇨ hair
handbag
happily ⇨ happy
happy
hat

heal ⇨ cure
hear
height
high ⇨ tall
hire
historic
historical ⇨ historic
history
holiday
holidays ⇨ holiday
home ⇨ house
homework
hood ⇨ bonnet
house
housework ⇨ homework
human
humane ⇨ human
humid ⇨ damp
husband ⇨ man
ill ⇨ sick
illegal
illegitimate ⇨ illegal
illicit ⇨ illegal
imaginary
imagination ⇨ fantasy
imaginative ⇨ imaginary
immoral
imply
impracticable ⇨ impractical
impractical
include
indoor ⇨ indoors
indoors
inedible
infant ⇨ baby
infer ⇨ imply
inflammable
inflict ⇨ afflict
in front of ⇨ before
in front of ⇨ opposite
inhuman ⇨ human
inhumane ⇨ human
institute
institution ⇨ institute
instruct ⇨ teach
insurance ⇨ assurance
insure ⇨ assure
interested
interesting ⇨ interested

in the end ⇨ **after all**
invaluable ⇨ **valuable**
irritated ⇨ **nervous**
irritation ⇨ **annoyance**
its
it's ⇨ **its**
jacket ⇨ **coat**
jealous ⇨ **jealousy**
jealousy
job
journal ⇨ **magazine** (1st entry)
journey
judicial
judicious ⇨ **judicial**
keep
lamp
lane ⇨ **footpath**
large ⇨ **big**
largely ⇨ **greatly**
lastly ⇨ **after all**
last of all ⇨ **after all**
late ⇨ **former**
later ⇨ **after** (1st entry)
lavatory ⇨ **toilet**
law ⇨ **rule**
lawful ⇨ **legal**
lawyer
lay
learn
leave behind ⇨ **forget**
lecture ⇨ **speech** (2nd entry)
lecturer ⇨ **teacher**
legal
legitimate ⇨ **legal**
lend ⇨ **borrow**
less
let ⇨ **hire**
library
licence
license ⇨ **licence**
lie ⇨ **lay**
lift ⇨ **carry** (1st entry)
light ⇨ **lamp**
like ⇨ **love**
likely ⇨ **alike**
listen to ⇨ **hear**
little (2 entries)
lively ⇨ **alive**
living ⇨ **alive**

loaf ⇨ **bread**
lone ⇨ **alone**
lonely ⇨ **alone**
loo ⇨ **toilet**
look at ⇨ **see**
look for ⇨ **search**
look forward to ⇨ **expect**
loose ⇨ **lose**
lorry ⇨ **van**
lose
love
luckily ⇨ **happy**
lucky ⇨ **happy**
luggage ⇨ **bag**
lunch ⇨ **dinner**
machine
magazine (2 entries)
magic
magical ⇨ **magic**
make
make ⇨ **brand**
male
man
manage ⇨ **control**
many
marriage ⇨ **wedding**
masculine ⇨ **male**
match ⇨ **game** (1st entry)
meal ⇨ **food**
memoirs ⇨ **memories**
memories
memory
mention ⇨ **comment**
meter
metre ⇨ **meter**
metro ⇨ **underground**
middle
migrate ⇨ **emigrate**
mistake
mistrust ⇨ **distrust**
moist ⇨ **damp**
moral
morale ⇨ **moral**
morals ⇨ **moral**
more
most ⇨ **more**
motor ⇨ **machine**
much
much ⇨ **many**

narrow
nation ⇨ **country** (2nd entry)
nauseous ⇨ **sick**
neither ⇨ **none** (1st entry)
nervous
newspaper
 ⇨ **magazine** (1st entry)
no
nobody ⇨ **none** (2nd entry)
noise ⇨ **sound**
none (2 entries)
none ⇨ **no**
non-flammable ⇨ **inflammable**
no-one ⇨ **none** (2nd entry)
north
northerly ⇨ **north**
northern ⇨ **north**
notable
note
notice
notice ⇨ **note**
notice ⇨ **remark**
noticeable ⇨ **notable**
now
observe ⇨ **notice**
obviously ⇨ **apparently**
occasion
ocean ⇨ **sea**
office
older ⇨ **elder**
oldest ⇨ **elder**
one
opportunity ⇨ **occasion**
opposed
opposite
opposite ⇨ **opposed**
other ⇨ **another**
others ⇨ **another**
outdoor
outdoors ⇨ **outdoor**
over ⇨ **above**
package ⇨ **parcel**
packet ⇨ **parcel**
pair ⇨ **couple**
pants
pants ⇨ **shorts**
paper ⇨ **magazine** (1st entry)
parcel
particular

particularly ⇨ **particular**
pass
pass ⇨ **spend**
path ⇨ **footpath**
pavement
pay
pay attention ⇨ **notice**
peculiar ⇨ **particular**
peculiarly ⇨ **particular**
people ⇨ **one**
petrol ⇨ **gas**
pillow ⇨ **cushion**
place
place ⇨ **square**
play
please
pocket ⇨ **sack**
polite ⇨ **gentle**
possibility ⇨ **occasion**
possible ⇨ **final**
possibly ⇨ **finally**
postpone ⇨ **cancel**
power
practicable ⇨ **practical**
practical
practice
practise ⇨ **practice**
precede ⇨ **proceed**
present
presently ⇨ **now**
pretend ⇨ **claim** (2nd entry)
prevent
prevent ⇨ **forbid**
price
price ⇨ **cost**
priceless
principal ⇨ **principle**
principle
prize ⇨ **price**
prize ⇨ **reward**
proceed
proclaim ⇨ **announce**
professor ⇨ **teacher**
program ⇨ **programme**
programme
pronounce ⇨ **announce**
proud ⇨ **arrogant**
prove
provinces ⇨ **country** (1st entry)

pub ⇨ bar
publish ⇨ edit
purse ⇨ handbag
quarrel ⇨ row
quiet ⇨ quite
quite
quite ⇨ fairly
rage ⇨ anger
raise
rare ⇨ scarce
rarely ⇨ scarcely
rather ⇨ fairly
reach ⇨ arrive
real ⇨ actual
really ⇨ actually
rear ⇨ back (2nd entry)
recommend ⇨ advocate
recover ⇨ cure
recovery ⇨ cure
refuse ⇨ deny
regard ⇨ see
regulation ⇨ rule
relation
relations
relationship ⇨ relations
relative ⇨ relation
remains ⇨ rest (1st entry)
remark
remark ⇨ comment
remember
remind ⇨ remember
rent ⇨ hire
resign ⇨ retire
rest (2 entries)
restive ⇨ restless
restless
retire
revenge ⇨ avenge
review
revue ⇨ review
reward
rise ⇨ raise
road
rob ⇨ steal
robber ⇨ thief
room ⇨ place
row
rug ⇨ carpet
rule

sack
safety
salary
salute
satisfactory
satisfying ⇨ satisfactory
say
scarce
scarcely
scene
scenery ⇨ scene
school
sea
search
search for ⇨ search
security ⇨ safety
see
seek ⇨ search
sensible
sensitive ⇨ sensible
serial
series ⇨ serial
serpent ⇨ snake
serviette
shade ⇨ shadow
shadow
ship
shirt
shop ⇨ magazine (2nd entry)
shop ⇨ store
shore ⇨ coast
shortly ⇨ briefly
shorts
shorts ⇨ pants
shout ⇨ cry (1st entry)
show ⇨ play
shrub ⇨ tree
sick
sidewalk ⇨ pavement
since ⇨ ago
since ⇨ because
sit ⇨ pass
sleeping ⇨ asleep
snake
sob ⇨ cry (2nd entry)
solicitor ⇨ lawyer
somebody ⇨ someone
someone
something

sometime ➪ **sometimes**
sometimes
somewhere
sound
south
southerly ➪ **south**
southern ➪ **south**
souvenir ➪ **memory**
speak
specially ➪ **especially**
speech (2 entries)
spend
sport ➪ **game** (2nd entry)
square
staircase ➪ **steps**
stairs ➪ **steps**
stand
start ➪ **begin**
state ➪ **country** (2nd entry)
stationary
stationery ➪ **stationary**
statistical ➪ **statistics**
statistics
stay ➪ **rest** (2nd entry)
steal
steps
still
stockings ➪ **tights**
stop ➪ **rest** (2nd entry)
store
store ➪ **magazine** (2nd entry)
storey
story ➪ **history**
story ➪ **storey**
strange
stranger
street ➪ **road**
strength ➪ **power**
studio ➪ **study**
study
study ➪ **learn**
subway
subway ➪ **underground**
suggest ➪ **advice**
suit
suite ➪ **suit**
supper ➪ **dinner**
support ➪ **stand**
surely ➪ **certainly**

surprised
surprising ➪ **surprised**
suspect ➪ **doubt**
suspenders
suspicious ➪ **doubtful**
sympathetic
take ➪ **bring**
take ➪ **pass**
talk ➪ **speak**
talk ➪ **speech** (2nd entry)
tall
taste
taste of ➪ **taste**
tax
tea ➪ **dinner**
teach
teach ➪ **learn**
teacher
tell ➪ **say**
terrified
terrifying ➪ **terrified**
test ➪ **prove**
testament
thanks ➪ **please**
thank you ➪ **please**
theatre
thief
thin ➪ **narrow**
though
tie
tights
tired
tiresome
tiring ➪ **tired**
tiring ➪ **tiresome**
toilet
tolerate ➪ **stand**
towel ➪ **serviette**
town
tree
trip ➪ **journey**
trousers ➪ **pants**
truck ➪ **van**
tube ➪ **underground**
tutor ➪ **teacher**
type ➪ **brand**
under
underground
underneath ➪ **under**

underpants ⇨ shorts
underpass ⇨ subway
understand ⇨ comprehend
understanding
  ⇨ comprehensive
uneatable ⇨ inedible
uninterested ⇨ disinterested
university ⇨ school
unlawful ⇨ illegal
unless ⇨ except
unsociable ⇨ unsocial
unsocial
valuable
value ⇨ worth
valueless ⇨ valuable
van
very ⇨ much
vest
vomit ⇨ sick
voyage ⇨ journey
wages ⇨ salary
waistcoat ⇨ vest
wait for ⇨ expect
want
warn ⇨ prevent
watch ⇨ see
WC ⇨ toilet
wear ⇨ carry (2nd entry)

wedding
weep ⇨ cry (2nd entry)
welcome ⇨ salute
west
westerly ⇨ west
western ⇨ west
whole
wife ⇨ woman
wilful ⇨ willing
will ⇨ testament
willing
win ⇨ earn
wine bar ⇨ café
wish ⇨ want
woman
wood
woods ⇨ wood
woollen ⇨ woolly
woolly
work ⇨ job
worried
worrying ⇨ worried
worth
worthless ⇨ priceless
yell ⇨ cry (1st entry)
yet ⇨ still
you ⇨ one